D1479151

Data Envelopment Analysis

Data Envelopment Analysis

Analysis

The Assessment of Performance

Michael Norman
and
Barry Stoker

JOHN WILEY & SONS

Chichester · New York · Brisbane · Toronto · Singapore

Other Wiley Editorial Offices

John Wiley & Sons, Inc., 605 Third Avenue,
New York, NY 10158-0012, USA

Jacaranda Wiley Ltd, G.P.O. Box 859, Brisbane,
Queensland 4001, Australia

John Wiley & Sons (Canada) Ltd, 22 Worcester Road,
Rexdale, Ontario M9W 1L1, Canada

John Wiley & Sons (SEA) Pte Ltd, 37 Jalan Pemimpin #05-04,
Block B, Union Industrial Building, Singapore 2057

Library of Congress Cataloging-in-Publication Data:

Norman, Michael
    Data envelopment analysis : the assessment of performance /
  Michael Norman and Barry Stoker.
        p.   cm.
    Includes bibliographical references and index.
    ISBN 0-471-92835-6 (ppc)
      1. Industrial productivity—Measurement.   2. Efficiency,
  Industrial—Measurement.   3. Government productivity—Measurement.
  I. Stoker, Barry.   II. Title.
  HD56.25.N67   1991
  658.5′036—dc20   90–28497
                                                                CIP

British Library Cataloguing in Publication Data:

Norman, Michael
    Data envelopment analysis : The assessment of
  performance.
    I. Title   II. Stoker, Barry
  003

    ISBN 0-471-92835-6

Typeset in 10/12pt Palatino
Printed and bound in Great Britain by Courier International Ltd, Tiptree, Essex

Dedicated to

Bridget and Barbara

Contents

List of Figures

List of Tables

Preface

In writing this book on Data Envelopment Analysis (DEA) we have had two objectives in mind:

- To introduce the business analyst to a very powerful tool for evaluating the performance of comparable organizational units, whether they are in the public or private sector, and to provide a working understanding of the technique;
- To assist the technical research analyst to achieve an understanding of the mathematical concepts underpinning DEA and to gain an appreciation of its practical interpretation and application.

We have tried to write the book that we ourselves would have appreciated when we first came across DEA. There were a number of learned papers, but no comprehensive volume that provided a step by step approach to the mathematical basis combined with a practical guide as to how to use DEA to solve real problems encountered by public and private organizations.

We strongly believe that analytical approaches have an important role in attacking strategic problems faced by senior managers. However, it is essential that the issues are carefully researched to ensure that the analysis is properly focused. All too often analytical studies are carried out as backroom research projects divorced from areas of real management concern. Although this book is about an analytical technique, we have placed great emphasis on its place in the context of management information and decision making. In particular, we show how organizational objectives dictate the use of the approach and we describe how the work can lead to management decisions, supported where appropriate by other techniques.

The book has been structured to allow the non-technical reader to learn about DEA without the need to wade through detailed mathematics. These have been confined to two specialist Chapters (3 and 5) and the Appendices.

Acknowledgements

We are indebted to many people whose suggestions have helped to improve the form and content of the book. We are also grateful to colleagues and clients who have worked with us on projects and who have encouraged us to put pen to paper.

We owe special thanks to Bernard Cullen, Robert Dyson, Maurice Gayton, Sue Lewis, Richard Mapleston, George Moore, Tani Nath, Steve Perry and Terry Sear.

Chapter 1

Performance, Efficiency and Data Envelopment Analysis

1.1 INTRODUCTION

People have been counting, and recording results, since time immemorial. It is a natural inclination to want to know 'How many?' and 'How much?' and of course William the Conqueror elevated such questions to become matters of national importance. Once the answers are recorded it is a straightforward step to begin to compare one set of numbers with another. This ability to compare is such an integral part of our daily life—'Which brand is cheaper?', 'Which marrow is longer?', 'Who scored more goals?'— that we barely give it a thought. In government and business, on the other hand, a great deal of effort goes into this process of: counting—measuring—comparing.

Governments use comparisons to detect changes from one period to another in such measures as: the number of registered unemployed; the value of exports and imports; and the ethnic mix in the population. They also need to be able to compare the relative effectiveness of alternative tax proposals. Companies also need to compare measures on a period by period basis, both to investigate deviations from plan and to determine if they are doing better or worse than their competitors.

Once we get beyond such global statistics and begin to compare the 'results' for smaller groupings, we inevitably encounter the problem of determining an equitable basis for the comparisons. There will be 'unquantifiable factors' and 'the human element' to consider, and even where these can somehow be taken into the equation there still remains the problem of accounting for a variety of characteristics that can sometimes represent conflicting objectives. Such then are some of the aspects of assessment that will form the subject matter of this book. We will not be so concerned with comparing 'How many...?' each member of a group has but rather 'How well are they doing?', together with the subsidiary question 'How much could they improve?'. In other words, we will be concerned with performance.

In the private sector, there is one overriding measure of performance— profit. However, the calculation of profit is hardly ever straightforward since it will depend on sets of accounting conventions concerning the treatment of such factors as long-term investment, depreciation, tax-deferrments, and monies set aside for bad debts. In addition, the measurement of profit *per se* gives no indication of the potential for improvement within an organization, even in profit terms. Further, the attainment of profit is in turn dependent on a number of other financial and operational outcomes, and management has to encourage and monitor performance across a wide front. In the public sector where profit is not (or is very rarely) an objective, it is necessary to delve more deeply to define outcome measures that can be used in an assessment of performance.

In the remainder of this chapter we shall be examining various approaches to the measurement of performance and the analytical techniques that are available. We shall then introduce Data Envelopment Analysis (DEA), a powerful new technique that not only supplements traditional approaches but also provides a more comprehensive insight into how well an organization is really performing. The remainder of the book describes DEA in more detail. A case study is used to illustrate the technique which is developed and explained in Chapters 2–6. Some simple mathematics is required in the development, but detailed mathematical expositions have been confined to Chapters 3 and 5 and the Appendices. Chapter 7 sets out the details of a procedure for successfully undertaking a DEA study and integrating the technique into management information and decision making processes. The final chapter describes several case studies that have been conducted by the authors.

1.2 PERFORMANCE ASSESSMENT IN THE PRIVATE SECTOR

Performance ratios are widely used throughout all sectors of business and commerce. The best known ratios are for financial and production management, but ratios have also been developed to assess marketing, purchasing and personnel management. Even in areas such as the accountancy and consulting professions use is made of measures of performance. Ratio measures are popular because a number on its own conveys little information; it needs to be compared with, or put into the context of, some other number, measuring either a similar quantity in another organization (or the same quantity for another time period) or a related quantity in the same organization. For example, it would not mean very much to an observer if Company A announced that it had manufactured 50 units of Product 1 in May. We learn more about the situation if we are told that in April they had manufactured 40 units. We continue to learn progressively more when we are told that:

(a) Company A employs 20 workers who are directly concerned with the manufacture of Product 1;
(b) Company A manufactured 30 units of Product 2 in both April and May;
(c) Company A employs 10 workers to manufacture Product 2;
(d) Company B manufactured 100 units of Product 1 in May;
(e) Company B employs 30 workers to manufacture Product 1.

We begin to build up a picture of 'how well' different companies and different production lines 'are performing'. Comparisons can then be made and management can decide whether or not any action need be taken.

There are also certain absolute measures of performance, usually financial, that are used to assess the continued viability of an organization. These measures are ratios of the type:

$$\frac{\text{Profits before tax}}{\text{Current liabilities}}; \quad \frac{\text{Working capital}}{\text{Total assets}}; \quad \frac{\text{Total liabilities}}{\text{Net capital employed}}.$$

A short term test for viability is the ratio

$$\frac{\text{Quick assets}}{\text{Current liabilities}}.$$

This is known as (the dynamic version of) the 'acid test' since it indicates how a company would react if it were called upon to settle its current liabilities.

Each of the above ratios, and literally hundreds like them, give a partial or incomplete picture of a company's health. In an attempt to reduce these into a single measure, some economists developed a viability indicator that has become known as the *z-score*. This is a composite measure comprising the weighted sum of some of the key financial ratios. A typical z-score might be computed as:

$$z\text{-score} = a + b\,\frac{(\text{Profits before tax})}{(\text{Current liabilities})} + c\,\frac{(\text{Current assets})}{(\text{Total liabilities})}$$
$$+ d\,\frac{(\text{Current liabilities})}{(\text{Total assets})}$$

where a, b, c and d are constants.

Taffler [1], carrying out research into z-scores, investigated two groups of companies over a period. The first group had either gone into receivership or voluntary liquidation, or had been compulsorily wound up, and the second group had remained solvent. The results of his discriminant analysis demonstrated how effective this form of measure could be as a predictor of the survival chances of a company.

A similar composite measure approach was taken by the Bank of England where the ratios they used were of the form:

$$\frac{\text{Current assets}}{\text{Gross total assets}};$$

$$\frac{\text{Cash flow (Profit before tax \& depreciation)}}{\text{Current liabilities}};$$

$$\frac{1000}{\text{Gross total assets (in £ '000)}};$$

$$\frac{\text{Funds flow (Funds from operations − Net increase in working capital)}}{\text{Total liabilities (Long term debt and current liabilities)}}$$

Each of these measures is aimed at giving a (single dimensional) indication of the strength of a company—without regard for its standing with its competitors. In this book we are concerned with the overall performance of an entity measured in comparison with the performance of several other entities. Hence, we will be concentrating not on 'whole companies' but on divisions within a company. For example, we might want to compare the performance of:

• Manufacturing units or product lines;
• Retail outlets;
• Branches of a financial organization;
• Hotels (within a group).

Organizations use a number of measures to assess their divisions, branches or outlets. One of the most powerful financial measures is the ratio 'return on investment'. This is used particularly when it is proposed to build, or purchase, a processing plant, shop or hotel, or to make another addition to the company's assets.

The manufacturing or marketing department will be required to furnish estimates of production levels or sales for a number of years ahead. The value of these will then be compared with the cost of investment (actual costs and opportunity costs) and a decision made on the desirability of making that investment.

When it comes to assessing past performance, measures are naturally related more to the profit and loss account rather than to the balance sheet. On the production side, and other non-revenue earning areas, the focus of the measures will be on the costs incurred while carrying out the work. For divisions, such as retail outlets, the focus will be more on how much profit has been generated. Where there are a number of similar divisions, such as a chain of shops, they can be compared one with another on the basis of gross or net contribution to group profits.

1.3 PERFORMANCE ASSESSMENT IN THE PUBLIC SECTOR

The public sector can be characterized as the provider of a range of services in the absence of a profit factor. In many cases—particularly in health, social services, education, Inland Revenue and defence—we are talking about very large expenditures, administered by a vast complex organization spread over a great number of locations. In most areas of public expenditure there is rarely a single overriding objective to take the place of the profit motive which is the raison d'etre of the private sector. Figure 1.1 shows these elements leading to the focus on control and management.

In central government it has long been recognized that in the process of control and management it is important to derive some sorts of measures,

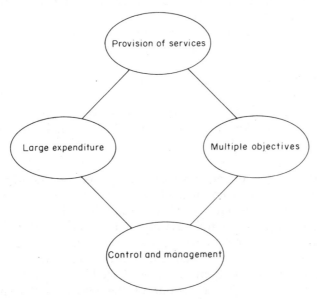

Figure 1.1 Elements in public sector management

or indicators, of the output of expenditure programmes. In its report on the 'Relationship of expenditure to needs' the Expenditure Committee (1971/72) noted that the achievement of accountable management

> 'depends upon identifying or establishing accountable units within government departments—units where output can be measured against costs or other criteria, and where individuals can be held personally responsible for their performance' [2].

In 1982 the Financial Management Initiative (FMI) was launched, with one of its objectives 'to promote in each department an organization and a system in which management at all levels have a clear view of their objectives and means to assess, and wherever possible measure, outputs or performance in relation to those objectives' [3].

The first step is to identify the activities carried out by the units within a department and then, in some way, relate them to the resources utilized. Two rather distinct types of activity can be identified:

- Administration and central support;
- Expenditure programmes.

In administration, measures have been developed for:

- Staff utilization, including ratios of actual numbers against work measurement assessed numbers;
- Productivity, usually in terms of average output per person—weighted, where appropriate, to cater for differing types and complexity of work load;
- Throughput, measured against either previously recorded levels or levels for equivalent units;
- Accuracy, i.e. errors as a proportion of cases dealt with;
- Customer satisfaction, usually inferred from numbers of complaints received.

Although these types of measures can be applied to any administrative unit, they are most prevalent at the local office level of departments such as Social Security, Customs and Excise, and Inland Revenue. Ways of measuring the output of central advisory units, other than those concerned with administrative functions, have proved more difficult to derive.

Measures to assess the performance of expenditure programmes are very much programme-specific. Some examples (listed by programme category) are included here to give a flavour of the measures that have been developed:

- Provision and maintenance of capital goods—maintenance expenditure per unit floor area;
- Provision of services and transfer payments—client/staff ratios, claimants by full time equivalent staff;
- Support and sponsorship—hectares of land reclaimed, occupancy rates, cost per job created;
- Research and development—numbers of publications and citations, royalty income;
- Regulation and enforcement—number of company accounts examined, crime clear up rate.

The Chartered Institute for Public Finance and Accountancy (CIPFA) has carried out a number of studies of local authority operations and has published comparative statistics on budgeted and actual expenditure. As part of its work it has developed a wide range of performance ratios, for example:

- Pupils per teacher;
- Net cost of Personal Social Services per 1000 population;
- Maintenance cost per km of roadway;
- Gross housing rents as a proportion of total costs;
- Revenue support for public passenger transport per 1000 population.

Perhaps the most fully developed of public sector performance ratios are the 'Performance Indicators' (PIs) used in the National Health Service. During 1985 a definitive set of some 450 PIs was established, covering acute services, support services, manpower, estate management, mental handicap and illness, and children's services. The PI system was enhanced by an expert system that helps users to work their way through a logic tree of PIs to highlight any outlier results and possible relationships between these outliers. Examples of PIs for acute services are:

- Hospitalization rate—

$$\frac{\text{Annual number of in-patient residents of a District Health Authority (DHA)}}{\text{Standardized resident population}}$$

where standardization is introduced to take account of differing area profiles of age mix, sex mix and mobility;

- Cost per case—

$$\frac{\text{Annual revenue in-patient expenditure of major acute hospitals in a DHA}}{\text{Annual number of in-patient cases}}$$

- Standardized throughput ratio (by speciality)—

$$\frac{\text{Actual throughput of in-patients per bed}}{\text{Expected throughput of in-patients per bed}}$$

The PIs are supplied, together with a micro-computer, as a working package for DHA and Unit (e.g. hospital) managers. They can be used to compare performance, on a measure by measure basis, with national averages or with other districts' performance. They are also used for monitoring or planning purposes by Regional Health Authorities and, centrally, by the Department of Health.

1.4 MULTIFACTORIAL ASPECTS OF PERFORMANCE

In the previous two sections, we have described some approaches to performance measurement in both the private and public sectors. In the former, indicators of the financial state of companies, and in particular the z-score, were discussed. The z-score approach is of interest since it attempts to give a comprehensive assessment of a company's viability. All the other measures that we have looked at are concerned either with certain facets of performance or with detailed operational aspects of an organization.

Detailed performance measures are very important at the micro level but they have limited value when comparing the operations of a number of composite units. For example, supposing a high street bank has identified three key performance ratios for its branches:

- Profit per (whole time equivalent) staff;
- Percentage increase in accounts;
- Proportion of transactions serviced by automatic transmission machines.

It would be operationally meaningless (not to say mathematically inaccurate) to simply add the three ratios to produce a composite overall measure. Some way needs to be found to accommodate all of these individual measures so that some sort of comprehensive assessment can be made. One approach, equivalent to the z-score model mentioned earlier, would be to construct an expression of the form:

$$a + b \text{ (ratio 1)} + c \text{ (ratio 2)} + d \text{ (ratio 3)},$$

where a, b, c, d are constants. These constants would be forms of weighting factors that reflected the 'relative importance' of the individual ratios.

A sophisticated version of the above approach has been taken by the Audit Commission in their development of a Management Performance Index (MPI). An example of this is given in their report into Housing Authorities' management of council housing [4]. The MPI is built step by step:

(i)   For each 'element of housing management' a regression analysis is carried out with staff cost (or numbers of staff) regressed against a set of common factors that have been shown, by correlation analysis, to be important.

(ii) The regression is repeated but on the best 25% subset of authorities— as determined by step (i).

(iii) Ratios are then calculated for each authority, for each management element, of their actual staff cost (or staff numbers) to best-practice staff costs/numbers, as determined by (ii).

(iv) These ratios are then weighted in such a way as to 'reflect their level of importance for potential economy, efficiency and effectiveness improvements'. The aggregation of these weighted ratios establishes the MPI.

The approaches taken by the Department of Health are described, together with a Data Envelopment Analysis project carried out for the Department, in Section 8.2.

It is clear from the above that generating a multifactorial measure of performance is difficult, both conceptually and mathematically. A more radical approach is called for.

1.5   EFFICIENCY, EFFECTIVENESS AND ECONOMY

Before proceeding, we must clarify some terminology so that we can be more precise in our language. In many papers written on the subject of performance measurement, there has been confusion and lack of consistency in the use of the terms efficiency, effectiveness, performance etc. Our definitions of these and related terms are as follows:

Effectiveness	The attainment of pre-determined goals (outcomes or outputs)
Economy	Keeping within pre-determined cost targets (inputs)
Efficiency	The use made of resources in the attainment of outputs, in the context of environmental factors.

We can combine these into the equation:

Achieved efficiency $\quad = \quad$ Effectiveness $\times$ Economy $\times$ Planned efficiency

or

$$\frac{\text{Actual outcome}}{\text{Actual inputs}} = \frac{\text{Actual outcome}}{\text{Planned outcome}} \times \frac{\text{Planned inputs}}{\text{Actual inputs}} \times \frac{\text{Planned outcome}}{\text{Planned inputs}}$$

where 'inputs' cover both resources and factors that aid or hinder the achievement of the 'Actual outcome'. Achieved efficiency is sometimes called 'value for money'.

Table 1.1 Production figures

	Budget		Achieved	
	Cost	Production	Cost	Production
Company A	50	180	60	200
Company B	50	180	40	160
Company C	50	180	50	180

Table 1.2 Performance factors

	Planned efficiency	Economy	Effectiveness	Achieved efficiency
Company A	$\frac{180}{50} = 3.60$	$\frac{50}{60} = 0.83$	$\frac{200}{180} = 1.11$	$\frac{200}{60} = 3.33$
Company B	$\frac{180}{50} = 3.60$	$\frac{50}{40} = 1.25$	$\frac{160}{180} = 0.89$	$\frac{160}{40} = 4.00$
Company C	$\frac{180}{50} = 3.60$	$\frac{50}{50} = 1.00$	$\frac{180}{180} = 1.00$	$\frac{180}{50} = 3.60$

A trivial example will illustrate the points. If we take the production figures in Table 1.1 and calculate the performance factors—Table 1.2—we can make a number of straightforward conclusions. Company A has been most effective—more cars produced, more customers served, more exam grades, more patients treated—but at the cost of economy—more overtime, more staff hired, smaller classes, more nursing hours. This is summarized by the comparison between achieved and planned efficiency. The results for Company B give the reverse picture. Company C is an accountant's dream!

In these simple, single-input single-output examples it is easy to see that management can make differing assessments depending on their point of view. In most cases, 'efficiency' is not planned as such, since there is no known relationship between inputs and outputs—that is, there is no known production function. Consequently, any assessment of efficiency is necessarily subjective. It is much easier to measure economy and effectiveness, at least on a factor by factor basis.

1.6   FRONTIER FUNCTIONS OF EFFICIENCY

Economists use the term 'productive efficiency' to describe how well an organizational unit is performing in utilizing resources to generate outputs or outcomes. Farrell, a pioneer in this field, demonstrated that 'overall efficiency' can be decomposed into 'allocative efficiency' and 'technical efficiency' [5]. This is illustrated in Figure 1.2, where it is assumed that output is produced by two factors I_1 and I_2, with the curve CC being an output isoquant. The line PP represents the cost minimization plane and, given this, the overall efficiency of unit X is measured by OQ/OX. Technical efficiency (T), measured as the radial distance that X is from the isoquant, and allocative efficiency (A), measured as the radial distance from the cost minimization plane, are given by:

$$T = \frac{OS}{OX} \text{ and } A = \frac{OQ}{OS}$$

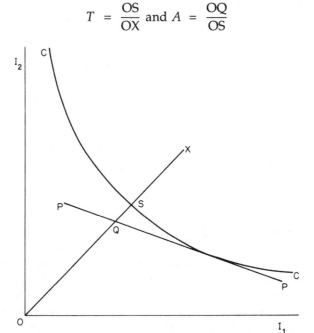

Figure 1.2   Efficiency measures

Thus we have that overall efficiency can be computed from A and T as follows:

$$E = \frac{OQ}{OX} = \frac{OQ}{OS} \times \frac{OS}{OX} = A \times T$$

There are two empirical approaches to the measurement of efficiency based on the above concepts of technical and allocative efficiency. The first, favoured by most economists, is parametric (either stochastic or deterministic). Here, the form of the production function (the isoquant in Figure 1.2) is either assumed to be known or is estimated statistically. The advantages of this approach are that any hypotheses can be tested with statistical rigour and that relationships between inputs and outputs follow known functional forms.

However, in many cases there is no known functional form for the production function and, indeed, it may be inappropriate to talk in terms of such a 'production' function. This is most clearly the case in public sector organizations such as health and education, but is also evident in private sector organizational units that are not, for example, concerned with taking unfinished goods (or raw materials), processing them and producing finished goods for sale or transfer.

In the non-parametric approach with which we shall be concerned in this book, no assumptions are made about the form of the production function. Instead, a best-practice function is built empirically from observed inputs and outputs. This will necessarily be piecewise linear and, as such, would be an approximation to the 'true' function, if such a one existed. Figure 1.3 shows observations for a number of similar units, A–J, where the axes represent input consumed per unit output produced. The efficiency 'frontier' is designated by the lines joining D to B, B to G and G to J; the frontier is assumed to extend parallel to the axes beyond D and J. Efficiencies for point C are calculated in an analogous manner to the approach shown in Figure 1.2. Here, we have:

Overall efficiency	=	OQ/OC
Technical efficiency	=	OS/OC
Allocative efficiency	=	OQ/OS

This is the basis for the development of the frontier approach to estimating technical efficiency. It is worth pausing to look more closely at basic differences of this approach with the parametric systems.

Consider the case of four management units (e.g. firms) producing only one unit of output. Each uses a different amount of the two factors of production (e.g. labour and raw material), although in fixed proportions.

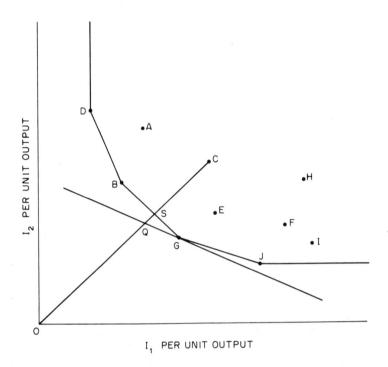

Figure 1.3 A simple efficiency frontier

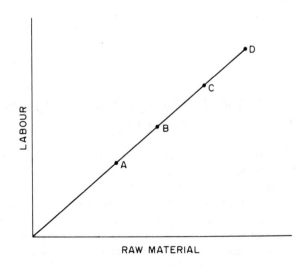

Figure 1.4 Comparative efficiencies

This simplistic case is shown in Figure 1.4. From the figure we deduce that unit A is the most efficient and, if we have no other management units to include in our analysis, we can give A a reference efficiency score and compute scores for B, C, D relative to that. Thus, if we attribute to A an efficiency score of 1, we can say that A 'is efficient relative to B, C, D'. We then have:

$$1 = \frac{OA}{OA} > \frac{OA}{OB} > \frac{OA}{OC} > \frac{OA}{OD},$$

and the ratios for B, C, D determine their own *relative efficiency* scores.

This is analogous to a Leontief single process input–output system. Farrell (cf. Figures 1.2 and 1.3) extended it to cover many processes and many inputs. In Figure 1.3 only unit G is both technically efficient *and* price efficient, whereas units D, B, J are technically efficient but not price efficient.

In the parametric approach the functional form usually chosen is Cobb–Douglas. In this context the Cobb–Douglas functions are estimated by 'averaging' statistical techniques, such as regression. Each unit is then compared with an average, but it is not immediately clear what this 'average' represents. It clearly does not refer to a firm of 'average size', nor indeed to a firm having 'average means at its disposal' (or 'average technology') since it assumed for these purposes that we are investigating the efficiency with which organizations utilize the resources available, and the environment in which it finds itself, in producing its outputs. In other words, we should have 'made allowances' for any encouraging or inhibiting factors enjoyed by the individual units.

In place of comparisons with some unspecified average, we are seeking to establish norms of best *achieved* practice to which those units that fall short can aspire. To this end, we pursue non-parametric extensions to frontier analysis and, in particular, the Data Envelopment Analysis approach.

1.7 THE EMERGENCE OF DATA ENVELOPMENT ANALYSIS

Considerable research effort has been expended in the development of more sophisticated methods of evaluating the efficiency of a unit in relation to the other units in its grouping. One of the major objections to the frontier approach has been that the frontier itself is determined by the extreme observations of the data set; thus the definition of the frontier could be sensitive to errors or inconsistencies in the data. A way around this, taking account of all observations, is to fit a constrained frontier around the data according to some functional form, such as Cobb–Douglas, with errors constrained to one sign. The fit itself (least squares for example) is achieved by linear or quadratic programming techniques.

It is not surprising that the topic of mathematical programming has been raised since we are dealing with some form of optimization when we determine our set of best (most efficient) units. As noted above, though, we are not happy with the restriction that we need to define the functional form of the process that generates outputs from the resources and environmental factors that serve as inputs. One further consideration is of the utmost importance—the need to take into account both multiple inputs *and* multiple outputs.

The breakthrough came in the research work undertaken by Charnes, Cooper and Rhodes (CCR). If Farrell's 1957 paper is taken as the seminal work, the CCR research reported in 1978 [6] is undoubtedly the basis for all subsequent developments in the non-parametric approach to evaluating technical efficiency. In a subsequent paper [7], Charnes and Cooper (1985) give their formal definition of efficiency:

'100% efficiency is attained for (a unit) only when:

(a) None of its outputs can be increased without either (i) increasing one or more of its inputs, or (ii) decreasing some of its other outputs;
(b) None of its inputs can be decreased without either (i) decreasing some of its outputs, or (ii) increasing some of its other inputs.'

This definition accords with the economist's concept of Pareto (or Pareto–Koopmans) optimality. If we have no way of establishing a 'true' or theoretical model of efficiency, that is some absolute standard, we have to adapt our definition so that it refers to levels of efficiency relative to known levels attained elsewhere in similar circumstances. Again, Charnes and Cooper [7] supply the definition:

'100% relative efficiency is attained by any (unit) only when comparisons with other relevant (units) do not provide evidence of *inefficiency* in the use of any input or output.'

In their original paper [6], CCR introduce the generic term 'Decision Making Units' (DMUs) to describe the collection of firms, departments, divisions or administrative units which have common inputs and outputs and which are being assessed for efficiency. We shall adopt this terminology since it neatly encompasses organizational units in both the public and private sectors. The focus for CCR's research was on decision making by 'not-for-profit' entities. This meant they could concentrate on multifactorial problems (particularly with reference to outputs), and they could discount economic weighting factors such as market prices. We shall show later, by means of references to completed studies, that the CCR approach is applicable to the private as well as the public sector. Consequently, we shall distinguish between the two only when it comes to specific aspects of interpretation.

The term Data Envelopment Analysis (DEA) has been used since the CCR paper [6] to describe their approach to efficiency evaluation, but in that paper they refer to DEA as 'a method for adjusting data to prescribed theoretical requirements such as optimal production surfaces, etc., prior to undertaking various statistical tests for public policy analysis'. In fact, the reference to public policy is unnecessary since what is described is the enveloping method discussed in the opening paragraph in this section. We shall use the term DEA in the commonly accepted sense of non-parametric assessment.

The mathematical formulations of DEA are developed elsewhere in the book but it is necessary at this point to describe the technique in general terms, as follows:

> 'The efficiency measure of a Decision Making Unit (DMU) is defined by its position relative to the frontier of best performance established mathematically by the ratio of weighted sum of outputs to weighted sum of inputs.'

CCR went to some lengths in their paper to relate their definition of efficiency, and their approach to its measurement, to traditional economic research. Their work was not universally accepted by the economists who, in general, continued to develop parametric methods. Grosskopf [8] describes how these developments 'have led many economists to believe that the non-parametric approach is obsolete, largely because of the restrictions placed on the technology in the early studies employing that approach'. These restrictions will be discussed in subsequent chapters, but suffice it to say at this point that Grosskopf proceeds to point out that the non-parametric approach is much more flexible than had been suggested and that it has been underestimated by economists. To support his argument he quotes Hildenbrand [9]:

> 'I find the conclusion of the present analysis (of alternative methods of modelling production) to be clear: it suggests a parameter-free approach based on technological information on the micro-level.... . The economic data...needed for the conventional econometric approach are often, in principle, unobtainable. In any case, these studies (using a parametric approach) start with an ad hoc specification which might not reflect the actual underlying structure.'

For the remainder of this book we shall be concerned solely with the non-parametric, linear programming, approach.

1.8   DEVELOPMENTS IN THE USA

Data Envelopment Analysis has provided a rich source of research material and this has been seized on by Doctoral students on both sides of the Atlantic. Until recently, most interest has been shown by academics and administrators in North America with a number of research papers and PhD theses being written on the subject. Many of the studies concern technical investigations and enhancements to the theoretical basis of DEA, but a number do address specific real life problems. When these problems have been in the private sector, there has been a natural reluctance to publish the studies and reports are few and far between. Consequently, we shall describe here two studies in the public service—hospital administration and armed forces recruitment—that in our view typify the power and usefulness of the DEA approach.

Sherman [10] describes his study as an empirical field-test of DEA as an approach to 'identifying and measuring hospital inefficiencies'. He first of all outlines the approaches traditionally used and compares them with DEA. Ratio analysis is widely used in both the private and public sectors, and we have already referred to examples of financial ratios and (UK) Health Service Performance Indicators. We have also referred to the other common technique—regression—which extends the one-input/one-output structure of a simple ratio to one-input/many-outputs or one-output/many-inputs. DEA takes this process to its logical conclusion of many-inputs/many-outputs.

The study investigated the medical–surgical areas of seven teaching hospitals in Massachusetts, using 1976 financial year data. This is a much smaller sample than would normally be used (see Chapter 7), but in the view of those involved, researchers and administrators, the results did provide sufficient information for them to make judgements about DEA. Two hospitals were identified as being inefficient in relation to the others. In the absence of a definitive measure of (absolute) efficiency, a means of checking this result had to be found. Sherman and his team decided to enlist a panel of experts, including managers and hospital accountants, to monitor the results and the output and input factors used in the evaluation. The experts agreed that the results were 'reasonable and believable', but a stronger test came when the director and chief financial officer of one of the hospitals identified as inefficient were approached.

It is always advisable to involve at an early stage the management of the units being investigated (see Chapter 7) but, although he waited until after the experiment, Sherman appears to have been lucky and received cooperation and assistance in interpreting the results. Some data problems were identified, and corrected, and the analysis carried out again. The hospital remained (marginally) inefficient but the remaining cause of the inefficiency, as highlighted by DEA, was accepted as a 'known problem'.

The DEA results were not in direct accordance with those from the Massachusetts state rate-setting commission's simple ratio technique. The latter involved analysing cost per patient, identifying as inefficient those hospitals with costs more than one standard deviation above the mean. Only one hospital was so identified by this method, and DEA found it to be efficient. However, it was readily accepted that the ratio provided only a limited view of the work of the hospital (ignoring, for example, the teaching element) and that DEA was much more comprehensive in its assessments—thus making it a fairer method of comparison.

The second American study—Lewin and Morey [11]—is particularly interesting because of the insights it provides concerning the interpretation of the results from a DEA exercise. The organization under investigation was the (US) Navy Recruitment Command, and 43 recruiting districts, spread over six regions, were analysed. Two types of analysis were undertaken. The first was a straightforward assessment of all 43 districts, which resulted in 18 proving to be inefficient. For each of these inefficient districts, the contribution of each factor to that inefficiency was noted and then summed over all the districts. This yielded aggregate 'potential levels of improvement' that could be achieved if data values were adjusted (outputs increased or inputs decreased) to bring inefficient districts in line with their (relatively) efficient counterparts.

The second analytical approach was to undertake DEA evaluations region by region, adjusting each district's data to make it as efficient as other districts in its own region and then carrying out an analysis on all districts. The deficiencies in performance identified in the regional assessments reflected the technical inefficiencies within the districts. Any inefficiencies identified in the second stage could be said to be due to managerial differences across regions and to their resource allocation strategies.

Lewin and Morey describe another way of viewing the amount by which an input factor needs to be reduced for a particular unit (district). Instead of merely identifying this as potential for cutting the provision of that resource, they show that it can be regarded as a resource under-utilization and as such it could be reallocated to a more efficient user of resources. There will clearly be limitations to the amount of extra resource any unit can accommodate but this sort of reallocation is a good general rule.

Lewin and Morey conclude their paper with a reference to analyses of districts over a period of 12 quarters. This approach can be very informative about the general performance of the organization which comprises the DMUs (see, for example, the first case study reported in Chapter 8). Using data from a series of time periods it can provide additional data points, thus increasing the amount of information that can be gleaned. This latter advantage is shown to good effect by Bowlin [12] in his paper on the use of DEA to study the maintenance activities of US Air Force fighter wings.

Amongst the plethora of US academic technical papers on DEA, there are a few further reports of practical applications. The most notable of these are by Lewin *et al.* (criminal superior courts) [13], Bessent *et al.* (school districts) [14], Banker and Morey (pharmacies) [15], Banker *et al.* (hospitals) [16], Banker (electric power generation plants) [17], and Charnes *et al.* (programmes for disadvantaged children) [18]. One paper on a private sector application stands alone at the time of writing—Banker and Morey (fast food restaurants) [19].

1.9   DEVELOPMENTS IN THE UK

It was almost the mid-1980s before any serious investigation of DEA was undertaken in the United Kingdom. Nor has there been a real flurry of activity in the universities, colleges and business schools. A few papers have appeared in specialist publications and presentations have been made at conferences and seminars under the auspicies of the Operational Research Society. But the cupboard is not quite as bare as it might seem at first glance since there are a number of major projects being undertaken in both the public and private sectors.

The (UK) Central Government has been the chief sponsor of DEA, with the Department of the Environment, the Manpower Services Commission, the Department of Education, and the Department of Health all commissioning studies. The Treasury produced a Working Paper reviewing DEA—its strengths, weaknesses and uses—and reported on some of the studies that had been undertaken.

One of the first published papers was that of Thanassoulis, Dyson and Foster [20] in which they reported on an investigation of the rate collection functions of metropolitan district councils. The data for 62 districts were analysed and in the results no bias emerged, which is as it should be if we are to have confidence in the objectivity of DEA as a means of assessment. In this study, the benefits of incorporating multiple inputs and outputs into the DEA analysis are not exploited since only one input factor was used. However, the work explored the application of the technique, and when the authors presented a version of their paper at an Operational Research Society Conference (see [20]) they brought DEA to the attention of a much wider audience.

There have been a few applications of DEA in the private sector, mainly in retailing and banking, but, as in the USA, the bulk of the studies has been for public service organizations. In education, the Department of Education undertook a joint research project with a team including the present authors to investigate the feasibility of using DEA to assess efficiency in secondary education. Existing data from Inner London schools were used in the study and the results were studied by educational planners and schools' inspectors. A similar, but independent, study was also undertaken by the same team for a Local Education Authority outside London. In this project a certain amount of extra data were collected because it was considered important to include particular additional factors.

Other UK studies in the public sector include:

- Department of Environment (DoE): (a) Rent offices in England; (b) DoE Regional offices
- Manpower Services Commission: Job Centres (several regional studies)
- National Institute of Economic and Social Research (NIESR): Police Authorities in England and Wales (reported in Levitt and Joyce [21])
- Home Office: Magistrates' Courts
- Ganley and Cubbin [22]: Prisons
- Cubbin, Domberger and Meadowcroft [23]: Competitive tendering—refuse collection
- Jesson, Mayston and Smith [24]: Local Education Authorities.

In Chapter 8 we report on some of our own projects, with detailed descriptions of those undertaken for clients in retail banking and the Department of Health. Our approach to these studies, and the techniques we employed to extract the maximum possible potential out of the use of DEA, drew heavily upon not only our own experience but also upon the research of others in the field. We are grateful for their generosity in sharing their knowledge with us.

1.10 SUMMARY

In this book we are concerned with one type of performance analysis. In essence, it is a mathematical technique that provides an objective assessment of the operational efficiency of each of a number of similar organizational units, relative to each other. As such, it is both very interesting and can provide some fascinating information, but that is not a sufficient reason for an organization to use it. There must be a definite need for the information that leads to both better managerial control and decision making. This need will be identified during the first stage of an information system evolution and this will generally be the starting point for a Data Envelopment Analysis exercise. In some cases it can be a lengthy process just getting to the point of knowing 'what it would be nice to know' and when it comes to analysing the data there will often be a requirement for a variety of techniques rather than just one that is pre-eminently suitable. This theme is developed in detail in Chapter 7.

Chapter 2

The Case Study—Introduction

2.1 MANAGEMENT ISSUES

The development of Chapters 2 to 6 will be based on a case study which will encapsulate both the performance related issues introduced in Chapter 1 and the mathematical development necessary to understand Data Envelopment Analysis. Our approach will be to allow the logic of the problem to dictate the method of analysis rather than to first present the mathematics of DEA and then to seek a use for it.

The case study concerns a national retailer with problems of performance assessment typical of those which the authors have encountered in their consultancy practice. The data came from a sample provided by a well known British company. For the purpose of the case study, we can regard the sample as representing the operation of the entire company. This comprises 45 shops spread nationally with a total annual turnover of £41.13 million. The annual turnover for each shop ranges from £0.19 million to £2.59 million.

The company accounts allow for the separate identification of costs incurred directly by the shops themselves (e.g. staff, premises, telephones) and centrally incurred costs not attributable directly to shops (e.g. buying, distribution, administration). Senior management use these costs to generate shop profitability figures according to the equation:

$$\text{Shop profit} = R - S - (R/T)\, C$$

where R = shop turnover, T = company turnover, S = direct shop costs and C = total central costs.

The total company profit before tax is £6.00 million and shop profits calculated on the above basis range from a loss of £0.14 million to a profit of £0.55 million.

The senior management, in line with all commercial organizations, run the company seeking not only to make a profit but also to continually increase profit. Whilst there may be some scope for improving profit through reducing central costs, the main opportunity lies in increasing the contribution to profit of the shops themselves through increased market penetration and greater efficiency.

Directives are issued and profit targets are set by senior management with a view to increasing shop profitability but the responsibility for its achievement lies with the shop managers. Consequently, they need to be able to measure the shop managers' achievements and the extent to which their directives are being carried out.

It could be argued that all activities carried out by the shops are with the ultimate objective of making a profit, and that shop profit is the only measure which gives an overall reflection of the value of those activities in terms of that objective. Shop profit is used for two main purposes:

(a) It allows management to assess the value of individual shops. They could decide to close unprofitable shops.
(b) It provides a base against which to target and measure improvement.

Targets are based on achieving a uniform percentage profit increase across shops in line with the overall company target. However, *ad hoc* adjustments are frequently made in the case of low-profit shops where senior management feel that the percentage target would be too lenient.

Managers of the less profitable shops are unhappy at being targeted on this basis, arguing that profitability is largely dictated by factors outside of their control, such as the length of time their shop has been in operation, local population, competition and pitch. Further arguments are raised regarding the way in which costs are apportioned. Some shop managers argue that they are good revenue earners but that this is negated in profit figures through high costs which are beyond their control. Examples of these are excessive repair and maintenance costs on premises and rental for leasehold shops, a charge not incurred by freehold shops.

Meanwhile, managers of the more profitable shops argue that their achievements are based on customer service and good management.

Senior management would like to use shop profit to encourage and reward shop managers directly through profit-related pay. However, they have deferred such a scheme fearing an adverse effect on morale if they impose it against the background of dissatisfaction with their current methods. They are now aware that no further progress will be made on the scheme until the underlying problem is analysed in greater detail. Consequently, they asked an internal team of analysts to collect data and investigate the claims of the shop managers. Data were collected under the following headings (see Table 2.1):

1 Staff cost
2 Non-staff controllable cost
3 Controllable cost (= 1+2)
4 Uncontrollable cost
5 Non-staff cost (= 2+4)
6 Total cost (= 1+2+4)
7 Revenue Gp1
8 Revenue Gp2
9 Revenue Gp3
10 Total revenue (= 7+8+9)
11 Revenue growth
12 Revenue % growth (= 11/10 as %)
13 Central overheads
14 Profit
15 Pitch
16 Age of shop (months)
17 Catchment population
18 Competition
19 Customer service

Total cost for each shop is given by item 6 and can be broken down into Staff cost and Non-staff cost. All Staff cost is controllable by the shop manager but a proportion of Non-staff cost is uncontrollable. Items 1 to 6 are different cost aggregations based on staff, non-staff, controllable and uncontrollable elements of cost. The revenue from three distinct product groups is separately identified by items 7, 8 and 9 with Total revenue identified by item 10. Item 11 identifies the growth in revenue in the last year and item 12 expresses this as a percentage of Total revenue. Items 13 and 14 are the apportionment of centrally incurred costs and resultant shop profit described above. Item 15 is an assessment of the quality of a shop's location. Item 18 is a count of the number of competitors within the shop's catchment area. Item 19 is a measure of the quality of the Customer service which the shop provides based on questionnaires returned by the customers themselves.

2.2 ANALYTICAL ISSUES

The analysts immediately encountered a problem familiar to many organizations. They needed to take account of many factors—profit, population, number of years in operation, competition, pitch and cost of

Table 2.1 Case study data

	1	2	3	4	5	6	7	8	9	10	11	12	13	14	15	16	17	18	19
BIRMINGHAM 1	194.10	29.63	223.73	71.62	101.25	295.35	220.39	432.24	145.37	798.00	140.65	17.63%	468.66	34.00	2	126	225677	11	660
BIRMINGHAM 2	119.65	24.04	143.69	35.96	60.00	179.65	105.12	561.90	179.92	846.93	88.41	10.44%	497.39	169.89	2	278	235391	12	462
BRADFORD	154.21	24.61	178.82	12.89	37.50	191.71	124.58	771.14	150.17	1045.89	166.95	15.96%	614.23	239.94	1	144	200020	9	599
BRENT CROSS	95.72	17.32	113.04	65.18	82.50	178.22	99.62	418.43	93.06	611.11	91.33	14.94%	358.89	73.99	1	90	333524	9	646
BRISTOL	140.92	30.82	171.74	29.18	60.00	200.92	177.24	386.07	115.20	678.51	133.02	19.60%	398.48	79.11	1	126	213974	13	549
BRIXTON	167.51	30.80	198.30	152.96	183.75	351.26	142.13	760.78	147.21	1050.12	183.12	17.44%	616.72	82.14	2	152	253383	7	618
BROMLEY	58.50	12.06	70.56	6.69	18.75	77.25	49.91	117.17	20.45	187.53	55.90	29.81%	110.14	0.15	2	44	63460	5	563
CHELTENHAM	385.54	46.95	432.49	114.30	161.25	546.79	275.59	1780.02	534.54	2590.15	271.21	10.47%	1521.15	522.21	1	600	90353	12	545
CRAWLEY	77.11	15.38	92.48	40.88	56.25	133.36	30.46	231.10	59.93	321.49	79.97	24.88%	188.80	-0.68	1	90	67719	8	439
CROYDON	154.21	28.02	182.23	65.73	93.75	247.96	214.89	358.15	151.86	1105.88	137.34	18.95%	425.72	51.21	2	98	211669	16	588
DUDLEY	167.51	21.44	188.95	31.06	52.50	220.01	39.76	834.45	231.67	724.89	134.48	12.16%	649.47	236.41	1	314	157084	18	541
EALING	156.87	23.62	180.49	17.63	41.25	198.12	118.87	578.46	114.21	811.54	115.92	14.28%	476.61	136.81	2	170	267773	9	604
FULHAM	335.02	46.63	381.65	80.87	127.50	462.52	544.62	1327.12	144.25	2015.99	291.85	14.48%	1183.96	369.51	1	162	279657	12	581
GLOUCESTER	79.77	13.70	93.46	12.55	26.25	106.02	92.64	229.41	80.65	402.70	95.20	23.64%	236.50	60.19	2	72	104454	9	603
HAMMERSMITH	178.14	37.47	215.61	63.78	101.25	279.39	145.94	880.28	342.50	1368.71	154.46	11.28%	803.82	285.49	2	296	385321	25	505
HARLOW	148.90	20.31	169.21	118.44	138.75	287.65	106.18	278.41	116.05	-500.63	80.88	16.15%	294.01	-81.03	2	90	81814	9	533
HIGH WYCOMBE	42.54	12.37	54.91	17.63	30.00	72.54	47.80	157.22	0.42	205.44	52.38	25.50%	120.65	12.25	2	90	56661	5	724
HOUNSLOW	164.85	26.98	191.83	63.02	90.00	254.85	127.96	380.07	79.38	587.42	106.40	18.11%	344.98	-12.41	1	116	123923	13	614
ILFORD	122.31	23.54	145.85	298.96	322.50	444.81	135.36	493.16	121.40	749.92	117.57	15.68%	440.42	-135.30	1	214	147296	7	672
KENSINGTON	148.90	29.90	178.80	112.60	142.50	291.40	198.81	973.34	276.08	1448.24	154.50	10.67%	850.53	306.31	2	260	435035	29	476
LEAMINGTON SPA	55.84	14.19	70.03	30.81	45.00	100.84	58.38	199.45	53.16	310.98	72.34	23.26%	182.63	27.51	1	62	31387	5	521

Table 2.1 *(cont.)*

LEICESTER	90.40	18.39	108.80	15.36	33.75	124.15	143.19	247.18	72.90	463.26	102.31	22.09%	272.07	67.04	1	98	189002	11	566
MAIDENHEAD	77.11	17.15	94.25	12.85	30.00	107.11	67.05	256.55	39.06	362.66	79.16	21.83%	212.98	42.57	1	80	32476	4	641
MANCHESTER 1	109.01	19.26	128.27	21.99	41.25	150.26	109.77	292.72	110.97	513.46	97.65	19.02%	301.55	61.65	2	90	160040	10	512
MANCHESTER 2	109.01	21.83	130.84	30.67	52.50	161.51	183.59	312.46	44.19	590.24	128.77	21.82%	346.64	82.09	1	72	174646	4	526
MILTON KEYNES	356.29	45.72	402.01	160.53	206.25	562.54	358.50	537.15	239.99	1135.64	193.29	17.02%	666.94	-93.85	1	90	92375	11	354
NEWCASTLE	382.88	23.23	406.11	70.52	93.75	476.63	346.44	1195.77	271.01	1813.22	242.55	13.38%	1064.88	271.72	1	170	210568	15	575
NORTHAMPTON	148.90	19.98	168.88	36.27	56.25	205.15	133.25	796.81	132.12	1062.17	198.09	18.65%	623.80	233.23	2	162	126483	5	606
OXFORD ST	183.46	31.58	215.05	133.42	165.00	348.46	306.47	543.64	173.43	1023.54	181.46	17.73%	601.11	73.97	2	126	456681	10	595
PLYMOUTH	252.59	31.73	284.32	35.77	67.50	320.09	270.30	641.70	262.12	1174.13	189.95	16.18%	689.55	164.49	1	144	180034	12	540
READING	268.55	26.72	295.27	48.28	75.00	343.55	211.72	1717.62	233.92	2163.26	255.53	11.81%	1270.45	549.27	1	188	125878	11	571
REDDITCH	138.26	18.14	156.40	26.86	45.00	183.26	171.95	754.72	10.43	937.10	122.47	13.07%	550.35	203.50	1	278	62916	5	508
REIGATE	74.45	15.03	89.48	11.22	26.25	100.70	46.53	302.10	91.93	440.56	70.74	16.06%	258.74	81.13	1	134	20000	7	571
SLOUGH	191.44	27.64	219.08	58.61	86.25	277.69	204.74	946.62	195.85	1347.21	161.32	11.97%	791.20	278.33	1	340	123856	7	569
SOLIHULL	111.67	19.63	131.30	36.62	56.25	167.92	139.17	337.28	94.89	571.34	84.37	14.77%	335.54	67.88	1	108	125878	11	599
ST. ALBANS	119.65	11.45	131.09	14.81	26.25	145.90	90.52	464.11	69.37	624.01	99.55	15.95%	366.47	111.64	1	224	51616	6	691
SUTTON COLDFIELD	199.42	29.52	228.93	37.98	67.50	266.92	235.19	757.47	280.45	1273.11	138.48	10.88%	747.68	258.52	2	456	90353	12	598
SWINDON	223.35	29.12	252.46	42.13	71.25	294.60	8.88	1110.26	333.19	1452.33	166.57	11.47%	852.93	304.80	1	242	146214	19	515
TONBRIDGE	71.79	11.31	83.10	22.44	33.75	105.54	105.75	330.65	0.99	437.39	80.54	18.41%	256.87	74.98	2	134	31004	2	609
VICTORIA	329.70	44.08	373.78	188.42	232.50	562.20	284.68	1023.68	294.55	1602.92	173.55	10.83%	941.37	99.35	1	358	421344	30	529
WATFORD	71.79	12.62	84.41	17.38	30.00	101.79	66.62	287.58	30.17	384.37	92.09	23.96%	225.74	56.85	1	72	74370	5	501
WINDSOR	63.81	9.97	73.78	23.78	33.75	97.56	56.89	255.36	0.99	313.24	57.86	18.47%	183.96	31.71	1	108	28519	4	651
WOLVERHAMPTON	172.83	28.62	201.44	20.13	48.75	221.58	167.30	673.36	150.73	991.39	152.47	15.38%	582.23	187.58	1	162	188667	11	533
WOOD GREEN	236.64	34.35	270.99	55.65	90.00	326.64	37.65	1352.99	133.53	1524.17	170.60	11.19%	895.12	302.41	1	162	244938	12	465
YORK	148.90	26.37	175.27	22.38	48.75	197.65	33.42	388.53	145.23	567.18	95.25	16.79%	333.10	36.44	1	80	104528	13	604

Table 2.2 Rankings by indicators

	Rank	Shop Profit	Rank	Profit / Yrs op	Rank	Profit / Capita	Rank	Profit / Capita / Competitor	Rank	Profit / Unit Cost	Rank	Shop Revenue	Rank	Revenue / Yrs op	Rank	Revenue / Capita	Rank	Revenue / Competitor	Rank	Revenue / Unit Cost
READING	1	549.27	1	2.92	2	4.36	2	48.00	1	1.60	2	2163.26	3	11.51	3	17.19	2	189.04	1	6.30
CHELTENHAM	2	522.21	13	0.87	1	5.78	1	69.36	11	0.96	1	2590.15	32	4.32	1	28.67	1	344.01	11	4.74
FULHAM	3	369.51	2	2.28	12	1.32	11	15.86	16	0.80	3	2015.99	2	12.44	16	7.21	12	86.51	16	4.36
KENSINGTON	4	306.31	8	1.18	24	0.70	7	20.42	6	1.05	8	1448.24	20	5.57	38	3.33	10	96.54	6	4.97
SWINDON	5	304.80	7	1.26	9	2.08	3	39.61	7	1.03	7	1452.33	17	6.00	12	9.93	3	188.72	7	4.93
WOOD GREEN	6	302.41	3	1.87	15	1.23	13	14.82	13	0.93	6	1524.17	5	9.41	19	6.22	15	74.67	13	4.67
HAMMERSMITH	7	285.49	12	0.96	22	0.74	9	18.52	8	1.02	9	1368.71	29	4.62	34	3.55	11	88.80	8	4.90
SLOUGH	8	278.33	16	0.82	7	2.25	12	15.73	9	1.00	10	1347.21	34	3.96	11	10.88	14	76.14	9	4.85
NEWCASTLE	9	271.72	5	1.60	14	1.29	8	19.36	20	0.57	4	1813.22	4	10.67	14	8.61	7	129.17	20	3.80
SUTTON COLDFIELD	10	258.52	28	0.57	5	2.86	4	34.33	10	0.97	11	1273.11	43	2.79	6	14.09	4	169.09	10	4.77
BRADFORD	11	239.94	4	1.67	16	1.20	17	10.80	2	1.25	17	1045.89	10	7.26	23	5.23	25	47.06	2	5.46
DUDLEY	12	236.41	19	0.75	11	1.50	6	27.09	5	1.07	14	1105.88	36	3.52	17	7.04	8	126.72	5	5.03
NORTHAMPTON	13	233.23	6	1.44	10	1.84	18	9.22	3	1.14	15	1062.17	14	6.56	15	8.40	29	41.99	3	5.18
REDDITCH	14	203.50	20	0.73	4	3.23	10	16.17	4	1.11	20	937.10	38	3.37	4	14.89	16	74.47	4	5.11
WOLVERHAMPTON	15	187.58	9	1.16	18	0.99	16	10.94	14	0.85	19	991.39	16	6.12	22	5.25	20	57.80	14	4.47
BIRMINGHAM 2	16	169.89	25	0.61	23	0.72	19	8.66	12	0.95	21	846.93	41	3.05	33	3.60	28	43.18	12	4.71
PLYMOUTH	17	164.49	10	1.14	19	0.91	15	10.96	24	0.51	12	1174.13	7	8.15	18	6.52	13	78.26	24	3.67
EALING	18	136.81	17	0.80	27	0.51	26	4.60	19	0.69	22	811.54	27	4.77	41	3.03	38	27.28	19	4.10
ST. ALBANS	19	111.64	33	0.50	8	2.16	14	12.98	17	0.77	27	624.01	44	2.79	8	12.09	17	72.54	17	4.28
VICTORIA	20	99.35	37	0.28	35	0.24	20	7.07	37	0.18	5	1602.92	31	4.48	31	3.80	9	114.13	37	2.85
BRIXTON	21	82.14	30	0.54	33	0.32	34	2.27	33	0.23	16	1050.12	12	6.91	29	4.14	36	29.01	33	2.99

Table 2.2 (cont.)

MANCHESTER 2	22	82.09	11	1.14	28	0.47	36	1.88	25	0.51	29	590.24	6	8.20	37	3.38	45	13.52	25	3.65
REIGATE	23	81.13	26	0.61	3	4.06	5	28.40	15	0.81	36	440.56	39	3.29	2	22.03	5	154.20	15	4.38
BRISTOL	24	79.11	24	0.63	30	0.37	25	4.81	30	0.39	26	678.51	22	5.38	40	3.17	30	41.22	30	3.38
TONBRIDGE	25	74.98	29	0.56	6	2.42	24	4.84	18	0.71	37	437.39	40	3.26	5	14.11	37	28.21	18	4.14
BRENT CROSS	26	73.99	15	0.82	36	0.22	35	2.00	26	0.42	28	611.11	13	6.79	45	1.83	43	16.49	26	3.43
OXFORD ST	27	73.97	27	0.59	38	0.16	38	1.62	34	0.21	18	1023.54	8	8.12	44	2.24	41	22.41	34	2.94
SOLIHULL	28	67.88	23	0.63	26	0.54	21	5.93	28	0.40	31	571.34	24	5.29	28	4.54	23	49.93	28	3.40
LEICESTER	29	67.04	22	0.68	31	0.35	30	3.90	23	0.54	35	463.26	28	4.73	43	2.45	39	26.96	23	3.73
MANCHESTER 1	30	61.65	21	0.68	29	0.39	32	3.85	27	0.41	33	513.46	18	5.71	39	3.21	35	32.08	27	3.42
GLOUCESTER	31	60.19	14	0.84	25	0.58	23	5.19	21	0.57	38	402.70	19	5.59	30	3.86	34	34.70	21	3.80
WATFORD	32	56.85	18	0.79	21	0.76	33	3.82	22	0.56	39	384.37	23	5.34	24	5.17	40	25.84	22	3.78
CROYDON	33	51.21	32	0.52	34	0.24	31	3.87	35	0.21	25	724.89	9	7.40	36	3.42	22	54.79	35	2.92
MAIDENHEAD	34	42.57	31	0.53	13	1.31	22	5.24	29	0.40	40	362.66	30	4.53	9	11.17	26	44.67	29	3.39
YORK	35	36.44	34	0.46	32	0.35	27	4.53	36	0.18	32	567.18	11	7.09	21	5.43	18	70.54	36	2.87
BIRMINGHAM 1	36	34.00	38	0.27	39	0.15	37	1.66	39	0.12	23	798.00	15	6.33	35	3.54	31	38.90	39	2.70
WINDSOR	37	31.71	36	0.29	17	1.11	28	4.45	31	0.33	42	313.24	42	2.90	10	10.98	27	43.93	31	3.21
LEAMINGTON SPA	38	27.51	35	0.44	20	0.88	29	4.38	32	0.27	43	310.98	26	5.02	13	9.91	24	49.54	32	3.08
HIGH WYCOMBE	39	12.25	39	0.14	37	0.22	39	1.08	38	0.17	44	205.44	45	2.28	32	3.63	42	18.13	38	2.83
BROMLEY	40	0.15	40	0.00	40	0.00	40	0.01	40	0.00	45	187.53	33	4.26	42	2.96	44	14.78	40	2.43
CRAWLEY	41	-0.68	41	-0.01	41	-0.01	41	-0.08	41	-0.01	41	321.49	35	3.57	26	4.75	32	37.98	41	2.41
HOUNSLOW	42	-12.41	42	-0.11	42	-0.10	42	-1.30	42	-0.05	30	587.42	25	5.06	27	4.74	19	61.62	42	2.30
HARLOW	43	-81.03	44	-0.90	44	-0.99	44	-8.91	44	-0.28	34	500.63	21	5.56	20	6.12	21	55.07	44	1.74
MILTON KEYNES	44	-93.85	45	-1.04	45	-1.02	45	-11.18	43	-0.17	13	1135.64	1	12.62	7	12.29	6	135.23	43	2.02
ILFORD	45	-135.30	43	-0.63	43	-0.92	43	-6.43	45	-0.30	24	749.92	37	3.50	25	5.09	33	35.64	45	1.69

resources—whilst at the same time presenting an overall picture. Unclear as to how to present the overall picture, they generated different indicators of performance each based on two factors, such as: profit per capita; profit per capita adjusted for competition; profit per year of operation; and profit per unit cost of resource. They then ranked shops according to each of the indicators and compared the rankings. Table 2.2 shows the results of this analysis.

The analysts were surprised at the extent to which different indicators can present a very different picture. Whilst a few shops have consistently high rankings and a few have consistently low rankings, the majority exhibit considerable variation depending on the indicator chosen. As a result, the analysts were even more unclear as to how to present the overall picture.

At this point, the shop managers were delighted with the analysts' progress because, in the majority of cases, a shop manager could identify an indicator which presented him in a reasonably good light. For example, the Milton Keynes manager now has documentary evidence for his claim to the best growth record in the entire company given the time his shop has been in operation. He agrees that his costs are high but argues that this has been essential to the growth achieved. He further argues that he would not look so bad even on a profit basis if he did not have to bear excessive building costs which he can do nothing about. Similarly, the Reigate manager now has support for his claim that he has achieved miracles given his exceptionally low catchment population.

It became essential that the analysis be completed to form an accurate overall picture, otherwise it would have a counterproductive effect on the company since a manager would use isolated statistics to argue more vehemently about the inadequacies of the shop profit measure currently used to assess his performance. As a result, he would refute criticism and resist pressure to effect changes to improve his shop's performance.

Seeking the overall picture whilst taking all important factors into account is the main theme around which this book is developed. However, before proceeding with further quantitative analysis, we need to review the advantages and disadvantages of the company's existing methods.

In terms of assessing the value of a shop, rather than that of a manager, the senior management approach has some merit. The external factors which influence a shop's profit cannot be changed; hence if a shop is not profitable it may well be best to close it. However, there is a need to determine whether the poor performance is due solely to external factors or whether there is scope for improved performance, for example through better management or through time when the shop has been in operation longer and become more established. Measuring shop profit alone cannot answer these questions.

In terms of assessing shop manager performance, the first step is to establish whether or not external factors do influence shop profit. If they do, it is almost certain that the growth potential is greater for some shop managers than for others and it is unfair to assess their performance on the basis of achieving a uniform growth target. Measuring shop profit alone gives no indication of realistic targets. Further, whatever target is set, there is still the question of what level of resource is required to achieve it. Again, shop profit does not inform this decision.

In summary, measuring shop profit alone does not indicate: (a) how well a shop is being managed where external factors influence its profitability; (b) the potential for improvement that may exist; (c) realistic targets; (d) which shops would benefit most from additional resources.

Alternatively, in the words of Chapter 1, we need to understand: 'How well are they doing?' and 'How much better could they do?'. The objective for our quantitative analysis is therefore to provide answers to these questions. Further, in order to relate directly to company objectives, our analysis must be primarily concerned with improving profit performance. Finally within this context, we have the problem with which the company's analysts were faced: to analyse the data in depth in order to understand the underlying relationships but at the same time present an overall picture.

2.3   A SIMPLE TWO-FACTOR COST EFFICIENCY MODEL

Profit is the difference between revenue and cost. Hence if we say a shop could have done better in terms of profit, it must be as a result of either:

(a)   achieving the same revenue at reduced cost through more efficient use of resources, or
(b)   achieving greater revenue through increased market penetration without incurring more than a directly proportional increase in cost.

We will look at these initially as two separate problems. Let us begin with the problem: 'For the level of revenue achieved, what level of cost should have been incurred?' We will refer to this as cost efficiency. One of the company analysts' ratios presented in Table 2.2 was Total revenue/Total cost. The analysts' ranking for this ratio tells us that Reading had the highest ratio. In other words, based on this ratio, Reading is the most efficient generator of revenue.

We could use this ratio to generate a measure of the other shops' efficiencies by comparing them directly to Reading's. For example, if we

Table 2.3 Cost efficiency

	Rank	Total revenue/ Total cost	Efficiency
READING	1	6.30	1.000
BRADFORD	2	5.46	0.866
NORTHAMPTON	3	5.18	0.822
REDDITCH	4	5.11	0.812
DUDLEY	5	5.03	0.798
KENSINGTON	6	4.97	0.789
SWINDON	7	4.93	0.783
HAMMERSMITH	8	4.90	0.778
SLOUGH	9	4.85	0.770
SUTTON COLDFIELD	10	4.77	0.757
CHELTENHAM	11	4.74	0.752
BIRMINGHAM 2	12	4.71	0.749
WOOD GREEN	13	4.67	0.741
WOLVERHAMPTON	14	4.47	0.711
REIGATE	15	4.38	0.695
FULHAM	16	4.36	0.692
ST. ALBANS	17	4.28	0.679
TONBRIDGE	18	4.14	0.658
EALING	19	4.10	0.651
NEWCASTLE	20	3.80	0.604
GLOUCESTER	21	3.80	0.603
WATFORD	22	3.78	0.600
LEICESTER	23	3.73	0.593
PLYMOUTH	24	3.67	0.583
MANCHESTER 2	25	3.65	0.580
BRENT CROSS	26	3.43	0.545
MANCHESTER 1	27	3.42	0.543
SOLIHULL	28	3.40	0.540
MAIDENHEAD	29	3.39	0.538
BRISTOL	30	3.38	0.536
WINDSOR	31	3.21	0.510
LEAMINGTON SPA	32	3.08	0.490
BRIXTON	33	2.99	0.475
OXFORD ST	34	2.94	0.466
CROYDON	35	2.92	0.464
YORK	36	2.87	0.456
VICTORIA	37	2.85	0.453
HIGH WYCOMBE	38	2.83	0.450
BIRMINGHAM 1	39	2.70	0.429
BROMLEY	40	2.43	0.386
CRAWLEY	41	2.41	0.383
HOUNSLOW	42	2.30	0.366
MILTON KEYNES	43	2.02	0.321
HARLOW	44	1.74	0.276
ILFORD	45	1.69	0.268

divide all shops' ratios by Reading's ratio, we achieve a scale of efficiency with maximum efficiency carrying a score of 1. This efficiency measure is shown in Table 2.3.

In line with our stated objective, we can use Reading's ratio to set, for any shop, either a revenue target for a given level of cost or a cost budget for a given level of revenue. We can justify the target, or budget, on the grounds that it is based on actual achieved performance. Further, we know the identity of the shop (Reading) which determines best performance. In future we will refer to a shop such as Reading as a 'reference shop'.

Two points need clarifying at this stage. The first is that by the term 'best performance', we mean best achieved performance, and we use this as a threshold against which to measure all other performance. This does not imply that the best cannot improve but does imply there is no demonstrable basis against which to measure the extent to which they can improve. Throughout the book, our analysis will always be concerned with measurement against demonstrable achievement.

The second point is that we are using the words 'target' and 'budget' to represent what is achievable. They could be appropriate in setting a manager's annual target or budget but only if the analysis is designed specifically for that purpose. For example, it would not be reasonable to target a manager on the basis of a model which assessed efficiency in terms of a shop's *Total revenue* relative to its market characteristics since current achievement could be a long way from best performance and a year may be an unreasonable timescale in which to redress the balance. It would, however, be reasonable to target a manager on the basis of a model which assessed efficiency in terms of *Revenue growth* achieved in the last year. We will return to this point in Chapter 6.

As a platform for further development, let us look at the above efficiency model graphically. Figure 2.1 shows, for all the shops, *Total revenue* plotted against *Total cost*. The straight line through Reading and the origin denotes all points equal in efficiency (under our current definition) to that of Reading. The line can be regarded as an efficiency frontier since all points below the line have a lower *Total revenue/Total cost* ratio and hence lower efficiency. In the figure, all other shops appear below this line, thus confirming that Reading is the most efficient of the shops.

Our efficiency measures in Table 2.3 can be determined directly from the graph. For example, the efficiency of Fulham (=0.692) is given by either of the ratios AB/AC or DE/DB. [Elementary geometry establishes that each of these ratios is equal to the ratio OE/OC and hence the two ratios themselves are equal.] The significance of the ratio AB/AC is that it expresses the *Total revenue* achieved by Fulham as a proportion of that which it would achieve at the same *Total cost* if it were efficient. Similarly the ratio DE/DB is the *Total cost* at which Fulham could achieve its current *Total revenue* if it were

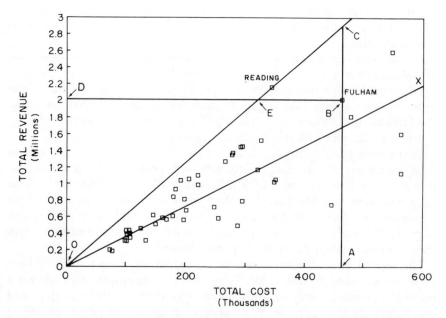

Figure 2.1 Efficiency: revenue versus cost

efficient expressed as a proportion of the cost at which it actually achieves it.

The point C represents the desired performance of Fulham if it is targeted to achieve the best *Total revenue* given its current level of *Total cost*. Alternatively, the point E represents the desired performance of Fulham if it is budgeted to operate at the lowest *Total cost* at which its current level of *Total revenue* can be achieved.

It should be noted that this development assumes constant returns to scale which implies that an increase in *Total cost* is matched by a proportionate increase in *Total revenue* irrespective of the value of *Total cost* from which the increase occurs. We will continue under this assumption for the present to avoid the additional complication of variable returns to scale in the initial development. We will return to consider increasing and decreasing returns to scale in Chapter 5.

A further point to note is that regression analysis, represented by the line OX in Figure 2.1, establishes a target level of *Total revenue* for a given level of *Total cost* based on average performance. It gives no information about best performance.

In terms of our analytical objectives, the above development provides suitable information on how well the shops are doing and what their potential is, thereby enabling us to set targets and budgets based on actual achievement. The method is still deficient, however, in terms of the number of factors which it takes into account. We could not confirm or deny any of the shop manager's arguments on the basis of our analysis to date. The next step, therefore, is to identify the additional factors which influence performance.

2.4   THE INFLUENCE OF OTHER FACTORS

If we have excluded a factor which influences performance from our efficiency measure, then our measure of efficiency must be biased in relation to that factor. We would expect, therefore, to observe a high statistical correlation between that factor and our measure of efficiency. However, we cannot conclude that a factor influences performance from the observation of a high statistical correlation alone. There must also be a logical causal relationship to explain why the factor influences performance. If we reject the existence of a causal relationship, this should be based on a logical explanation of the statistical relationship.

Table 2.4   Correlations of factors with cost efficiency

Factor	Correlation
Profit	0.86002
Revenue Gp2	0.61688
Revenue % growth	−0.53137
Total revenue	0.52867
Central overheads	0.52867
Age of shop (months)	0.49182
Revenue growth	0.40681
Uncontrollable cost	−0.39918
Non-staff cost	−0.34921
Revenue Gp3	0.34264
Staff cost	0.18650
Controllable cost	0.17996
Competition	0.16306
Customer service	−0.11465
Catchment population	0.09529
Non-staff controllable cost	0.09423
Pitch	−0.08051
Total cost	−0.04119
Revenue Gp1	0.03733

   A useful first step is to collect data on possible influencing factors as the company analysts did and then evaluate the correlation of each factor with the current efficiency measure (this will be referred to as Step 1). Table 2.4 shows the value of the correlation of each of the data items in Table 2.2

with the current efficiency measure. The table is presented in descending order of the strength of correlation. The inter-factor correlations are shown in Table 2.5 and will be used to supplement the arguments below.

Let us consider the logic behind the higher correlations observed in Table 2.4.

Profit—The high correlation here is attributable to the fact that for any shop, the lower its *Total cost* relative to its *Total revenue*, the higher its *Profit*. Hence higher efficiency is associated with greater profitability. However, efficiency causes profitability rather than the reverse.

Revenue Gp2—A causal relationship here would imply that less cost is required to generate a unit of revenue from product group 2 than from other product groups. However, for this to be the case there must be a matching negative correlation between efficiency and revenue from another product group, which is not the case. It is therefore likely that the revenue group correlations currently observed are merely effects of the correlations between revenue from product groups and *Total revenue*. [It will be seen in Chapter 4 that a causal relationship here does become apparent once other influences are taken into account.]

Revenue % growth—A causal relationship here would imply that more resource is required per unit of revenue for shops with a higher percentage growth. This is consistent with there being additional promotion and selling effort required to achieve higher growth. Further, as the correlation is negative, the relationship cannot be attributed to the correlation between *Revenue growth* and *Total revenue*.

Total revenue—A causal relationship could exist if there were significantly increasing returns to scale. In that event, there would also be a strong relationship between efficiency and *Total cost*, which is not present in this case. This is further confirmed by Figure 2.1, where there is no obvious suggestion of either increasing or decreasing returns to scale. The correlation with *Total revenue* can therefore only be representative of variation in revenue which is not explained by cost.

Age of shop—There is no obvious reason why an older shop should require more resource to generate a unit of *Total revenue*. The relationship is likely to be the effect of the high correlation between *Age of shop* and *Total revenue*, which in turn is correlated with our efficiency measure.

Non-staff cost—This is negatively correlated with our efficiency measure whilst *Staff cost* is weakly positively correlated. This would imply a causal

Table 2.5 Correlations between factors

	1	2	3	4	5	6	7	8	9	10	11	12	13	14	15	16	17	18	19	
	1.000	0.840	0.999	0.431	0.523	0.915	0.747	0.796	0.773	0.881	0.883	-0.608	0.881	0.540	-0.227	0.511	0.348	0.487	-0.298	1 Staff cost
		1.000	0.869	0.520	0.628	0.858	0.701	0.663	0.758	0.772	0.774	-0.572	0.772	0.421	-0.091	0.494	0.549	0.599	-0.364	2 Non-staff controllable cost
			1.000	0.447	0.541	0.922	0.753	0.794	0.782	0.883	0.885	-0.613	0.883	0.536	-0.216	0.517	0.373	0.505	-0.309	3 Controllable cost
				1.000	0.991	0.758	0.409	0.267	0.369	0.348	0.353	-0.307	0.348	-0.148	0.007	0.263	0.393	0.311	-0.059	4 Uncontrollable cost
					1.000	0.823	0.481	0.345	0.453	0.436	0.441	-0.368	0.436	-0.070	-0.008	0.316	0.443	0.376	-0.110	5 Non-staff cost
						1.000	0.726	0.694	0.730	0.794	0.798	-0.580	0.794	0.327	-0.155	0.491	0.442	0.503	-0.251	6 Total cost
							1.000	0.471	0.442	0.626	0.757	-0.326	0.626	0.315	-0.043	0.271	0.419	0.278	-0.128	7 Revenue Gp1
								1.000	0.743	0.973	0.866	-0.736	0.973	0.883	-0.208	0.675	0.335	0.441	-0.210	8 Revenue Gp2
									1.000	0.829	0.705	-0.684	0.829	0.626	-0.035	0.739	0.410	0.672	-0.321	9 Revenue Gp3
										1.000	0.922	-0.739	1.000	0.834	-0.168	0.694	0.408	0.510	-0.243	10 Total revenue
											1.000	-0.534	0.922	0.709	-0.162	0.458	0.408	0.365	-0.198	11 Revenue growth
												1.000	-0.739	-0.623	0.124	-0.724	-0.419	-0.561	0.182	12 Revenue % growth
													1.000	0.834	-0.168	0.694	0.408	0.510	-0.243	13 Central overheads
														1.000	-0.121	0.634	0.233	0.337	-0.149	14 Profit
															1.000	-0.035	0.228	0.041	0.134	15 Pitch
																1.000	0.175	0.421	-0.108	16 Age of shop (months)
																	1.000	0.678	-0.134	17 Catchment population
																		1.000	-0.337	18 Competition
																			1.000	19 Customer service

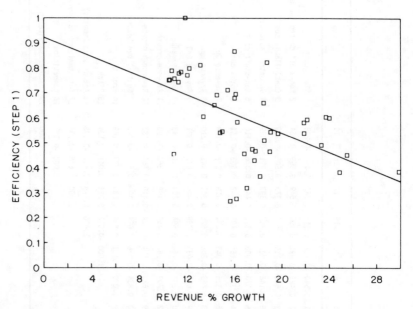

Figure 2.2 Step 1 efficiency versus revenue percentage growth

relationship indicating that expenditure on staff appears to be more revenue productive than other expenditure.

Hence in examining the relationships between our efficiency measure and other factors, the strongest causal relationship which we can identify at this stage is with *Revenue % growth*. A graph of this relationship is shown in Figure 2.2.

2.5 INCORPORATING AN ADDITIONAL FACTOR—A GRAPHICAL APPROACH

Let us now consider the implications of the relationship between our efficiency measure and *Revenue % growth*. It establishes that the value of the ratio of *Total revenue* to *Total cost* (our efficiency measure) is higher where a greater proportion of *Total revenue* is attributable to growth. In other words, greater cost must be associated with generating one unit of *Revenue growth* than with maintaining one unit of *Total revenue*. Therefore, in order to reflect this in our measure of efficiency, we must take separate account of *Total revenue* and *Revenue growth*. However, we cannot establish which element of cost went into *Revenue growth* and which to maintaining *Total revenue*. Hence we are left to assess efficiency where two distinct outputs are produced from a single input.

We can produce a graphical representation of the problem by again assuming constant returns to scale and plotting each of these two outputs divided by the input. The resulting graph is shown in Figure 2.3. The boundary formed by the straight line joining the two shops, Reading and Northampton, together with horizontal and vertical lines to the axes, envelops the remaining shops in a manner such that any point on the boundary performs better than any point within the boundary. This can be demonstrated, for example, by the Newcastle shop in Figure 2.3. By increasing the Newcastle shop's outputs in the same proportion, we move along the extension of the line OA until we arrive at the point B on the boundary. This is the basis of the Farrell method referred to in Section 1.6. Farrell [5] refers to the envelope as the 'unit isoquant'. We will refer to the envelope as the efficiency frontier—hence the term frontier analysis. In this case our frontier is determined by only two shops. In general, it could be determined by any number of shops; for example, see Figure 3.4.

For the reasons given above, the frontier represents a standard of best performance. Let us consider what the frontier means in terms of achieved performance. Clearly the points on the frontier determined by the shops Reading and Northampton represent demonstrable achieved performance. Further, Reading's performance is superior to that represented by any

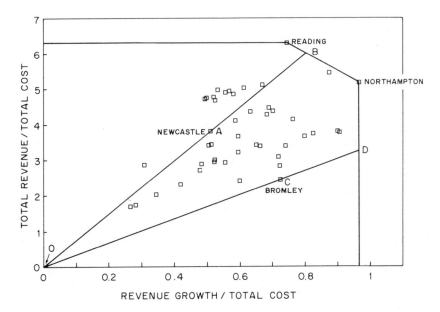

Figure 2.3 Frontier analysis

point on the horizontal line from Reading to the axis and Northampton's performance is superior to that represented by any point on the vertical line from Northampton to the axis. Hence any point on either of these two lines must be achievable. In the case of the straight line joining Reading and Northampton, we assume that given the end points are achievable, the points on the line between are achievable. This is a reasonable assumption implying that for shops operating at maximum efficiency, there is trade-off between the two outputs represented by the straight line. Hence, subject only to the latter assumption, the frontier is a frontier of best performance substantiated by actual achieved performance. This statement will remain true for all analyses conducted in the course of this book and is of critical importance in gaining management acceptance for the analysis and results.

We can also use the graphical representation of Figure 2.3 to update our measure of efficiency to reflect accurately the distinction between *Total revenue* and *Revenue growth*. Referring again to the performance of the Newcastle shop, we have already observed that by increasing its outputs in the same proportion, we move along the extension of the line OA until we arrive at the point B on the frontier. We can therefore measure the Newcastle shop's efficiency as the ratio OA/OB, that is, the output per unit input currently being achieved expressed as a proportion of that which is achievable.

Further, we can set an output target for the Newcastle shop to be the output which, given its current level of input, would give it the same output/input ratio as the point B. Alternatively, we could set a budget for the Newcastle shop as the input which, given its current output, would give it the same output/input ratio as the point B. Further, as with our previous efficiency measure, we can define 'reference shops', in this case Reading and Northampton upon whose actual achieved performance the target point B is based.

Note that whereas in the case of the original efficiency measure all shops had the same reference shop, this is no longer the case. Newcastle has two reference shops, but we can see from Figure 2.3 that Bromley's efficiency is established by reference to the point D which is determined by Northampton's performance only.

Note, too, that the cases of Newcastle and Bromley are also different in another respect. In the case of Newcastle, suppose we were to seek a further increase in either one of the output/input ratios from that given by our target point B. This can only be achieved by moving from the target point B. However, we cannot move beyond the frontier as this would be beyond the bounds of demonstrable achieved performance. Remaining on the frontier necessitates a trade-off between the outputs, which becomes a question of *objectives* rather than *efficiency*.

The same argument is not true for Bromley since the *Total revenue/Total*

Table 2.6 Step 2 efficiency measure

	Step-two efficiency score	Step-one efficiency score
READING	1.000	1.000
NORTHAMPTON	1.000	0.822
BRADFORD	0.980	0.866
WATFORD	0.937	0.600
GLOUCESTER	0.930	0.603
LEICESTER	0.853	0.593
REDDITCH	0.844	0.812
MANCHESTER 2	0.826	0.580
DUDLEY	0.807	0.798
TONBRIDGE	0.796	0.658
KENSINGTON	0.792	0.789
WOLVERHAMPTON	0.791	0.711
REIGATE	0.788	0.695
SWINDON	0.784	0.783
HAMMERSMITH	0.779	0.778
SLOUGH	0.774	0.770
ST. ALBANS	0.768	0.679
MAIDENHEAD	0.765	0.538
SUTTON COLDFIELD	0.760	0.757
CHELTENHAM	0.756	0.752
BIRMINGHAM 2	0.752	0.749
FULHAM	0.751	0.692
BROMLEY	0.749	0.386
HIGH WYCOMBE	0.748	0.450
LEAMINGTON SPA	0.743	0.490
WOOD GREEN	0.743	0.741
EALING	0.701	0.651
BRISTOL	0.686	0.536
MANCHESTER 1	0.673	0.543
PLYMOUTH	0.663	0.583
NEWCASTLE	0.634	0.604
CRAWLEY	0.621	0.383
WINDSOR	0.617	0.510
BRENT CROSS	0.598	0.545
SOLIHULL	0.591	0.540
CROYDON	0.574	0.464
BRIXTON	0.559	0.475
OXFORD ST	0.554	0.466
YORK	0.528	0.456
BIRMINGHAM 1	0.508	0.429
VICTORIA	0.454	0.453
HOUNSLOW	0.439	0.366
MILTON KEYNES	0.373	0.321
HARLOW	0.314	0.276
ILFORD	0.300	0.268

cost ratio can be increased without detriment to the *Revenue growth / Total cost* ratio by moving from the point D until the point representing the Northampton shop itself is reached.

Hence the target for Bromley is based on the Northampton shop rather than the point D. However, the efficiency measure for Bromley must remain the ratio OC/OD. The reason for this is discussed in depth in Chapter 3. We refer to the additional improvement possible in *Total revenue / Total cost* in moving from the point D to the point representing the Northampton shop as the 'slack' for that output.

The methodology just described allows us to calculate a new efficiency score for each shop which we will refer to as the Step 2 efficiency measure. The Step 2 scores are shown in Table 2.6 together with the original efficiency score. We are now in a similar position to that encountered when we produced the original efficiency measure. We have a measure of efficiency but need to know which further factors, if any, should be taken into account. We must therefore perform a correlation analysis for our Step 2 measure, identical to that conducted earlier for the original measure. Table 2.7 shows the value of the correlations in descending order of strength.

Table 2.7 Correlations of factors with Step 2 efficiency measure

Factor	Correlation
Uncontrollable cost	−0.65944
Non-staff cost	−0.64242
Profit	0.58094
Total cost	−0.43175
Non-staff controllable cost	−0.26972
Revenue Gp2	0.22178
Controllable cost	−0.20138
Staff cost	−0.19070
Revenue Gp1	−0.17448
Competition	−0.16067
Catchment population	−0.15084
Total revenue	0.12112
Central overheads	0.12112
Age of shop (months)	0.11225
Revenue growth	0.10513
Revenue % growth	0.05389
Revenue Gp3	−0.04331
Customer service	−0.02655
Pitch	−0.01444

However, we will postpone an in-depth analysis of the correlations until Chapter 4. What is immediately apparent from the correlations is that the component parts of cost and revenue appear to be significant. Hence, irrespective of the exact way in which we decide to proceed, it is clear that our analysis methodology must cater for additional outputs and inputs. It is this problem which we will address first.

In generating our Step 2 efficiency measure, we were able to proceed graphically. Once an additional factor is added this will no longer be possible and we will be totally dependent on mathematics. Provided that we can establish a mathematical analogy between the two-dimensional case and cases with higher numbers of dimensions, our interpretation of the results will be aided by our conceptual understanding of the two-dimensional case.

This will therefore be the theme for developing our methodology. Chapter 3 begins with the mathematics of the two-dimensional case and then generalises the approach to cater for more dimensions. Chapter 3 will be useful to the reader who wishes to gain an appreciation of the underlying mathematics, but the reader wishing to follow only the general development of the case study may prefer to proceed directly to Chapter 4.

Chapter 3

Simple Mathematical Development

3.1 THE EFFICIENCY FRONTIER—GENERAL CASE

The mathematical development centres around the mathematics of our efficiency measure generated from the graphical development based on the Farrell approach shown in Figure 2.3.

Let us begin by summarizing the graphical development. We began by plotting each output divided by the input. From the resultant graph we were able to define a frontier of best achieved performance. For any shop not on the frontier, we can identify a target point on the frontier which represents what that shop could be achieving. We measure the efficiency of each shop in relation to its target point. We can identify 'reference shops' for each inefficient shop. These are the shops whose performance determines the inefficient shop's target point.

In the case of the Newcastle shop, the target was the point B on the frontier and the Newcastle shop's efficiency was given by the ratio OA/OB. Our mathematical requirement therefore is to calculate the ratio OA/OB.

This will be done by reference to Figure 3.1 which replicates the appropriate features of Figure 2.3. Simple geometry establishes that the ratio OA/OB is the same as the ratio OC/OD. The point D is given by the line BD obtained by extending the line joining Northampton and Reading to the Y-axis. The point C is given by the intercept on the Y-axis of the line AC drawn parallel to BD through the point A (Newcastle). The equation of the line BD is

$$Y = 10.050 - 5.046X \tag{3.1}$$

where Y is *Total revenue/Total cost*, X is *Revenue growth/Total cost*, -5.046 is the slope of the line, and 10.050 is the value of the intercept of the line on the Y-axis (OD). The equation of the line AC is

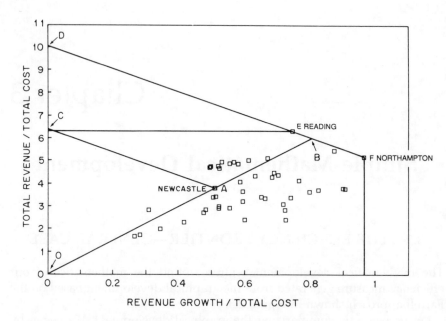

Figure 3.1 Newcastle efficiency calculation

$$Y = 6.372 - 5.046X \tag{3.2}$$

where 6.372 is the value of the intercept of the line on the Y-axis (OC). Hence our measure of Newcastle's efficiency is given by

$$\frac{OA}{OB} = \frac{OC}{OD} = \frac{6.372}{10.050} = 0.634$$

which is the value shown in Table 2.6.

Let us explore these equations further. For the purpose of generalization, let us denote the coordinates of the shops Newcastle, Reading and Northampton as $(X(\text{Ne}), Y(\text{Ne}))$, $(X(\text{R}), Y(\text{R}))$ and $(X(\text{Nh}), Y(\text{Nh}))$ respectively. Then, by substitution and adjustment using equation 3.2 we have

$$OC = 6.372 = Y(\text{Ne}) + 5.046\, X(\text{Ne}) \tag{3.3}$$

and by substitution and adjustment using equation 3.1 we have

$$OD = 10.050 = Y(\text{R}) + 5.046\, X(\text{R}) \tag{3.4}$$

$$OD = 10.050 = Y(\text{Nh}) + 5.046\, X(\text{Nh}) \tag{3.5}$$

Dividing all three of these equations by OD (=10.050) and switching the left and right hand sides of the equations gives us

$$0.0995\, Y(Ne) + 0.502\, X(Ne) = \frac{OC}{OD} = \frac{6.372}{10.050} = 0.634$$

$$0.0995\, Y(R) + 0.502\, X(R) = \frac{OD}{OD} = 1$$

$$0.0995\, Y(Nh) + 0.502\, X(Nh) = \frac{OD}{OD} = 1$$

We originally obtained the X and Y values by dividing each shop's outputs by its input. Let us define $O_1(Ne)$ and $O_2(Ne)$ to be the Newcastle shop's outputs and $I(Ne)$ to be its input and assume similar notation for the other shops. Hence we have

$$Y(Ne) = \frac{O_1(Ne)}{I(Ne)} \quad \text{and} \quad X(Ne) = \frac{O_2(Ne)}{I(Ne)}$$

Similar relationships exist for the Reading and Northampton shops. Substituting these in the above equations gives

$$\frac{0.0995\, O_1(Ne) + 0.502\, O_2(Ne)}{I(Ne)} = 0.634$$

$$\frac{0.0995\, O_1(R) + 0.502\, O_2(R)}{I(R)} = 1$$

$$\frac{0.0995\, O_1(Nh) + 0.502\, O_2(Nh)}{I(Nh)} = 1$$

Finally, we can constrain the denominator of the first of these equations to 1 by dividing both the numerator and denominator of the equations by the value of $I(Ne)$ (=476.63). This gives

$$\frac{0.000208\, O_1(Ne) + 0.00105\, O_2(Ne)}{0.00210\, I(Ne)} = 0.634$$

$$\frac{0.000208\, O_1(R) + 0.00105\, O_2(R)}{0.00210\, I(R)} = 1$$

$$\frac{0.000208\, O_1(Nh) + 0.00105\, O_2(Nh)}{0.00210\, I(Nh)} = 1$$

The purpose of this constraint is to accord with the solution procedure described in Appendix A.

Thus we have expressed our efficiency measure for Newcastle (0.634) as the ratio of a weighted sum of its outputs and a weighted sum of its inputs whilst restricting the value of the weighted sum of inputs to 1. Further, the value of the weighted sum ratio obtained using the same weights for either of Newcastle's reference shops, Reading or Northampton, is 1.

Note that all other shops lie below and to the left of the line BD and by analogy with the Newcastle analysis would have a weighted sum ratio less than 1 with the above weights. Hence the shops with a weighted sum ratio of 1 match exactly the reference shops identified for Newcastle's by the graphical approach and no shop has a weighted sum ratio greater than 1.

Also, since all of the inputs and outputs have positive values, it is clear by direct inspection of the ratios that, if we increase either of the output weights or decrease the input weight in order to increase the value of the ratio for Newcastle, then an identical change to either the Reading or Northampton ratio will cause it to exceed the value 1. Hence the weights obtained maximize the value of a weighted sum ratio of this form when the constraint is imposed that the same weighted ratio of any other shop's outputs to inputs must not exceed the value 1.

In summary, we have demonstrated that our graphical efficiency measure for the Newcastle shop obtained from Figure 2.3 is equivalent to the value of the ratio of a weighted sum of its outputs and a weighted sum of its inputs where the weights are selected to maximize the value of the ratio subject to the value of the same weighted ratio of any other shop's outputs and inputs not exceeding 1. This is identical to the Data Envelopment Analysis (DEA) formulation set out in Appendix A and relates to the general statement in Section 1.7.

The name Data Envelopment Analysis stems directly from the graphical process which we have observed in that the frontier envelops the other data points. In fact, the frontier is often referred to as the envelope.

Let us now consider further how the weights should be interpreted. If we return to equations 3.3, 3.4 and 3.5, we see that the coefficients of Y and X in each case are respectively 1 and 5.046, where the latter is the negative of the slope of the line BD. In the subsequent development to generate the ratio of weighted sums, the output weights were maintained in this proportion. In other words, the ratio of the output weights is equal to the slope of the line on the frontier which contains the point against which efficiency is measured. As already pointed out in Chapter 2, this slope represents the trade-off between the two outputs at that point. Hence the efficiency score indicates what is required for a shop to operate at maximum efficiency with its outputs maintained in their existing proportion whilst the ratio of the output weights indicates the rate of trade-off between the outputs of a shop which will maintain that efficiency.

Note that any other shop within the triangle OEF would also be measured with respect to a point on the line EF, and hence a further consequence of the above result is that all shops in the triangle OEF have weights in the same proportion. Further, if there were another shop within this sector and also on the line AC, equations 3.3, 3.4 and 3.5 for this shop would be identical to those for Newcastle, resulting in an identical efficiency score being achieved. Hence efficiency contours exist and are parallel to the frontier.

It is critical to recognize that the weights represent the trade-offs which apply across a frontier segment rather than the common misconception that they reflect the importance of particular inputs or outputs. However, by virtue of the fact that these weights maximize the weighted sum ratio within the constraints imposed, we can be certain that no shop will ever be presented in a better light by any alternative method of weighting, and clearly this will include the case where weights are chosen to reflect the importance of inputs and outputs. Equivalently, we can be certain that DEA will never overestimate improvement potential relative to that identified by any other weighting method.

3.2 THE EFFICIENCY FRONTIER—AN ALTERNATIVE VIEW

We can develop mathematics relating to our efficiency measure from another perspective. Again, if we consider the efficiency of the Newcastle shop, we can consider the mathematics of its target point B on the line EF. Using the same notation as in Section 3.1, we have by definition,

$$(X(R), Y(R)) = \left(\frac{O_2(R)}{I(R)}, \frac{O_1(R)}{I(R)} \right)$$

$$= \left(\frac{255.53}{343.55}, \frac{2163.26}{343.55} \right) = (0.744, 6.297)$$

and

$$(X(Nh), Y(Nh)) = \left(\frac{O_2(Nh)}{I(Nh)}, \frac{O_1(Nh)}{I(Nh)} \right)$$

$$= \left(\frac{198.09}{205.15}, \frac{1062.17}{205.15} \right) = (0.966, 5.178)$$

The point $(X(B), Y(B))$ lies on the line EF which is given by equation 3.1 in Section 3.1; hence $(X(B), Y(B))$ satisfies

$$Y(B) = 10.050 - 5.046 \, X(B)$$

The point $(X(B), Y(B))$ also lies on the line OB. OB has a zero intercept since it passes through the origin and its slope is given by the coordinates of the point A (Newcastle) since it passes through that point also. Hence the equation of the line OB is

$$Y = \frac{1813.22}{242.55} X = 7.476 X$$

and hence $(X(B), Y(B))$ must also satisfy

$$Y(B) = 7.476 \, X(B)$$

Combining these two equations gives

$$7.476 \, X(B) = 10.050 - 5.046 \, X(B)$$

Hence $X(B) = 0.803$ and $Y(B) = 7.476 \times 0.803 = 6.000$.

It is a fact of elementary mathematics that if a point Z lies on the line PQ, we can express the coordinates of the point Z in terms of the coordinates of the points P and Q in the form

$$(X(Z), Y(Z)) = K_1 \times (X(P), Y(P)) + K_2 \times (X(Q), Y(Q))$$

where $K_1 + K_2 = 1$. Hence we can express the coordinates of the point B in terms of Newcastle's reference shops, Reading and Northampton, in the form

$$(X(B), Y(B)) = K_1 \times (X(R), Y(R)) + K_2 \times (X(Nh), Y(Nh))$$

From this we deduce

$$X(B) = K_1 \times X(R) + (1 - K_1) \times X(Nh)$$

that is

$$0.803 = K_1 \times 0.743 + (1 - K_1) \times 0.966$$

$$= K_1 \times (0.743 - 0.966) + 0.966$$

Hence

$$K_1 = \frac{0.803 - 0.966}{0.743 - 0.966} = \frac{-0.163}{-0.222} = 0.735$$

and hence $K_2 = 0.265$. Thus we have

$$(X(B), Y(B)) = 0.735 \times (X(R), Y(R)) + 0.265 \times (X(Nh), Y(Nh))$$

or equivalently

$$\left(\frac{O_2(B)}{I(B)}, \frac{O_1(B)}{I(B)}\right) = 0.735 \times \left(\frac{O_2(R)}{I(R)}, \frac{O_1(R)}{I(R)}\right) + 0.265 \times \left(\frac{O_2(Nh)}{I(Nh)}, \frac{O_1(Nh)}{I(Nh)}\right)$$

Since the values of K_1 and K_2 are guaranteed to sum to one, we can add an extra dimension within the brackets, as follows

$$\left(\frac{O_2(B)}{I(B)}, \frac{O_1(B)}{I(B)}, 1\right) =$$
$$0.735 \times \left(\frac{O_2(R)}{I(R)}, \frac{O_1(R)}{I(R)}, 1\right) + 0.265 \times \left(\frac{O_2(Nh)}{I(Nh)}, \frac{O_1(Nh)}{I(Nh)}, 1\right)$$

which rearranged gives

$$\frac{1}{I(B)} \times (O_2(B), O_1(B), I(B)) =$$
$$\frac{0.735}{I(R)} \times (O_2(R), O_1(R), I(R)) + \frac{0.265}{I(Nh)} \times (O_2(Nh), O_1(Nh), I(Nh))$$

and further rearranged gives

$$(O_2(B), O_1(B), I(B)) = \frac{0.735 \times I(B)}{I(R)} \times (O_2(R), O_1(R), I(R))$$
$$+ \frac{0.265 \times I(B)}{I(Nh)} \times (O_2(Nh), O_1(Nh), I(Nh))$$

Hence we now have a relationship of the form

$$(O_2(B), O_1(B), I(B)) = L_1 \times (O_2(R), O_1(R), I(R))$$
$$+ L_2 \times (O_2(Nh), O_1(Nh), I(Nh)) \qquad (3.6)$$

where

$$L_1 = \frac{0.735 \times I(B)}{I(R)} \quad \text{and} \quad L_2 = \frac{0.265 \times I(B)}{I(Nh)}$$

Hence we can express the performance of the point B as a weighted average of the performances of Reading and Northampton. The averaging can be broken down into two distinct phases. The first phase converts the performances of the Reading and Northampton shops to the same scale of operation as the point B. In other words, their inputs are made equal to that of the point B and their outputs are adjusted in the same proportion. The second phase then finds the linear combination of these revised performances which yields the same output mix as the point B.

Whilst this may sound complex, it is merely a replica of the process by which we established our graphical representation. The data points on the graph were established by dividing each output by its associated input so that each point on the graph could be viewed on a common scale. We then selected a point on the line joining Reading and Northampton (equivalent to selecting a linear combination) to correspond to a specific output mix. What we have now established is a means of expressing this mathematically through the weights L_1 and L_2.

As yet, we have not defined $O_2(B)$, $O_1(B)$ and $I(B)$. However, we have selected the point B to act as a target point for the Newcastle shop in that it has the same output mix but a higher output to input ratio than the Newcastle shop. The efficiency measure OA/OB expresses the output to input ratio of the Newcastle shop as a proportion of the output to input ratio of the point B. We established in Section 3.1 that OA/OB had the value 0.634. The target point B can be arrived at either by reducing the input of the Newcastle shop to the proportion 0.634 of its current value or by increasing each output so that its current value is the proportion 0.634 of the final value.

Hence we can have for *reduced input*

$$(O_2(B), O_1(B), I(B)) = (O_2(Ne), O_1(Ne), 0.634 \times I(Ne))$$

whence

$$L_1 = \frac{0.735 \times I(B)}{I(R)} = \frac{0.735 \times 0.634 \times I(Ne)}{I(R)}$$

$$= \frac{0.735 \times 0.634 \times 476.63}{343.55}$$

$$= 0.646$$

and

$$L_2 = \frac{0.265 \times I(B)}{I(Nh)} = \frac{0.265 \times 0.634 \times I(Ne)}{I(Nh)}$$

$$= \frac{0.265 \times 0.634 \times 476.63}{205.15}$$

$$= 0.391$$

and for *increased output*

$$(O_2(B), O_1(B), I(B)) = \left(\frac{O_2(Ne)}{0.634}, \frac{O_1(Ne)}{0.634}, I(Ne)\right)$$

whence

$$L_1 = \frac{0.735 \times I(B)}{I(R)} = \frac{0.735 \times I(Ne)}{I(R)}$$

$$= \frac{0.735 \times 476.63}{343.55}$$

$$= 1.020$$

and

$$L_2 = \frac{0.265 \times I(B)}{I(Nh)} = \frac{0.265 \times I(Ne)}{I(Nh)}$$

$$= \frac{0.265 \times 476.63}{205.15}$$

$$= 0.616$$

Hence for reduced input we can rewrite equation 3.6 as

$$(O_2(Ne), O_1(Ne), 0.634 \times I(Ne)) = 0.646 (O_2(R), O_1(R), I(R)) + 0.391$$
$$\times (O_2(Nh), O_1(Nh), I(Nh))$$

and for increased output we can rewrite equation 3.6 as

$$\left(\frac{O_2(Ne)}{0.634}, \frac{O_1(Ne)}{0.634}, I(Ne)\right) = 1.020 (O_2(R), O_1(R), I(R)) + 0.616$$
$$\times (O_2(Nh), O_1(Nh), I(Nh))$$

We have therefore established that we can find a weighted combination of the performances of the Reading and Northampton shops such that the weighted combination produces exactly the same output as the Newcastle shop but consumes only 0.634 of the input of the Newcastle shop. Alternatively, we can amend the weighted combination (dividing by 0.634) such that the output of the Newcastle shop is only 0.634 of the output of the weighted combination whilst their inputs are exactly the same.

Figure 3.2 shows the effect if we define our target point with reference to a different pair of shops. If we use Reading and Bradford, the extension of the line OA meets the line joining Reading and Bradford at B'. We can see by inspection that the ratio OA/OB' is larger than the ratio OA/OB. We can also see by inspection that a similar result would be obtained whatever alternative pair of shops was chosen. Hence the value of 0.634 is the smallest value of this ratio which exists for any pair of shops. So we can be certain that 0.634 is the minimum proportion of the Newcastle shop's input which could be attained by any weighted combination of the performances of other shops which achieves the same level of output. Alternatively, 0.634 is the minimum value which could be obtained in expressing the Newcastle shop's current outputs as a proportion of a weighted combination of other shops which consumes the same input.

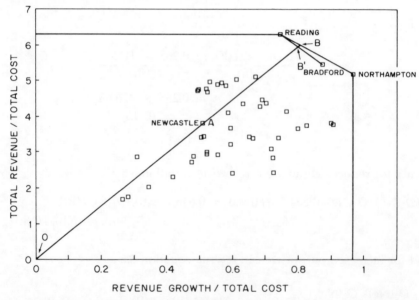

Figure 3.2 Alternative shop combinations

Hence in Section 3.1 and the current section, we have established two views of the efficiency measure 0.634. On the one hand 0.634 is the maximum of the ratio of a weighted sum of outputs to a weighted sum of inputs, whilst on the other hand, it indicates a minimum proportion in the sense described above. We can refer to each of these views as the dual of the other. Such terminology will help us establish a closer link with the full mathematical development in Appendix A. Further, it is potentially confusing to use the term 'weights' in the context of both the weighted output to input ratio and the weighted combination of shop performances. We will therefore refer to the latter as dual weights.

3.3 THE BOUNDARIES OF THE EFFICIENCY FRONTIER

We noted in Chapter 2 that there was a fundamental difference in calculating the target for Bromley. This is shown in Figure 3.3 which replicates the appropriate features of Figure 2.3. The difference arises from the fact that in moving along the line OC to increase Bromley's output/input ratios in the same proportion, the frontier is met at the point D. There is no information based on achieved performance in the region of the point D regarding the trade-off between outputs. This is because there is no shop with a lower value *Total revenue/Total cost* than Northampton which has a higher value of *Revenue growth/Total cost*.

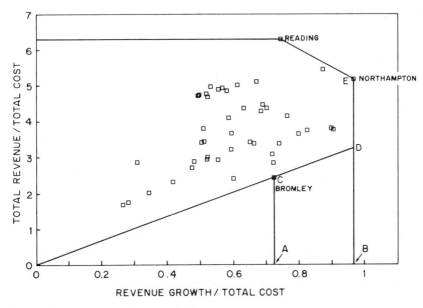

Figure 3.3 Bromley efficiency calculation

We stated in Chapter 2 that our efficiency measure is the ratio OC/OD but that in addition to improving its performance to the point D, Bromley could be expected to achieve a further increase in *Total revenue/Total cost* without a decrease in *Revenue growth/Total cost*, thus making its target the point representing the Northampton shop rather than the point D.

Let us consider the logic behind this statement. A shop can achieve its target either by maintaining its existing level of output at reduced cost or by increasing its existing level of output at no additional cost. Taking the former case, if Bromley reduces its input whilst maintaining output, it can do so until the output/input ratios match those of the point D. Any further reduction of input without changing the outputs would move Bromley's performance beyond the frontier and hence beyond the bounds of demonstrable achieved performance. However, at this point, it is possible, based on the Northampton shop's performance, to achieve an increase in *Total revenue / Total cost* without increase in *Total cost* or reduction in *Revenue growth / Total cost*. Since *Total cost* is the same in each ratio, it is clear that this can only be achieved through an increase in *Total revenue* without a reduction in *Revenue growth*. Hence our efficiency measure OC/OD gives us the maximum decrease in input which can be achieved without detriment to output. At this point we have an additional 'slack' value in the output *Total revenue*.

Taking the latter case, if Bromley increases its output whilst maintaining its current level of input, it can do so until the output/input ratios match those of the point D. Any further increase in output without increase in *Total cost* or changing the balance between the outputs would again move Bromley's performance beyond the frontier and hence beyond the bounds of demonstrable achieved performance. However, as before, it is then possible, based on the Northampton shop's performance, to achieve an increase in *Total revenue / Total cost* without increase in *Total cost* or reduction in *Revenue growth / Total cost*. Again, since *Total cost* is the same in each ratio, it is clear that this can only be achieved through an increase in *Total revenue* without a reduction in *Revenue growth*. Hence our efficiency measure OC/OD gives us the maximum increase in output which can be achieved without increasing *Total cost* or altering the balance between outputs. At this point we have an additional 'slack' value in the output *Total revenue*.

We can develop this theme mathematically using similar methods to those in the case of Newcastle. Referring to Figure 3.3, we can see by simple geometry that our efficiency measure for Bromley, OC/OD, is the same as the ratio OA/OB. OA and OB are the X-coordinates of Bromley and Northampton respectively. Hence our efficiency measure for Bromley is given by

$$\frac{OC}{OD} = \frac{OA}{OB} = \frac{0.724}{0.966} = 0.749$$

which is the value shown in Table 2.6.

Let us denote the coordinates of the shops Bromley and Northampton as $(X(B), Y(B))$ and $(X(Nh), Y(Nh))$ respectively. Then,

$$OA = 0.724 = 0 \, Y(B) + 1 \, X(B)$$

$$OB = 0.966 = 0 \, Y(Nh) + 1 \, X(Nh)$$

Dividing both of these equations by OB (=0.966) and switching the left hand side and right hand sides of the equations gives us

$$0 \, Y(B) + 1.036 \, X(B) = \frac{OA}{OB} = \frac{0.724}{0.966} = 0.749$$

$$0 \, Y(Nh) + 1.036 \, X(Nh) = \frac{OB}{OB} = 1$$

Denoting *Total cost* by I, *Total revenue* by O_1, *Revenue growth* by O_2 and using an analogous notation to the Newcastle case, we have

$$\frac{0 \, O_1(B) + 1.036 \, O_2(B)}{I(B)} = 0.749$$

$$\frac{0 \, O_1(Nh) + 1.036 \, O_2(Nh)}{I(Nh)} = 1$$

Again, we can constrain the value of the denominator to 1 by dividing both the numerator and denominator of these equations by the value of $I(B)$ (=77.25). This gives us

$$\frac{0 \, O_1(B) + 0.0134 \, O_2(B)}{0.0129 \, I(B)} = 0.749$$

$$\frac{0 \, O_1(Nh) + 0.0134 \, O_2(Nh)}{0.0129 \, I(Nh)} = 1$$

As in the Newcastle case, we have now expressed our efficiency measure for Bromley as the ratio of a weighted sum of its outputs to a weighted sum of its inputs whilst restricting the value of the weighted sum of inputs to 1. Note, however, that in this case the weight for *Total revenue/Total cost* is zero. As in the Newcastle case, the output weights are in proportion to the slope of the line on the frontier which contains the point against which Bromley's efficiency is measured, thus giving us the value of the trade-off between the outputs at this point. The zero value therefore reflects our earlier discussion that an increase in *Total Revenue/Total cost* (O_1/I) can be achieved without a corresponding decrease in *Revenue growth/Total cost* (O_2/I). In general, therefore, a slack value in an output will be matched by a zero weight for that output in the ratio of weighted sums.

The value of Bromley's input (*Total cost*) is 77.25. Following our discussion above, if we choose to decrease input and maintain output, we can decrease input to a factor of 0.749 (the efficiency score) of its original value (77.25 × 0.749 = 57.89), following which there is a slack value which can only be achieved by an increase in *Total revenue* (O_1) without a reduction in *Revenue growth* (O_2). Let $s(O_1)$ be the value of this slack. The value of $s(O_1)/I$ is given by the length of the line DE (=1.938). Hence $s(O_1)/57.89 = 1.938$, and hence $s(O_1) = 112.218$.

Alternatively, if we choose to increase output and maintain input, then both outputs can be increased in proportion to a factor of 1.334 (= 1/0.749, i.e. we divide by the efficiency score) of their original values while input is maintained at 77.25. Following this there is a slack value which can only be achieved by an increase in *Total revenue* (O_1) without a reduction in *Revenue growth* (O_2). Again, if we let $s(O_1)$ be the value of this slack, then the value of $s(O_1)/I$ is given by the length of the line DE (=1.938).

In view of the fact that the input at this point is higher than in the former case, this leads to a higher slack value, as follows: $s(O_1)/77.25 = 1.938$, and hence $s(O_1) = 149.728$.

3.4   THE RECIPROCAL FORMULATION

In Sections 3.1 and 3.2, we formed two equivalent views of efficiency. We can form yet another view, but in order to achieve this we need to change the nature of our two dimensional problem. Suppose, therefore, that we had undertaken a different line of analysis and had chosen to assess a manager's performance in terms of the *Revenue growth* that he achieves. Suppose further, that we had identified that the two most important inputs which affect *Revenue growth* were *Total revenue* and *Staff cost*. Note that here we are regarding *Total revenue* as an input in the sense that lack of it inhibits a manager's ability to achieve *Revenue growth*, whilst in the previous case it was an output in the sense that maintaining it consumes a resource.

We can proceed in a manner similar to that of our analysis of Figure 2.3 by plotting each input divided by the output. The result of this is shown in Figure 3.4. This analysis will differ from that in Figure 2.3 in that we have inverted our measure from output divided by input to input divided by output. This affects our interpretation of the graph in that, in Figure 3.4, best performance is now in the direction of the bottom left hand corner of the graph whereas in Figure 2.3 best performance was in the direction of the top right hand corner of the graph. Note that Figure 3.4 also provides a better illustration than Figure 2.3 of how a number of shops can determine the frontier.

By direct analogy with Figure 2.3, our efficiency measure for Crawley is

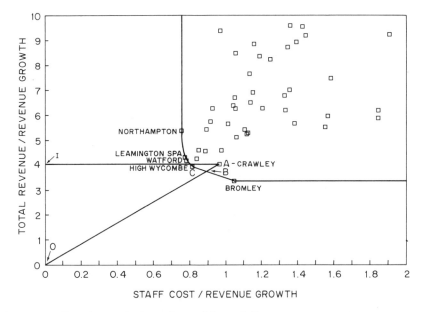

Figure 3.4 Frontier analysis: reciprocal formulation

OA/OB which we can see is greater than 1. Hence under this formulation, efficient units still have an efficiency score of 1 but inefficient units have scores which are greater than 1. This approach leads to an alternative DEA formulation with the weighted sum of inputs forming the numerator instead of the denominator. In Appendix A we show that the two formulations generate equivalent measures of efficiency with the efficiency measure from one being the reciprocal of the efficiency measure of the other. However, we also show that the choice of formulation does alter the calculation of dual weights and slack values and that, strictly, the formulation in Section 3.1 applies only to input minimization whilst the reciprocal formulation applies only to output maximization.

3.5   EXPANSION BEYOND TWO DIMENSIONS

The purpose of our simple mathematical development has been to produce results for the graphical example which arose originally in Figure 2.3 and to derive an equivalent mathematical model in a form which will generalize to cater for additional inputs and outputs. Our model formulations in Sections 3.1 and 3.2 meet this objective.

The generalization of the weighted sum ratio derived in Section 3.1 gives us precisely the same definition of efficiency as is presented in the original paper on DEA produced in 1978 by Charnes, Cooper and Rhodes (CCR)[6]. The CCR paper uses this definition of efficiency as a starting point and then establishes:

(a)   the equivalence of a set of alternative mathematical models to evaluate efficiency which correspond to the original, dual and reciprocal model formulations which we derived in Sections 3.1 to 3.4;

(b)   a solution procedure;

(c)   the existence of slack values equivalent to our development in Section 3.3;

(d)   interpretation of the models in terms of a multidimensional efficiency frontier;

(e)   the relationship between input or output weights and the trade-off characteristics of the efficiency frontier equivalent to our result in Section 3.1.

In Appendix A, we present the mathematics essential to generating results. Readers interested in establishing rigorous proofs of the results quoted should refer to the CCR paper itself.

Tables 3.1 and 3.2 set out the results obtained using the CCR method based on minimizing input for a given level of output. It can be seen that all values obtained for Newcastle and Bromley match those derived in the simple mathematical analysis. In particular, the dual weights for Newcastle and the slack for Bromley correspond with those derived graphically for the reduced input case. For all future analysis, we can therefore replace our graphical approach with the CCR approach.

3.6 UNCONTROLLABLE INPUTS

Let us consider the implications of choosing our efficiency measure in Section 3.4 to be OA/OB. Certainly, as before, we can maintain input (*Total revenue* and *Staff cost*) and increase output (*Revenue growth*) causing performance to move along the line AO from A until the point B is reached. However, we cannot do the same by maintaining output and reducing input because *Total revenue* is an historical fact which cannot be changed. The same would be true of environmental factors such as population and competition. We will refer to such inputs as 'uncontrollable inputs'. The manager can, however, change *Staff cost*. Consequently, if the objective is to maintain output and reduce input, performance can only move along the line AI which intercepts the frontier at the point C and our efficiency measure becomes the ratio IA/IC.

Table 3.1 Weights from Step 2 cost efficiency model

	Efficiency score	Weights		
		Revenue growth	Total revenue	Total cost
BIRMINGHAM 1	0.508	0.001700	0.000337	0.003386
BIRMINGHAM 2	0.749	0.000000	0.000884	0.005566
BRADFORD	0.980	0.002619	0.000519	0.005216
BRENT CROSS	0.598	0.002817	0.000558	0.005611
BRISTOL	0.686	0.005154	0.000000	0.004977
BRIXTON	0.559	0.001429	0.000283	0.002847
BROMLEY	0.749	0.013407	0.000000	0.012946
CHELTENHAM	0.752	0.000000	0.000290	0.001829
CRAWLEY	0.621	0.007766	0.000000	0.007499
CROYDON	0.574	0.004177	0.000000	0.004033
DUDLEY	0.807	0.002282	0.000452	0.004545
EALING	0.701	0.002534	0.000502	0.005047
FULHAM	0.751	0.001086	0.000215	0.002162
GLOUCESTER	0.930	0.009769	0.000000	0.009433
HAMMERSMITH	0.778	0.000000	0.000568	0.003579
HARLOW	0.314	0.001746	0.000346	0.003476
HIGH WYCOMBE	0.748	0.014276	0.000000	0.013785
HOUNSLOW	0.439	0.001970	0.000390	0.003924
ILFORD	0.300	0.001129	0.000224	0.002248
KENSINGTON	0.789	0.000000	0.000545	0.003432
LEAMINGTON SPA	0.743	0.010270	0.000000	0.009917
LEICESTER	0.853	0.008342	0.000000	0.008055
MAIDENHEAD	0.765	0.009669	0.000000	0.009336
MANCHESTER 1	0.673	0.006892	0.000000	0.006655
MANCHESTER 2	0.826	0.006412	0.000000	0.006191
MILTON KEYNES	0.373	0.000893	0.000177	0.001778
NEWCASTLE	0.634	0.001053	0.000209	0.002098
NORTHAMPTON	1.000	0.002447	0.000485	0.004875
OXFORD ST	0.554	0.001441	0.000286	0.002870
PLYMOUTH	0.663	0.001569	0.000311	0.003124
READING	1.000	0.000000	0.000462	0.002911
REDDITCH	0.844	0.002740	0.000543	0.005457
REIGATE	0.788	0.004986	0.000988	0.009931
SLOUGH	0.774	0.001808	0.000358	0.003601
SOLIHULL	0.591	0.002990	0.000593	0.005955
ST. ALBANS	0.768	0.003441	0.000682	0.006854
SUTTON COLDFIELD	0.757	0.000000	0.000595	0.003746
SWINDON	0.783	0.000000	0.000539	0.003394
TONBRIDGE	0.796	0.004757	0.000943	0.009475
VICTORIA	0.453	0.000000	0.000282	0.001779
WATFORD	0.937	0.010174	0.000000	0.009824
WINDSOR	0.617	0.005146	0.001020	0.010250
WOLVERHAMPTON	0.791	0.002266	0.000449	0.004513
WOOD GREEN	0.741	0.000000	0.000486	0.003061
YORK	0.528	0.002540	0.000503	0.005060

Table 3.2 Other information from Step 2 cost efficiency model

	Slacks		Reference shops		Dual weights	
	Revenue growth	Total revenue				
BIRMINGHAM 1	0	0	NORTHAMPTON	READING	0.639	0.055
BIRMINGHAM 2	11.63598	0	READING		0.392	
BRADFORD	0	0	NORTHAMPTON	READING	0.598	0.190
BRENT CROSS	0	0	NORTHAMPTON	READING	0.264	0.153
BRISTOL	0	34.74757	NORTHAMPTON		0.672	
BRIXTON	0	0	NORTHAMPTON	READING	0.814	0.086
BROMLEY	0	112.2180	NORTHAMPTON		0.282	
CHELTENHAM	34.74750	0	READING		1.197	
CRAWLEY	0	107.3442	NORTHAMPTON		0.404	
CROYDON	0	11.52790	NORTHAMPTON		0.693	
DUDLEY	0	0	NORTHAMPTON	READING	0.053	0.485
EALING	0	0	NORTHAMPTON	READING	0.276	0.240
FULHAM	0	0	NORTHAMPTON	READING	0.740	0.569
GLOUCESTER	0	107.7572	NORTHAMPTON		0.481	
HAMMERSMITH	7.217436	0	READING		0.633	
HARLOW	0	0	NORTHAMPTON	READING	0.299	0.084
HIGH WYCOMBE	0	75.44472	NORTHAMPTON		0.264	
HOUNSLOW	0	0	NORTHAMPTON	READING	0.510	0.021
ILFORD	0	0	NORTHAMPTON	READING	0.399	0.151
KENSINGTON	16.56867	0	READING		0.669	
LEAMINGTON SPA	0	76.92259	NORTHAMPTON		0.365	
LEICESTER	0	85.34341	NORTHAMPTON		0.516	
MAIDENHEAD	0	61.81952	NORTHAMPTON		0.400	
MANCHESTER 1	0	10.14528	NORTHAMPTON		0.493	
MANCHESTER 2	0	100.2288	NORTHAMPTON		0.650	

Table 3.2 (cont.)

	Slacks		Reference shops		Dual weights	
	Revenue growth	Total revenue				
MILTON KEYNES	0	0	NORTHAMPTON	READING	0.814	0.125
NEWCASTLE	0	0	NORTHAMPTON	READING	0.391	0.646
NORTHAMPTON	0	0	NORTHAMPTON		1.000	
OXFORD ST	0	0	NORTHAMPTON	READING	0.834	0.064
PLYMOUTH	0	0	NORTHAMPTON	READING	0.706	0.196
READING	0	0	READING		1.000	
REDDITCH	0	0	NORTHAMPTON	READING	0.162	0.354
REIGATE	0	0	NORTHAMPTON	READING	0.257	0.077
SLOUGH	0	0	NORTHAMPTON	READING	0.030	0.608
SOLIHULL	0	0	NORTHAMPTON	READING	0.232	0.150
ST. ALBANS	0	0	NORTHAMPTON	READING	0.356	0.114
SUTTON COLDFIELD	11.89835	0	READING		0.589	
SWINDON	4.981214	0	READING		0.671	
TONBRIDGE	0	0	NORTHAMPTON	READING	0.398	0.007
VICTORIA	15.79023	0	READING		0.741	
WATFORD	0	109.4179	NORTHAMPTON		0.465	
WINDSOR	0	0	NORTHAMPTON	READING	0.287	0.004
WOLVERHAMPTON	0	0	NORTHAMPTON	READING	0.487	0.219
WOOD GREEN	9.434784	0	READING		0.705	
YORK	0	0	NORTHAMPTON	READING	0.389	0.071

Hence, where an uncontrollable input exists, we measure efficiency against
a different point on the frontier and obtain a different value for the measure
according to whether our objective is to increase output or to decrease input.
The points against which the two efficiencies are measured differ only in
respect of the change in the relative proportions of the inputs enforced by
the need to reduce one and keep the other constant. Note further that, as
can be seen in the case of Crawley in Figure 3.4, the reference shops in the
two cases may also be different.

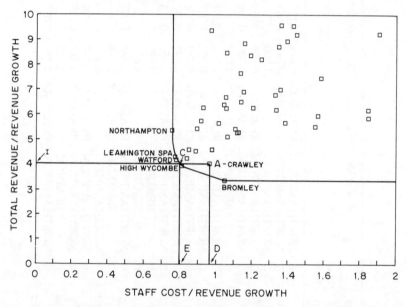

Figure 3.5 Efficiency calculation: uncontrollable input

We now need to develop the uncontrollable input case mathematically.
This will be done by reference to Figure 3.5 which replicates the essential
features of Figure 3.4.

Our efficiency measure for Crawley is

$$\frac{IA}{IC} = \frac{OD}{OE} = \frac{0.964}{0.799} = 1.206$$

Let us represent the coordinates of points as follows: Crawley
$(X(Cr), Y(Cr))$, Watford $(X(W), Y(W))$, High Wycombe $(X(H), Y(H))$ and the
point C $(X(C), Y(C))$. The equation of the line on the frontier between High
Wycombe and Watford is

$$Y = 10.209 - 7.742\,X$$

We can rearrange this equation to give

$$X = 1.319 - 0.129\, Y$$

High Wycombe, the point C and Watford all lie on this line. Hence, substituting their coordinates and rearranging the equation gives

$$X(C) = 1.319 - 0.129\, Y(C) \tag{3.7}$$

$$X(W) = 1.319 - 0.129\, Y(W) \tag{3.8}$$

$$X(H) = 1.319 - 0.129\, Y(H) \tag{3.9}$$

Hence using equation 3.7 we can express our efficiency measure as follows:

$$\frac{IA}{IC} = \frac{X(Cr)}{X(C)} = \frac{X(Cr)}{1.319 - 0.129\, Y(C)}$$

and since $Y(C) = Y(Cr)$ by the definition of uncontrollable input, we have

$$1.206 = \frac{IA}{IC} = \frac{X(Cr)}{1.319 - 0.129\, Y(Cr)}$$

Also, equations 3.8 and 3.9 give

$$1 = \frac{X(W)}{X(W)} = \frac{X(W)}{1.319 - 0.129\, Y(W)}$$

$$1 = \frac{X(H)}{X(H)} = \frac{X(H)}{1.319 - 0.129\, Y(H)}$$

Using analogous notation for inputs and outputs to that used earlier, we have for Crawley

$$Y(Cr) = \frac{I_2(Cr)}{O(Cr)} \quad \text{and} \quad X(Cr) = \frac{I_1(Cr)}{O(Cr)}$$

Under this definition, I_2 represents the uncontrollable input, *Total revenue*. Similar relationships exist for Watford and High Wycombe. Substituting these in the above equations gives

$$\frac{I_1(\text{Cr})}{1.319\ O(\text{Cr})\ -\ 0.129\ I_2(\text{Cr})} = 1.206$$

$$\frac{I_1(\text{W})}{1.319\ O(\text{W})\ -\ 0.129\ I_2(\text{W})} = 1$$

$$\frac{I_1(\text{H})}{1.319\ O(\text{H})\ -\ 0.129\ I_2(\text{H})} = 1$$

Finally, we can again constrain the denominator of the first equation to 1 by dividing the numerators and denominators of each equation by the value of the denominator of the first equation (= $1.319 \times 79.57 - 0.129 \times 321.49$ = 63.94). This gives

$$\frac{0.0156\ I_1(\text{Cr})}{0.0206\ O(\text{Cr})\ -\ 0.00202\ I_2(\text{Cr})} = 1.206$$

$$\frac{0.0156\ I_1(\text{W})}{0.0206\ O(\text{W})\ -\ 0.00202\ I_2(\text{W})} = 1$$

$$\frac{0.0156\ I_1(\text{H})}{0.0206\ O(\text{H})\ -\ 0.00202\ I_2(\text{H})} = 1$$

Hence we have expressed the efficiency of Crawley as a modified ratio of weighted inputs and output. Only the controllable input remains in the numerator whilst the uncontrollable input is incorporated in the denominator. Using the same set of weights, the value of the ratio of weighted inputs and output for the efficient shops Watford and High Wycombe is 1.

Note that despite the modified form of the ratio, the input weights are preserved in proportion to the slope of the line joining Watford and High Wycombe and hence in proportion to the implied trade-off at the point against which efficiency is measured.

A generalization of this formulation to cover any number of inputs and outputs is explained in Appendix A. Tables 3.3 and 3.4 show the results of a DEA run using the above formulation. In particular, the efficiency score, weights and reference shops obtained for Crawley match those obtained in the development above.

We have now developed our efficiency measure sufficiently to return to the analysis of the case study in the next chapter.

Table 3.3 Weights from uncontrollable input model

	Efficiency score	Weights Revenue growth	Total revenue	Staff cost
BIRMINGHAM 1	1.836	0.007110	0.000000	0.009459
BIRMINGHAM 2	1.801	0.011312	0.000000	0.015049
BRADFORD	1.229	0.005990	0.000000	0.007969
BRENT CROSS	1.394	0.010949	0.000000	0.014567
BRISTOL	1.400	0.008479	0.000189	0.009936
BRIXTON	1.217	0.005461	0.000000	0.007265
BROMLEY	1.000	0.041576	0.007061	0.017095
CHELTENHAM	1.891	0.003687	0.000000	0.004905
CRAWLEY	1.206	0.020625	0.002020	0.015640
CROYDON	1.491	0.008249	0.000183	0.009666
DUDLEY	1.657	0.007436	0.000000	0.009893
EALING	1.800	0.008626	0.000000	0.011476
FULHAM	1.527	0.003426	0.000000	0.004558
GLOUCESTER	1.080	0.014047	0.000838	0.013535
HAMMERSMITH	1.534	0.006474	0.000000	0.008613
HARLOW	2.449	0.012365	0.000000	0.016450
HIGH WYCOMBE	1.000	0.030998	0.003036	0.023506
HOUNSLOW	2.061	0.009399	0.000000	0.012504
ILFORD	1.384	0.008505	0.000000	0.011315
KENSINGTON	1.282	0.006473	0.000000	0.008611
LEAMINGTON SPA	1.000	0.015284	0.000340	0.017909
LEICESTER	1.151	0.010868	0.000242	0.012735
MAIDENHEAD	1.271	0.014065	0.000313	0.016481
MANCHESTER 1	1.481	0.011596	0.000258	0.013588
MANCHESTER 2	1.105	0.008647	0.000192	0.010133
MILTON KEYNES	2.452	0.005173	0.000000	0.006883
NEWCASTLE	2.100	0.004123	0.000000	0.005485
NORTHAMPTON	1.000	0.005731	0.000127	0.006716
OXFORD ST	1.345	0.005511	0.000000	0.007332
PLYMOUTH	1.769	0.005265	0.000000	0.007004
READING	1.398	0.003913	0.000000	0.005206
REDDITCH	1.502	0.008165	0.000000	0.010863
REIGATE	1.400	0.014137	0.000000	0.018808
SLOUGH	1.579	0.006199	0.000000	0.008247
SOLIHULL	1.761	0.011853	0.000000	0.015768
ST. ALBANS	1.599	0.010045	0.000000	0.013364
SUTTON COLDFIELD	1.916	0.007221	0.000000	0.009607
SWINDON	1.784	0.006003	0.000000	0.007987
TONBRIDGE	1.186	0.012416	0.000000	0.016518
VICTORIA	2.527	0.005762	0.000000	0.007666
WATFORD	1.000	0.014457	0.000862	0.013930
WINDSOR	1.467	0.017284	0.000000	0.022994
WOLVERHAMPTON	1.508	0.006558	0.000000	0.008725
WOOD GREEN	1.845	0.005862	0.000000	0.007798
YORK	2.080	0.010499	0.000000	0.013967

Table 3.4 Other results from uncontrollable input model

	Slacks		Reference shops		Dual weights	
	Total revenue	Staff cost				
BIRMINGHAM 1	80.4365	0	NORTHAMPTON		1.30357	
BIRMINGHAM 2	671.426	0	NORTHAMPTON		0.80357	
BRADFORD	185.179	0	NORTHAMPTON		1.03571	
BRENT CROSS	169.265	0	NORTHAMPTON		0.64285	
BRISTOL	0	0	LEAMINGTON SPA	NORTHAMPTON	0.63249	0.70924
BRIXTON	82.9990	0	NORTHAMPTON		1.125	
BROMLEY	0	0	BROMLEY		1	
CHELTENHAM	2148.29	0	NORTHAMPTON		2.58928	
CRAWLEY	0	0	HIGH WYCOMBE	WATFORD	1.12533	0.40721
CROYDON	0	0	LEAMINGTON SPA	NORTHAMPTON	0.22340	0.95193
DUDLEY	637.608	0	NORTHAMPTON		1.125	
EALING	341.988	0	NORTHAMPTON		1.05357	
FULHAM	688.830	0	NORTHAMPTON		2.25	
GLOUCESTER	0	0	LEAMINGTON SPA	WATFORD	0.64004	0.61329
HAMMERSMITH	829.348	0	NORTHAMPTON		1.19642	
HARLOW	164.029	0	NORTHAMPTON		1	
HIGH WYCOMBE	0	0	HIGH WYCOMBE		1	
HOUNSLOW	34.8621	0	NORTHAMPTON		1.10714	
ILFORD	165.368	0	NORTHAMPTON		0.82142	
KENSINGTON	794.667	0	NORTHAMPTON		1	
LEAMINGTON SPA	0	0	LEAMINGTON SPA		1	
LEICESTER	0	0	LEAMINGTON SPA	NORTHAMPTON	1.27729	0.12815
MAIDENHEAD	0	0	LEAMINGTON SPA	NORTHAMPTON	1.02127	0.13487
MANCHESTER 1	0	0	LEAMINGTON SPA	NORTHAMPTON	0.19537	0.65887
MANCHESTER 2	0	0	LEAMINGTON SPA	NORTHAMPTON	1.43925	0.19242

Table 3.4 (cont.)

	Slacks		Reference shops	Dual weights
	Total revenue	Staff cost		
MILTON KEYNES	243.217	0	NORTHAMPTON	2.39285
NEWCASTLE	1076.65	0	NORTHAMPTON	2.57142
NORTHAMPTON	0	0	NORTHAMPTON	1
OXFORD ST	67.9808	0	NORTHAMPTON	1.23214
PLYMOUTH	275.298	0	NORTHAMPTON	1.69642
READING	1108.88	0	NORTHAMPTON	1.80357
REDDITCH	421.113	0	NORTHAMPTON	0.92857
REIGATE	85.7904	0	NORTHAMPTON	0.5
SLOUGH	761.319	0	NORTHAMPTON	1.28571
SOLIHULL	209.448	0	NORTHAMPTON	0.75
ST. ALBANS	144.230	0	NORTHAMPTON	0.80357
SUTTON COLDFIELD	1016.39	0	NORTHAMPTON	1.33928
SWINDON	997.461	0	NORTHAMPTON	1.5
TONBRIDGE	6.53545	0	NORTHAMPTON	0.48214
VICTORIA	1699.25	0	NORTHAMPTON	2.21428
WATFORD	0	0	WATFORD	1
WINDSOR	4.39806	0	NORTHAMPTON	0.42857
WOLVERHAMPTON	262.094	0	NORTHAMPTON	1.16071
WOOD GREEN	1124.52	0	NORTHAMPTON	1.58928
YORK	117.384	0	NORTHAMPTON	1

Chapter 4

The Case Study—Building and Interpreting DEA Models

4.1   THE STEPWISE APPROACH

The objective of the analysis on which we embarked in Chapter 2 was to identify factors which influence shop performance and to construct a single measure of cost efficiency which takes these factors into account, enabling us to determine for each shop the level of cost which should have been incurred given the level of revenue it achieved.

Our initial simple measure of efficiency was *Total revenue / Total cost*. This measure identified a single reference shop, Reading. We then observed through examining correlations with this measure of efficiency, that the achievement of *Revenue growth* requires significantly more resource than simply maintaining *Total revenue*. We therefore used DEA with two outputs, *Total revenue* and *Revenue growth*, and one input, *Total cost*, to calculate a new efficiency measure which took this fact into account. A second reference shop, Northampton, emerged based on its economical growth.

We ended Chapter 2 by examining correlations with this new efficiency measure and the observation that the correlations suggest the need to consider the component parts of cost and revenue in measuring cost efficiency. It was explained earlier in Chapter 2 that because our efficiency measure is essentially one of revenue divided by cost, factors correlated with revenue or cost may exhibit a correlation with efficiency as a result. This can apply to the component parts of revenue and cost themselves. In considering whether cost or revenue should be broken down into its component parts, therefore, a clearer picture often emerges by observing the correlation between efficiency and the component parts expressed as proportions of the total since these proportions are less likely to be correlated with cost or revenue. We will therefore include such proportions in all further analysis.

We use the approach of Chapter 2 to establish an iterative procedure through which we can build our complete model, and at each step we use the techniques developed in Chapter 3 to measure efficiency in terms of the important factors identified up to that step. We can then identify another important factor by examining factors which are correlated with that measure of efficiency and applying judgement in terms of cause and effect. We then incorporate that factor into our measure and repeat the process until no further important factors emerge. At that stage, we will have constructed a measure which accounts for all the identifiable factors which influence performance.

We will refer to this approach as the Stepwise Approach and this will be our basis for constructing models throughout the remainder of the book.

4.2 FACTORS INFLUENCING PERFORMANCE— APPLYING THE STEPWISE APPROACH

Table 4.1 summarizes the application of this approach in building the cost efficiency model. The table shows, for each step, the factors in the model together with the correlations of all factors with the efficiency measurement at that step.

We will not discuss at every step factors exhibiting correlations which reflect natural relationships with the constituent parts of efficiency rather than causal relationships. These factors were identified in the discussion in Chapter 2 and are the same at each step and so have been excluded from all subsequent discussion.

In examining correlations at Step 2, there is little to choose numerically between breaking *Total cost* down into *Controllable cost* and *Uncontrollable cost* or *Staff cost* and *Non-staff cost*. Our judgement in selecting the breakdown of *Total cost* into *Controllable cost* and *Uncontrollable cost* is based not only on the marginally higher correlation but the existence of the uncontrollable element itself. It was established in Chapter 3 that measurement in respect of uncontrollable factors is at a different point on the frontier; hence it is more important to make this distinction first. This does not preclude the need for a further breakdown of controllable cost into its staff and non-staff elements emerging at a later stage.

At Step 3, the high positive correlation observed between efficiency and the proportion of *Total revenue* which was derived from Group 2 products (% *Gp2 revenue of total*) together with the negative correlations observed for the proportions relating to the other product groups strongly suggest a causal relationship. In other words, we are saying that Group 2 product revenue

Table 4.1 Correlations for cost efficiency model

		Step 1	Step 2	Step 3	Step 4	Step 5
OUTPUTS	Total revenue	*	*	*		
	Revenue growth		*	*	*	*
	Revenue Gp2				*	*
	Revenue Gp1+3				*	*
INPUTS	Total cost	*	*			
	Uncontrollable cost			*	*	*
	Controllable cost			*	*	
	Non-staff controllable cost				*	
	Staff cost					*
Age of shop (months)		0.492	0.112	0.119	0.193	0.228
Catchment population		0.095	−0.151	0.003	0.151	0.125
Central overheads		0.529	0.121	0.098	0.199	0.284
Customer service		−0.115	−0.027	0.056	−0.046	−0.036
Non-staff controllable cost		0.094	−0.270	−0.285	−0.073	−0.047
Uncontrollable cost		−0.399	−0.659	−0.272	−0.262	−0.192
Pitch		−0.081	−0.014	0.087	0.146	0.085
Profit		0.860	0.581	0.457	0.506	0.502
Revenue Gp1		0.037	−0.174	−0.191	0.052	0.191
Revenue Gp2		0.617	0.222	0.200	0.225	0.285
Revenue Gp3		0.343	−0.043	−0.061	0.117	0.191
Revenue growth		0.407	0.105	0.084	0.216	0.313
Revenue % growth		−0.531	0.054	0.076	−0.036	−0.038
Staff cost		0.186	−0.191	−0.295	−0.147	0.029
Competition		0.163	−0.161	−0.161	−0.055	−0.036
Non-staff cost		−0.349	−0.642	−0.292	−0.250	−0.182
Total revenue		0.529	0.121	0.098	0.199	0.284
Total cost		−0.041	−0.432	−0.335	−0.216	−0.067
Controllable cost		0.180	−0.201	−0.298	−0.142	0.022
Revenue Gp1 % of Total revenue		−0.507	−0.262	−0.255	−0.055	0.004
Revenue Gp2 % of Total revenue		0.488	0.410	0.414	0.084	0.054
Revenue Gp3 % of Total revenue		−0.095	−0.276	−0.290	−0.055	−0.082
Staff cost % of Total cost		0.568	0.607	0.116	0.175	0.214
Non-staff cost % of Total cost		−0.568	−0.607	−0.116	−0.175	−0.214
Uncontrollable % of Total cost		0.525	0.649	0.160	0.218	0.217
Controllable % of Total cost		−0.525	−0.649	−0.160	−0.218	−0.217
Staff cost % of Controllable cost				−0.184	−0.161	0.007
Non-staff cost % of Controllable cost				0.184	0.161	−0.007

can be achieved at a lower unit cost than other product group revenue. This could be for any of a number of reasons ranging from the obvious such as higher markup, to the less obvious such as less staff time used in promotion and selling, less storage or display space or lower stockholding costs. It is not possible within the limitations of our current data to identify the exact reasons; but nevertheless, results such as this can lead to important findings in terms of product profitability.

On the basis of this finding, we have accounted for revenue mix in our efficiency measure, but it is important to recognize the significance of doing this. We are not addressing the question of what the revenue mix should be, merely the efficiency of each shop in using resources to achieve the revenue mix which it generates. This statement reflects the theme of Section 1.5, in that we are measuring achieved efficiency whilst planned revenue mix is a question of objectives and actual revenue mix is a question of effectiveness in achieving the planned revenue mix. Clearly, the question of what the revenue mix should be is important in the context of corporate objectives, and depending on the objectives, there may be reasons why we should not account for revenue mix in the model despite our findings. We will return to this subject in Chapter 6.

A further question arises as to which constituent parts of revenue should be represented in the model. As a general rule in applying DEA, we suggest that a factor should be broken down into as few constituent parts as possible, consistent with allowing for the components which have been demonstrated to have a significant effect on efficiency. Since we interpreted the above correlations to mean that *Revenue Gp2* could be achieved at a lower unit cost whilst drawing no distinction between Groups 1 and 3, the above rule implies that the breakdown should be Group 2 and Other.

Discussion of the reason for this rule would preempt the discussion in Section 4.3, so we will return to this issue again in that section. However, as in the case of selecting our cost breakdown, if there is in fact a significant difference between the unit costs associated with Group 1 and Group 3 revenue and this has been obscured by the dominance of the effects of Group 2 revenue, then this would emerge in examining correlations at a later stage of the analysis—at which stage a further breakdown of revenue could be made.

At Step 4, the only correlations which warrant consideration are those between efficiency and the component part proportions which reflect the breakdown of *Total cost* into *Staff cost*, *Non-staff controllable cost* and *Uncontrollable cost*.

Following the incorporation of this breakdown at Step 5, the most striking correlations are those with component parts of total cost. However, at this stage, this breakdown has already been made. In all other cases, the high correlations between efficiency and the component part percentages of a

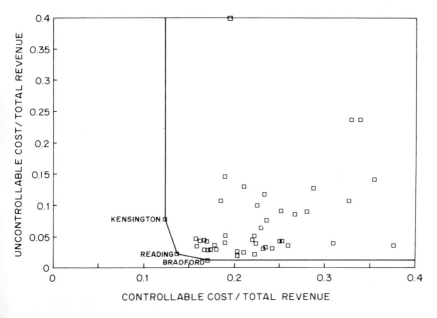

Figure 4.1 Controllable and uncontrollable costs

factor which were present prior to including the component parts in the efficiency measure were no longer present for the new efficiency measure once the breakdown was made. Figure 4.1 may help to explain this. It appears that a group of shops with particularly high values of *Uncontrollable cost* to *Total revenue* also have high values of *Controllable cost* to *Total revenue*. This would require detailed investigation beyond the scope of our present analysis but is consistent with trying to put too large a shop in these locations relative to the market potential. We will comment further on this point in Chapter 6.

Of the remaining factors, only *Age of shop* exhibits a sufficiently high correlation to warrant possible inclusion in the model. Figure 4.2 inspects the relationship more closely. It can be seen that much is contributed to the relationship by the particularly poor performance of three of the newer shops. The greater variation in efficiency for newer shops would indicate that the relationship is more likely to exist as a result of management uncertainty about the level of resource to allocate to newer shops, rather than the fact that newer shops are genuinely more expensive to run. For this reason the inclusion of *Age of shop* as a factor in the model would not be justified. We can therefore regard the current model as our final model of cost efficiency. We will say more about targeting and the use of the model in Chapter 6.

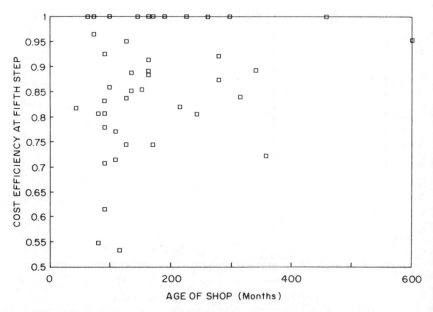

Figure 4.2 Efficiency versus age of shop

In arriving at our final model, the features of our approach have been that we have been able to rigorously justify our choice of factors to include in the model and to establish consistency with simpler analyses which will aid our interpretation of the results. It is encouraging that our final measure is correlated with profit. However, it is far from identical to profit and, unlike profit, is able to inform us of improvement potential.

Note that factors such as *Population* and *Competition* do not influence efficiency under our current definition. Even if we compute proxy market share statistics (*Total revenue / Catchment population*) or competitor weighted market share (*Total revenue* x *Competition / Catchment population*) there is still no indication of a relationship with efficiency. Hence, whilst *Catchment population* and *Competition* may restrict overall business potential, they have no impact on the level of resource which must be consumed per unit of business achieved.

4.3 INTERPRETING EFFICIENCY—SPECIFIC ASPECTS OF PERFORMANCE

The stepwise approach also helps us to interpret why particular shops are efficient. Table 4.2 shows the efficiency scores obtained at each step of the analysis and separates out the units introduced as efficient at each step.

At Step 1 it is clear that the Reading shop is efficient because it produces more revenue per unit of cost than any other shop.

At Step 2 we established that a greater cost was required to generate one unit of revenue growth than to maintain one unit of revenue. The Northampton shop was identified as efficient at this step because it had the highest revenue growth per unit of cost. Also, as shown in Figure 2.3, the implied trade-off between the performances of the Reading and Northampton shops exceeds the performances of all other shops; hence no other shop was identified as efficient at this step.

At Step 3, two new reference shops, Bradford and Kensington, were introduced as a result of breaking *Total cost* down into *Controllable cost* and *Uncontrollable cost*. A glance at Table 2.1 will show that this is because Kensington has especially low *Controllable cost* in relation to its *Total revenue* and Bradford has particularly low *Uncontrollable cost* in relation to its *Total revenue*.

Clearly it is no longer possible to produce a complete graphical representation of the model at Step 3 to include *Total revenue*, *Revenue growth* and the cost breakdown. However, Figure 4.1 shows graphically the situation if we ignore *Revenue growth*. This is equivalent to the DEA result which would have been obtained at Step 2 if staff costs had been split before *Revenue growth* had been introduced. We can see from Figure 4.1 that Kensington has the lowest ratio of *Controllable cost* to *Total revenue* and Bradford has the lowest ratio of *Uncontrollable cost* to *Total revenue*. We can also see that the implied trade-offs between the performances of these two shops and Reading exceed the performances of all other shops such that no other shop forms part of the efficiency frontier.

Although we cannot produce the whole picture, the results of Step 3 tell us that Northampton is the only other shop required such that the trade-offs between the performances of the resultant set of four shops exceed the performance of all other shops across the whole three dimensional space. Further, we have identified that each of the four shops is best in a specific aspect of performance, in that Reading has the best ratio of *Total revenue* to *Total cost*, Northampton has the best ratio of *Revenue growth* to *Total cost*, Bradford has the best ratio of *Total revenue* to *Uncontrollable cost* and Kensington has the best ratio of *Total revenue* to *Controllable cost*. In general, the best performer in terms of the ratio of any single output to any single input will be efficient. [Appendix B shows that this result can be simply deduced from the mathematical formulation in Appendix A.]

It is this result that lies behind the rule suggested during the stepwise approach in Section 4.2; namely that a factor should be broken down into as few constituent parts as possible, consistent with allowing for the components which have been demonstrated to have a significant effect on efficiency.

Table 4.2 Steps in constructing cost efficiency model

		Step 1	Step 2	Step 3	Step 4	Step 5
OUTPUTS	Total revenue	*				
	Revenue growth		*	*	*	*
	Revenue Gp1				*	*
	Revenue Gp1+3				*	*
INPUTS	Total cost	*				
	Uncontrollable cost					
	Controllable cost		*	*		
	Non-staff controllable cost				*	*
	Staff cost			*	*	*
	READING	1.00	1.00	1.00	1.00	1.00
	NORTHAMPTON	0.82	1.00	1.00	1.00	1.00
	BRADFORD	0.87	0.98	1.00	1.00	1.00
	KENSINGTON	0.79	0.79	1.00	1.00	1.00
	GLOUCESTER	0.60	0.93	0.98	1.00	1.00
	LEICESTER	0.59	0.85	0.87	1.00	1.00
	MANCHESTER 2	0.58	0.83	0.84	1.00	1.00
	SUTTON COLDFIELD	0.76	0.76	0.75	1.00	1.00
	HAMMERSMITH	0.78	0.78	0.83	0.99	1.00
	PLYMOUTH	0.58	0.66	0.62	0.93	1.00
	LEAMINGTON SPA	0.49	0.74	0.88	0.92	1.00
	ST. ALBANS	0.68	0.77	0.75	0.76	1.00
	NEWCASTLE	0.60	0.63	0.62	0.73	1.00

Table 4.2 (cont.)

	Step 1	Step 2	Step 3	Step 4	Step 5
WATFORD	0.60	0.94	0.93	0.93	0.96
CHELTENHAM	0.75	0.75	0.79	0.87	0.95
OXFORD ST	0.47	0.55	0.74	0.91	0.95
HIGH WYCOMBE	0.45	0.75	0.81	0.81	0.93
BIRMINGHAM 2	0.75	0.75	0.78	0.90	0.92
FULHAM	0.69	0.75	0.76	0.88	0.91
SLOUGH	0.77	0.77	0.82	0.89	0.89
WOOD GREEN	0.74	0.74	0.75	0.86	0.89
REIGATE	0.69	0.79	0.77	0.86	0.89
WOLVERHAMPTON	0.71	0.79	0.78	0.88	0.88
REDDITCH	0.81	0.84	0.84	0.86	0.87
CROYDON	0.46	0.57	0.64	0.84	0.86
BRIXTON	0.47	0.56	0.81	0.83	0.85
TONBRIDGE	0.66	0.80	0.83	0.84	0.85
DUDLEY	0.80	0.81	0.80	0.84	0.84
BRISTOL	0.54	0.69	0.66	0.82	0.84
MANCHESTER 1	0.54	0.67	0.65	0.83	0.83
ILFORD	0.27	0.30	0.75	0.81	0.82
BROMLEY	0.39	0.75	0.78	0.78	0.82
BRENT CROSS	0.54	0.60	0.77	0.80	0.81
MAIDENHEAD	0.54	0.77	0.75	0.75	0.81
SWINDON	0.78	0.78	0.78	0.80	0.81
CRAWLEY	0.38	0.62	0.74	0.74	0.78
SOLIHULL	0.54	0.59	0.62	0.76	0.77
BIRMINGHAM 1	0.43	0.51	0.55	0.68	0.74
EALING	0.65	0.70	0.68	0.74	0.74
VICTORIA	0.45	0.45	0.53	0.58	0.72
WINDSOR	0.51	0.62	0.67	0.70	0.71
MILTON KEYNES	0.32	0.37	0.43	0.56	0.71
HARLOW	0.28	0.31	0.44	0.53	0.62
YORK	0.46	0.53	0.49	0.54	0.55
HOUNSLOW	0.37	0.44	0.48	0.53	0.53

If at Step 4, we were to break *Total revenue* down into its three constituent parts by product group, in addition to identifying the best performer in terms of *Revenue Gp2* relative to cost, we would identify best performers in terms of Group 1 revenue relative to cost and Group 3 revenue relative to cost. If the unit costs of generating Group 1 and Group 3 revenue are similar, then specific achievement in one or the other is not very meaningful and would be detrimental to our assessment of performance as we would cause the efficiency of other shops to be measured relative to reference shops identified on this basis.

Alternatively, if we break *Total revenue* down into only two constituent parts, namely *Revenue Gp2* and *Revenue Gp1+3*, then as we have established that the unit costs in generating each of these types of revenue are different, it is important to have an example of best performance in each area.

Before discussing the shops identified as efficient at Step 4, we will examine the concept of efficiency in greater depth since, as the dimensionality of the analysis increases, it becomes difficult and often impossible to explain why a shop is efficient by using simple graphs or in terms of being best in any particular aspect of performance.

4.4 INTERPRETING EFFICIENCY—TRADE-OFF BETWEEN ASPECTS OF PERFORMANCE

Shops may be efficient without being best in terms of any single output to single input ratio. For example, Reading is second best in terms of both ratios illustrated in Figure 4.1, performing worse than Kensington in terms of one ratio and worse than Bradford in terms of the other. However, as can be seen from the graph, Reading is still efficient in this analysis because its performance is better than the performance which would be implied for the same input mix by the trade-off between Kensington and Bradford (i.e. the straight line that would join them in the graph).

Figure 3.4 (p. 57) illustrates a more complex case where a number of shops perform better than the implied trade-off between the best performers in terms of each individual ratio. If we refer to these best performers as the extremes, then the efficiency frontier is determined by identifying the shops which give the best trade-off from each extreme and then the shops which give the best trade-off from each of the new shops identified, and so on until a closed set of shops has been identified. Each efficient shop determines the direction of the frontier within a locality, the extent of which depends on the relative performance of the other shops.

It does not follow that the next shop identified in moving away from an extreme will be the second best in terms of a ratio and the next third best and so on. This is evident from the fact that the next shop is identified in

Table 4.3 Rankings of ratio values

	1	2	3	4	5	6	Total rank	Efficiency
BRADFORD	25	9	9	1	1	1	46	1.00
READING	27	1	11	13	2	13	67	1.00
GLOUCESTER	11	33	4	5	14	3	70	1.00
NORTHAMPTON	22	5	1	23	11	10	72	1.00
WOLVERHAMPTON	21	22	26	2	3	4	78	0.88
LEICESTER	7	36	8	4	22	6	83	1.00
REIGATE	24	21	19	8	7	8	87	0.86
ST. ALBANS	35	16	25	9	5	5	95	0.76
SUTTON COLDFIELD	3	23	39	6	13	21	105	1.00
DUDLEY	30	6	30	16	8	17	107	0.84
MANCHESTER 2	5	34	5	14	30	19	107	1.00
PLYMOUTH	10	37	31	3	15	11	107	0.93
REDDITCH	36	4	21	26	6	14	107	0.86
EALING	33	24	34	7	4	7	109	0.74
FULHAM	13	17	23	17	20	22	112	0.88
SWINDON	31	7	32	19	9	20	118	0.80
WATFORD	37	19	2	29	19	12	118	0.93
HAMMERSMITH	2	11	29	22	26	30	120	0.99
KENSINGTON	1	2	13	32	33	39	120	1.00
MAIDENHEAD	38	29	15	18	12	9	121	0.75
SLOUGH	12	8	28	25	21	27	121	0.89
MANCHESTER 1	16	35	24	11	27	16	129	0.83
BROMLEY	41	43	18	10	16	2	130	0.78
BIRMINGHAM 2	8	13	38	21	23	28	131	0.90
TONBRIDGE	34	12	6	31	25	23	131	0.84
BRISTOL	18	38	22	12	28	15	133	0.82
CHELTENHAM	9	10	37	24	24	31	135	0.87
NEWCASTLE	26	25	40	15	18	24	148	0.73
LEAMINGTON SPA	20	27	3	34	34	32	150	0.92
WOOD GREEN	45	3	35	37	10	25	155	0.86
BRENT CROSS	17	15	16	39	35	38	160	0.80
OXFORD ST	4	31	14	35	42	40	166	0.91
SOLIHULL	14	30	33	27	31	33	168	0.76
HIGH WYCOMBE	43	26	7	40	32	26	174	0.81
CROYDON	6	41	27	28	39	34	175	0.84
YORK	40	39	42	20	17	18	176	0.54
BRIXTON	29	14	10	43	41	42	179	0.83
WINDSOR	44	18	20	41	29	29	181	0.70
ILFORD	15	20	17	45	45	45	187	0.81
BIRMINGHAM 1	19	42	36	30	36	35	198	0.68
CRAWLEY	42	32	12	42	38	36	202	0.74
VICTORIA	23	28	45	38	40	43	217	0.58
HOUNSLOW	39	40	41	36	37	37	230	0.53
MILTON KEYNES	28	45	43	33	43	41	233	0.56
HARLOW	32	44	44	44	44	44	252	0.53

KEY 1 Revenue Gp1+3/Controllable cost   4 Revenue Gp1+3/Uncontrollable cost
      2 Revenue Gp2/Controllable cost   5 Revenue Gp2/Uncontrollable cost
      3 Revenue growth/Controllable cost   6 Revenue growth/Uncontrollable cost

Table 4.4 Computed trade-offs of shop ratios

	A	B	C	(1) Trade-off A vs B	Rank (1)	(2) Trade-off A vs C	Rank (2)	(3) Trade-off A vs 0.3(1) + 0.7(2)
BRADFORD	1.54	0.9336	12.949	−0.059	7	−0.016	3	−0.029
GLOUCESTER	1.85	1.0185	7.5824	−0.097	1	0.006	10	−0.025
KENSINGTON	2.66	0.8641	1.3720	−0.067	5	−0.006	5	−0.024
MANCHESTER 2	2.12	0.9841	4.1983	−0.005	22	−0.032	1	−0.024
NORTHAMPTON	1.57	1.1729	5.4615	−0.072	3	−0.001	8	−0.022
LEICESTER	1.99	0.9404	6.6625	−0.060	6	0.008	12	−0.022
OXFORD ST	2.23	0.8438	1.3600	−0.005	21	−0.009	4	−0.013
LEAMINGTON SPA	1.59	1.0330	2.3480	−0.069	4	0.021	24	−0.008
HAMMERSMITH	2.27	0.7163	2.4217	−0.044	9	0.017	18	−0.006
CROYDON	2.01	0.7536	2.0893	0.051	38	−0.021	2	−0.002
WATFORD	1.15	1.0909	5.2993	−0.077	2	0.035	38	0.001
SUTTON COLDFIELD	2.25	0.6049	3.6458	−0.018	17	0.010	14	0.002
ILFORD	1.76	0.8061	0.3932	0.007	28	0.001	9	0.002
BRIXTON	1.46	0.9234	1.1972	−0.015	18	0.011	15	0.003
BRENT CROSS	1.70	0.8079	1.4012	−0.029	12	0.018	20	0.003
FULHAM	1.80	0.7647	3.6089	−0.029	13	0.019	22	0.004
SLOUGH	1.83	0.7363	2.7522	0.027	32	−0.004	6	0.005
TONBRIDGE	1.28	0.9692	3.5886	0.004	26	0.009	13	0.005
READING	1.51	0.8654	5.2924	−0.020	16	0.019	21	0.007
BRISTOL	1.70	0.7745	4.5587	−0.022	15	0.020	23	0.007
MANCHESTER 1	1.72	0.7612	4.4398	−0.043	10	0.030	31	0.008
BIRMINGHAM 2	1.98	0.6152	2.4582	−0.032	11	0.029	30	0.008
CHELTENHAM	1.87	0.6270	2.3727	−0.044	8	0.035	37	0.011
PLYMOUTH	1.87	0.6680	5.3100	−0.044	8	0.035	36	0.011
SOLIHULL	1.78	0.6425	2.3037	−0.023	14	0.027	27	0.012
REIGATE	1.55	0.7905	6.3065	−0.002	23	0.022	25	0.015

Table 4.4 (cont.)

	A	B	C	(1) Trade-off A vs B	Rank (1)	(2) Trade-off A vs C	Rank (2)	(3) Trade-off A vs 0.3(1) + 0.7(2)
BIRMINGHAM 1	1.63	0.6286	1.9639	−0.009	19	0.028	28	0.017
HIGH WYCOMBE	0.88	0.9539	2.9714	0.066	41	−0.002	7	0.018
CRAWLEY	0.98	0.8647	1.9565	0.051	36	0.006	11	0.020
WOLVERHAMPTON	1.58	0.7569	7.5730	−0.008	20	0.033	35	0.021
DUDLEY	1.44	0.7117	4.3296	0.012	29	0.026	26	0.021
NEWCASTLE	1.52	0.5972	3.4396	0.002	25	0.035	39	0.025
REDDITCH	1.17	0.7830	4.5594	0.044	35	0.018	19	0.026
VICTORIA	1.55	0.4643	0.9210	−0.001	24	0.039	42	0.027
SWINDON	1.35	0.6597	3.9535	0.020	31	0.030	32	0.027
MAIDENHEAD	1.13	0.8399	6.1581	0.060	40	0.014	16	0.028
MILTON KEYNES	1.49	0.4808	1.2040	0.004	27	0.039	41	0.028
WINDSOR	0.78	0.7841	2.4328	0.071	42	0.014	17	0.031
HARLOW	1.31	0.4779	0.6828	0.018	30	0.037	40	0.031
ST. ALBANS	1.22	0.7593	6.7242	0.051	37	0.028	29	0.035
HOUNSLOW	1.08	0.5546	1.6883	0.040	34	0.034	36	0.036
EALING	1.29	0.6422	6.5743	0.038	33	0.046	44	0.044
WOOD GREEN	0.63	0.6295	3.0656	0.092	43	0.031	33	0.049
YORK	1.02	0.5434	4.2567	0.059	39	0.045	43	0.049
BROMLEY	1.00	0.7922	8.3607	0.118	44	0.031	34	0.057

KEY   A Revenue Gp1+3/Controllable cost
        B Revenue growth/Controllable cost
        C Revenue growth/Uncontrollable cost

terms of trade-off which will exclude the second best if it performs poorly in terms of the other ratio.

The same concept applies in multidimensional cases. For example, in three dimensions we may visualize a triangle formed by the best performers in terms of each of three single output to single input ratios. In most cases, there will be shops whose performance exceeds the performance implied for the same input and output mix by points within the triangle. Hence an efficiency frontier will be formed above the triangle with the efficient shops being identified on a trade-off basis similar to that in two dimensions.

Hence our concept of efficiency is that of identifying a multidimensional surface formed by a set of best performing shops. Each efficient shop determines the shape of the surface locally. The surface as a whole quantifies best performance for every possible mix of input and output activity within the range which can be observed in practice. Each extreme of the surface quantifies best performance with regard to a single output to input ratio. As we move away from an extreme, we do so in a manner which sacrifices as little as possible in respect of this ratio whilst combining as good a performance as possible in other output to input ratios. The further we move from all extremes, the greater the overall balance of good performance in every aspect.

In the light of the concept, let us consider the four additional shops identified as efficient at Step 4 during the construction of the cost efficiency model, namely: Gloucester, Leicester, Manchester 2 and Sutton Coldfield. Since our concept of efficiency can relate to individual ratios of output and input values, we can evaluate these ratios to use as a base against which to consider these shops. Such ratios are, of course, similar in nature to those constructed by the company analysts and shown in Table 2.2. The rankings of the ratio values are shown in Table 4.3.

Gloucester is the third best achiever in terms of *Revenue growth* to *Uncontrollable cost*. The best and second best achievers in this respect are Bradford and Bromley respectively. Bradford performs better than Bromley in terms of all the ratios. Gloucester performs better than Bradford in terms of *Revenue Gp1+3* to *Controllable costs* and *Revenue growth* to *Controllable costs*, and worse in terms of all other ratios.

Relating this to the concept of efficiency developed above, Bradford is the extreme in terms of *Revenue growth* to *Uncontrollable cost*. Bromley is the next best but is not efficient since it is worse than Bradford in every respect; hence no positive trade-off can exist between *Revenue growth* to *Uncontrollable cost* and any other aspect of Bromley's performance relative to Bradford's performance.

However, in terms of Gloucester's performance relative to Bradford's performance, there is a positive trade-off between *Revenue growth* to *Uncontrollable cost* and each of *Revenue Gp1+3* to *Controllable cost* and

Revenue growth to *Controllable cost*. Identifying Gloucester as efficient is equivalent to stating that this combined trade-off is greater than the combined trade-off which would be implied by the performances of any other set of shops relative to Bradford's performance.

This cannot be verified by direct inspection of the data but can be verified by actually computing the trade-offs in these ratios which are implied by the performance of each of the other shops relative to Bradford's performance. Table 4.4 shows, for each shop, the value of *Revenue Gp1+3* to *Controllable cost* (A), *Revenue growth* to *Controllable cost* (B) and *Revenue growth* to *Uncontrollable cost* (C), the computed trade-off between A and B (1) and A and C (2) implied by its performance relative to Bradford's performance and the ranking of that trade-off compared with that for other shops.

It can be seen that Gloucester is not the highest ranked shop in terms of either trade-off (1) or trade-off (2) taken individually. For trade-off (1) the best value is given by Kensington, and for trade-off (2) the best value is given by Northampton. However, for a range of linear combinations of trade-offs (1) and (2) [illustrated by $0.3 \times (1) + 0.7 \times (2)$], Gloucester is the highest ranked. This case is identical to one envisaged earlier when discussing the concept of multidimensional efficiency. The shops Bradford, Kensington and Northampton form a triangle, the sides of which determine best performance. The points within the triangle are given by all linear combinations of the trade-offs (1) and (2). Our computations confirm that the trade-off implied by Gloucester's performance relative to Bradford's performance exceeds that implied by a region within the triangle. Further, there is no other shop whose performance relative to Bradford's performance implies a greater trade-off within this region. Hence Gloucester is one of the efficient shops.

4.5 INTERPRETING EFFICIENCY—AREAS OF EFFICIENCY

Our analysis for Gloucester identifies an area within which the evaluation of efficient performance is influenced by the performance of the Gloucester shop. We can refer to this as Gloucester's area of efficiency. We can use the rankings of the ratio values in Table 4.3 to identify areas of efficiency for the other shops which were identified as efficient at Step 4 in the construction of the cost efficiency model.

Leicester is the fourth best achiever in terms of *Revenue Gp1+3* to *Uncontrollable cost*. The three better performers in terms of this ratio perform worse than Leicester in terms of *Revenue Gp1+3* to *Controllable cost* and *Revenue growth* to *Controllable cost*. Its area of efficiency is therefore associated with high values of the three ratios mentioned.

Sutton Coldfield is the third best achiever in terms of *Revenue Gp1+3* to *Controllable cost*. It is not as good as Kensington or Hammersmith in terms of this ratio but is better than either of these shops in terms of *Revenue Gp1+3* to *Uncontrollable cost*. This defines a similar area of efficiency for Sutton Coldfield as was defined for Leicester. However, Sutton Coldfield is better than Leicester in terms of *Revenue Gp1+3* to *Controllable cost* but is worse in terms of *Revenue growth* to *Controllable cost*.

Manchester 2 is the fifth best achiever in terms of *Revenue Gp1+3* to *Controllable costs*. It is better than the fourth best, Oxford, in most other respects and is better than Sutton Coldfield in terms of *Revenue growth* to *Controllable cost*. Note that Manchester 2 is better than Leicester in terms of both these ratios but is worse than Leicester in terms of *Revenue Gp1+3* to *Uncontrollable cost*.

Hence all four of the additional efficient shops have a similar area of efficiency with a particular leaning toward *Revenue Gp1+3*. In fact this is what we would expect as a result of our analysis within the stepwise construction of the model. The correlation analysis at the end of Step 3 identified *Revenue Gp2* as 'cheap' revenue in that it was generally associated with higher efficiency scores in the Step 3 model and hence, by definition, lower unit costs. Best performers in terms

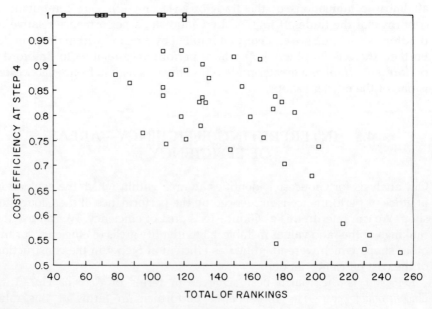

Figure 4.3 Efficiency versus total of rankings

of *Revenue Gp2* will therefore already have been identified in earlier steps as best performers in terms of *Total revenue*. The newly identified shops will therefore be the best performers in terms of *Revenue Gp1+3*.

Hence the stepwise approach will always provide a guideline to the area of efficiency of the shops. This is convenient because it is usually of practical value to understand a shop's area of efficiency at least in broad terms and it is desirable that this can be done without an exhaustive analysis such as that above on every occasion. In Chapter 6, we will present a further guide to understanding a shop's area of efficiency and we will postpone until then the discussion of the five additional efficient shops introduced at the final step in the construction of the cost efficiency model.

As a final observation on interpreting efficiency, the total of the six ratio rankings in Table 4.3 has been calculated for each shop and included in the table. The table is presented in order of the Total Rank value. A graph of the relationship between the DEA efficiency score at Step 4 and the total of the rankings is shown in Figure 4.3. The eight efficient shops appear high in the table, which further supports the concept of DEA as an overall performance measure. DEA, however, has the advantage over a pure ranking method that it evaluates trade-offs and improvement potential.

4.6 INCORPORATING THE INFLUENCE OF MARKET FACTORS—ISSUES ARISING

So far, we have used DEA to assess only the cost efficiency of each shop, that is, the level of cost at which its existing level of revenue should have been achieved. We noted in concluding Section 4.2 that factors such as population and competition do not influence this assessment.

If, instead, we wish to assess revenue potential, our mathematical formulation will allow us to reverse the process and assess the level of revenue which should be achieved given the cost input. However, if we do this, we have no indication of whether the potential market exists to allow that revenue to be achieved. Hence it is essential that, if the model is to be used in this manner, factors which establish the market potential, such as *Catchment population* and *Competition*, are incorporated into the model. We will refer to efficiency in this sense as 'market efficiency'.

If we construct a market efficiency model by simply incorporating *Catchment population* and *Competition* into our existing cost efficiency model, in the knowledge that these factors appear to have no impact on cost efficiency, we face another problem. Figure 4.4 illustrates a simplified version of the problem in the form of a graph representing a DEA model

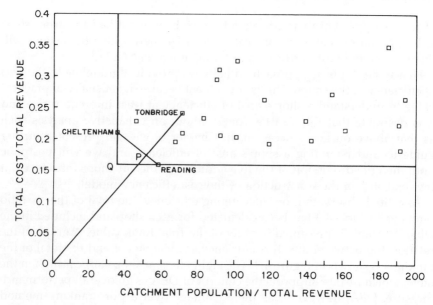

Figure 4.4   Cost efficiency versus market efficiency

with two inputs (*Total cost* and *Catchment population*) and one output (*Total revenue*). Hence the X-axis represents market penetration and the Y-axis represents efficient use of resources. If we consider the performance of the Tonbridge shop, DEA would lead us to target the point P as the appropriate trade-off between the performances of the most cost-efficient shop, Reading, and the shop with the greatest market penetration, Cheltenham. However, if as above we maintain that there is no relationship between the efficient use of resources and market penetration, then no such trade-off exists and the performance given by the point Q should be achievable.

Hence as a general theoretical rule, where there are two aspects of performance between which there is no trade-off, a shop should be capable of simultaneously achieving the best observed performance in each of these aspects. Incorporation of both aspects into the same DEA model will lead to an underestimation of true performance potential (e.g. the difference between P and Q above). The correct theoretical approach in such a case is to model each aspect separately and to combine the performance targets which result from each model. Where each aspect is multidimensional, this approach will result in the construction of two separate DEA models with distinct inputs. In the context of our case study, this means constructing a separate market efficiency model to determine potential revenue in terms of market characteristics only and then using the cost efficiency model to determine the resource required to support the potential revenue identified.

However, the correct theoretical approach could weaken one of the great strengths of DEA pointed out in Chapter 2—that the frontier against which performance is measured is substantiated by actual achieved performance. In the separate model approach, although the target for a shop within each model is based on achieved performance, the combination of these targets might represent a level of performance which no single shop has actually achieved. For example, the separate components of the target point Q in Figure 4.4 can be substantiated by the achieved performances of the Reading and Cheltenham shops but the combination of these components exceeds the achieved performance of either of these shops.

By contrast, the point P, which would be the target if we used a combined model, can be interpreted as an averaging of the performances of the Reading and Cheltenham shops. It will be much harder on this evidence to convince the manager of the Tonbridge shop that he should aspire to the standard of performance represented by the point Q rather than that of the point P. We must, however, balance against this the consideration that the managers should be encouraged to aspire to the performance represented by the point Q if the results of our analysis suggest it is achievable. This is particularly true in the case of shops such as Cheltenham and Reading where improvement potential would be identified for one of the components by a separate model approach but the combined model approach would identify no improvement potential at all.

A further point which is specific to our case study also requires discussion in this context. *Total revenue* is an appropriate output in addressing the efficient use of resources since each shop manager can control the level of resources assigned in conducting existing business. However, the shop manager can currently do nothing to control the historical decisions which have determined the current market penetration and for which a previous manager may have been responsible. The shop manager can only control *Revenue growth*. Hence this should be the only output in assessing manager performance in terms of market penetration. As the cost efficiency model already includes *Total revenue* as an output, a conflict with management accountability would arise if we were to construct a combined model in this case.

In our view, the ability to correctly reflect accountability outweighs the arguments surrounding achieved performance and makes the construction of separate models the preferred approach in this case. However, as there were points in favour of each approach, we will, for completeness, construct models using both approaches and compare the results.

4.7 INCORPORATING THE INFLUENCE OF MARKET FACTORS—BUILDING THE MODELS

We can construct the separate market efficiency model by repeating the approach used for the cost efficiency model but excluding resource related factors from consideration. However, we cannot construct the combined model by simply extending the build-up already used for the cost efficiency model since we have already established the absence of correlation between market factors and the final cost efficiency measure. It is nevertheless important to include only those factors which genuinely aid or impede market penetration. Hence our approach will be to construct the separate model first and then to replicate the factors used in this model within the combined model. Note that even if we were constructing only the combined model, the absence of correlation between market factors and cost efficiency would make it necessary to first consider the construction of separate models in order to identify the influencing factors.

Let us now consider the construction of a separate market efficiency model. We established above that *Revenue growth* should be the only output in this model. A number of additional issues arise at Step 1 of the model construction.

Table 4.5 shows the correlations of other factors with *Revenue growth*. The correlation with *Total revenue* is considerably higher than the correlations with other market factors, indicating that greater growth is achievable from a larger customer base. Hence we incorporate *Total revenue* into this model as an input rather than an output.

If we proceed as in the case of our previous model, we can generate efficiency scores for the single output *Revenue growth* and the single input *Total revenue*. We would then consider the correlations with this measure which are shown in Table 4.6. However the correlations in this instance exhibit a major peculiarity in that a large negative correlation now exists with *Total revenue*. The reason for this is that the relationship between *Revenue growth* and *Total revenue* exhibits significantly decreasing returns to scale which is not accounted for in the efficiency measure. This is illustrated in Figure 4.5. The true relationship is illustrated by the curve whilst the relationship assumed under constant returns to scale is illustrated by the straight line. Hence although shops with larger *Total revenue* can achieve higher *Revenue growth*, they achieve a lower growth in proportion to their existing revenue base. Using an efficiency measure which assumes constant returns to scale will, therefore, in general cause the shops with a higher *Total revenue* to have lower efficiency scores, and this is the cause of the negative correlations.

Our DEA development to date has assumed constant returns to scale. Incorporating variable returns to scale is the subject of Chapter 5 and

Table 4.5 Correlations of factors with revenue growth

Factor	Correlation
Total revenue	0.92187
Central overheads	0.92187
Controllable cost	0.88480
Staff cost	0.88288
Revenue Gp2	0.86590
Total cost	0.79798
Non-staff controllable cost	0.77407
Revenue Gp1	0.75683
Profit	0.70897
Revenue Gp3	0.70489
Revenue % growth	−0.53413
Age of shop (months)	0.45823
Non-staff cost	0.44122
Catchment population	0.40801
Competition	0.36508
Uncontrollable cost	0.35337
Customer service	−0.19840
Pitch	−0.16183

Table 4.6 Correlations of factors with constant-returns market efficiency measure

Factor	Correlation
Total revenue	−0.73909
Central overheads	−0.73909
Revenue Gp2	−0.73602
Age of shop (months)	−0.72431
Revenue Gp3	−0.68353
Profit	−0.62263
Controllable cost	−0.61347
Staff cost	−0.60831
Total cost	−0.58011
Non-staff controllable cost	−0.57173
Competition	−0.56078
Revenue growth	−0.53413
Catchment population	−0.41876
Non-staff cost	−0.36792
Revenue Gp1	−0.32626
Uncontrollable cost	−0.30712
Customer service	0.18162
Pitch	0.12443

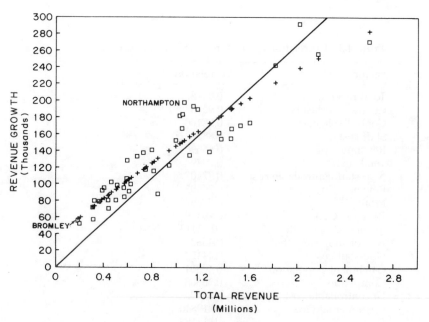

Figure 4.5   Revenue growth versus total revenue

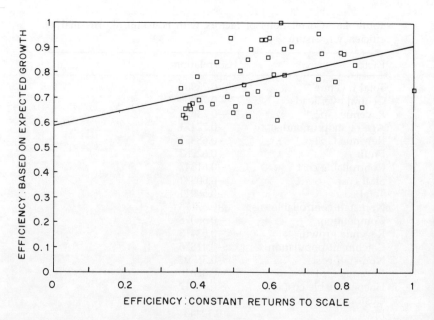

Figure 4.6   Comparison of market efficiency scores

further development of the model to account for variable returns to scale will be considered then. However, we can complete the development of the model in this chapter using our constant returns to scale methodology and it will be instructive to compare the results of this approach with that of Chapter 5.

We can make an assessment of the impact of decreasing returns to scale using the curve fitted in Figure 4.5 as a measure of *Expected growth* and examining the efficiency measure *Revenue growth / Expected growth*. In other words, we substitute *Expected growth* (derived from *Total revenue*) for *Total revenue* in the model formulation. We then continue our stepwise model build-up as before. Table 4.7 shows the correlations associated with each step of the model construction. Note that having accounted for decreasing

Table 4.7 Market efficiency model: correlations at each step

		Step 1	Step 2	Step 3
OUTPUTS	Revenue growth	*	*	*
INPUTS	Expected growth	*	*	*
	Competition		*	*
	Catchment population			*
Age of shop (months)		−0.40069	−0.08051	−0.01530
Catchment population		0.07856	0.45808	0.13300
Central overheads		0.02233	0.36987	0.34409
Customer service		−0.01486	−0.19048	−0.11838
Non-staff controllable cost		0.18048	0.52196	0.34731
Uncontrollable cost		0.07832	0.30436	0.16355
Pitch		−0.03038	−0.01443	−0.16480
Profit		−0.11430	0.12893	0.20597
Revenue Gp1		0.40730	0.59032	0.47933
Revenue Gp2		−0.05582	0.25862	0.27045
Revenue Gp3		−0.07666	0.33428	0.26766
Revenue growth		0.38920	0.62255	0.53911
Revenue % growth		0.43665	0.09599	0.07168
Staff cost		0.17535	0.48230	0.39939
Competition		−0.22127	0.33192	0.13542
Non-staff cost		0.09917	0.35773	0.20252
Total revenue		0.02233	0.36987	0.34409
Total cost		0.16396	0.49125	0.36237
Controllable cost		0.17841	0.49327	0.39997
Revenue Gp1 % of Total revenue		0.47524	0.32287	0.21082
Revenue Gp2 % of Total revenue		−0.39943	−0.40286	−0.20201
Revenue Gp3 % of Total revenue		0.00511	0.19285	0.03801

returns to scale, there is now virtually no correlation between the Step 1 efficiency score and *Total revenue*.

The efficiency scores at Step 1 compared with the equivalent measure generated under the assumption of constant returns to scale are shown in Table 4.8 and graphically in Figure 4.6. Although there is some correlation between the two sets of scores, the results for any particular shop can vary substantially.

A number of issues arose in deciding which other factors to introduce. The Step 1 efficiency scores exhibit a strong positive correlation with *Revenue Gp1 % of total* and a strong negative correlation with *Revenue Gp2 % of total*. This suggests that the breakdown of revenue by product group is important. However, using our current approach, the revenue breakdown would need to be incorporated within the regression relationship which estimates *Expected growth*. To achieve this would require assumptions to be made about the mathematical form of the relationship and it is far from clear what these assumptions should be. We must therefore accept this as a limitation of the current approach and delay the inclusion of revenue breakdown in our model until the methodology of Chapter 5 is introduced.

Age of shop emerged as the next strongest relationship. However, it is not completely clear that this is a causal relationship. Clearly the age of a shop will determine the extent to which a shop has been able to build up revenue, but this has already been accounted for in introducing *Total revenue* as an input. The negative correlation between *Age of shop* and the efficiency measure at Step 1 indicates that higher growth relative to *Total revenue* is possible in newer shops. This might be because newer shops have greater unfulfilled market potential and it is easier to grow in these markets. If so, it might be that the unfulfilled potential is better expressed in terms of market factors such as *Competition*, *Catchment population* and *Pitch* but the relationship with *Age of shop* appears stronger because it is a proxy for all market factors.

With this in mind, we have allowed the other market factors to be introduced into the model first. It should be noted that *Catchment population* and *Competition* are correlated in that the higher population areas have attracted greater competition. This has the result that the effect of one is to some extent outweighed by the other, which weakens the observed correlations and hence the case for the inclusion of *Catchment population* and *Competition* in the model. The inclusion of *Competition* at Step 1 is therefore a marginal decision if based on the strength of correlation alone, but following this the inclusion of *Catchment population* is clearly indicated.

At Step 3, it becomes clear that there is no longer a correlation between the efficiency scores at that step and *Age of shop*, which suggests that *Age of shop* was indeed a proxy for *Catchment population* and *Competition*. At this point, although there could be a hint of a relationship with *Pitch*,

Table 4.8 Market efficiency: constant returns and decreasing returns

	Efficiency decreasing returns	Efficiency constant returns
NORTHAMPTON	1.000	0.626
MANCHESTER 2	0.957	0.732
OXFORD ST	0.940	0.595
FULHAM	0.939	0.486
BRIXTON	0.932	0.585
MILTON KEYNES	0.931	0.571
BRISTOL	0.906	0.658
CROYDON	0.896	0.636
PLYMOUTH	0.894	0.543
GLOUCESTER	0.882	0.793
LEICESTER	0.877	0.741
WATFORD	0.875	0.804
BIRMINGHAM 1	0.862	0.591
BRADFORD	0.852	0.535
NEWCASTLE	0.840	0.449
CRAWLEY	0.832	0.835
WOLVERHAMPTON	0.807	0.516
HOUNSLOW	0.793	0.608
MANCHESTER 1	0.789	0.638
READING	0.783	0.396
MAIDENHEAD	0.775	0.732
LEAMINGTON SPA	0.765	0.780
ILFORD	0.751	0.526
CHELTENHAM	0.735	0.351
BROMLEY	0.732	1.000
YORK	0.725	0.563
ST. ALBANS	0.715	0.535
TONBRIDGE	0.713	0.618
EALING	0.703	0.479
SLOUGH	0.689	0.402
SWINDON	0.675	0.385
REDDITCH	0.674	0.438
WOOD GREEN	0.668	0.375
BRENT CROSS	0.664	0.501
HARLOW	0.663	0.542
HIGH WYCOMBE	0.663	0.855
DUDLEY	0.660	0.408
VICTORIA	0.656	0.363
HAMMERSMITH	0.653	0.379
SOLIHULL	0.640	0.495
KENSINGTON	0.627	0.358
REIGATE	0.624	0.539
SUTTON COLDFIELD	0.616	0.365
WINDSOR	0.610	0.620
BIRMINGHAM 2	0.521	0.350

Table 4.9 Market efficiency model: efficiency scores at each step

		Step 1	Step 2	Step 3
OUTPUTS	Revenue growth	*	*	*
INPUTS	Total revenue	*	*	*
	Competition		*	*
	Catchment population			*
	NORTHAMPTON	1.000	1.000	1.000
	FULHAM	0.939	1.000	1.000
	VICTORIA	0.656	1.000	1.000
	MILTON KEYNES	0.931	0.978	1.000
	NEWCASTLE	0.840	0.972	1.000
	CHELTENHAM	0.735	0.860	1.000
	REIGATE	0.624	0.624	1.000
	OXFORD ST	0.940	0.980	0.980
	READING	0.783	0.833	0.968
	MAIDENHEAD	0.775	0.775	0.961
	MANCHESTER 2	0.957	0.957	0.957
	BRIXTON	0.932	0.954	0.954
	BRISTOL	0.906	0.944	0.944
	CROYDON	0.896	0.943	0.943
	PLYMOUTH	0.894	0.942	0.943
	TONBRIDGE	0.713	0.713	0.933
	LEAMINGTON SPA	0.765	0.765	0.932
	KENSINGTON	0.627	0.917	0.917
	BIRMINGHAM 1	0.862	0.896	0.896
	LEICESTER	0.877	0.894	0.894
	SWINDON	0.675	0.814	0.887
	BRADFORD	0.852	0.884	0.884
	GLOUCESTER	0.882	0.882	0.882
	HAMMERSMITH	0.653	0.880	0.880
	WATFORD	0.875	0.875	0.875
	WOLVERHAMPTON	0.807	0.844	0.844
	CRAWLEY	0.832	0.832	0.832
	ST. ALBANS	0.715	0.715	0.833
	HOUNSLOW	0.793	0.823	0.823
	REDDITCH	0.674	0.674	0.808
	MANCHESTER 1	0.789	0.802	0.802
	WINDSOR	0.610	0.610	0.772
	ILFORD	0.751	0.757	0.757
	YORK	0.725	0.752	0.752
	BROMLEY	0.732	0.732	0.732
	DUDLEY	0.660	0.703	0.727
	SLOUGH	0.689	0.713	0.723
	EALING	0.703	0.723	0.723
	WOOD GREEN	0.668	0.708	0.708
	SUTTON COLDFIELD	0.616	0.650	0.704
	BRENT CROSS	0.664	0.676	0.676
	HARLOW	0.663	0.669	0.669
	HIGH WYCOMBE	0.663	0.663	0.663
	SOLIHULL	0.640	0.657	0.657
	BIRMINGHAM 2	0.521	0.544	0.544

Table 4.10 Comparison of cost, market and combined efficiency scores .

	Combined	Cost	Market	
NORTHAMPTON	1.000	1.000	1.000	EFFICIENT COST,
NEWCASTLE	1.000	1.000	1.000	MARKET & COMBINED
READING	1.000	1.000	0.968	
MANCHESTER 2	1.000	1.000	0.957	
PLYMOUTH	1.000	1.000	0.943	
LEAMINGTON SPA	1.000	1.000	0.932	
KENSINGTON	1.000	1.000	0.917	EFFICIENT COST
LEICESTER	1.000	1.000	0.894	& COMBINED
BRADFORD	1.000	1.000	0.884	
GLOUCESTER	1.000	1.000	0.882	
HAMMERSMITH	1.000	1.000	0.880	
ST. ALBANS	1.000	1.000	0.833	
SUTTON COLDFIELD	1.000	1.000	0.704	
CHELTENHAM	1.000	0.954	1.000	
FULHAM	1.000	0.913	1.000	EFFICIENT MARKET
REIGATE	1.000	0.887	1.000	& COMBINED
MILTON KEYNES	1.000	0.708	1.000	
OXFORD ST	1.000	0.951	0.980	EFFICIENT
CROYDON	1.000	0.858	0.943	COMBINED ONLY
VICTORIA	0.807	0.722	1.000	EFFICIENT
				MARKET ONLY
BROMLEY	0.993	0.817	0.732	
WATFORD	0.991	0.964	0.875	
WOLVERHAMPTON	0.951	0.883	0.844	
BIRMINGHAM 2	0.940	0.922	0.544	
MAIDENHEAD	0.928	0.806	0.961	
HIGH WYCOMBE	0.926	0.926	0.663	
SWINDON	0.921	0.806	0.887	
BRISTOL	0.917	0.838	0.944	
WOOD GREEN	0.914	0.891	0.708	
SLOUGH	0.909	0.892	0.723	
BRIXTON	0.901	0.853	0.954	
MANCHESTER 1	0.889	0.832	0.802	
REDDITCH	0.876	0.874	0.808	NOT
BRENT CROSS	0.872	0.806	0.676	EFFICIENT
DUDLEY	0.867	0.841	0.727	
TONBRIDGE	0.852	0.852	0.933	
SOLIHULL	0.848	0.771	0.657	
CRAWLEY	0.841	0.780	0.832	
YORK	0.833	0.548	0.752	
BIRMINGHAM 1	0.821	0.745	0.896	
ILFORD	0.820	0.820	0.757	
EALING	0.776	0.743	0.723	
WINDSOR	0.761	0.715	0.772	
HARLOW	0.699	0.616	0.669	
HOUNSLOW	0.675	0.533	0.823	

it is difficult to justify the inclusion of any other factor in the model. In practice, our preference would be to carry out further investigation of the relationships between *Age of shop, Competition, Catchment population* and *Pitch* before accepting this as the final model. In particular, we would want the measures themselves to come under close scrutiny in terms of whether, in some cases, better quality measures could be made available (e.g. *Pitch* only has two possible values) or whether alternative measures might be more appropriate (e.g. counts of the flow of people past a shop may be a better measure of potential business than *Catchment population*).

Table 4.9 shows the efficiency scores at each stage of the model build-up. Table 4.10 shows the final results in direct comparison with those obtained if we extend the cost efficiency model to include *Catchment population* and *Competition*. There are 19 efficient shops in the combined model. Two of these shops, Newcastle and Northampton, are efficient in both the cost and market efficiency models. Of the remainder, all but Oxford Street and Croydon are efficient in either the cost efficiency model or the market efficiency model. One shop, Victoria, is efficient in the market efficiency model but not in the combined model. [Note that the latter result can happen only where a sub-model is not an exact subset of a larger model. For an efficient shop in a true sub-model, the weights from the sub-model together with zero weights for the factors not in the sub-model establish the shop's efficiency in the full model. In this case, we do not have a true sub-model since *Total revenue* is an output in the combined model and an input (with transformation applied) in the market efficiency model.]

Hence in terms of the shops which define the efficiency frontiers, there is a good degree of consistency between the separate and combined model approaches. However, the variation in the efficiency scores reflects our earlier discussion of how the approaches will lead to different views on achievable targets. We will comment further on this in Chapter 6 when we review the important issue of what we have learnt about the shops themselves.

Chapter 5

Accommodating Returns to Scale—Simple Mathematical Development and Results

5.1 STATEMENT OF THE PROBLEM

In Chapter 4, we encountered the problem of returns to scale in the context of examining *Revenue growth* in relation to *Total revenue*. Figure 4.5 illustrated that although higher *Revenue growth* can be derived from a higher *Total revenue*, the amount of *Revenue growth* which is achievable per unit of *Total revenue* becomes lower as *Total revenue* increases. This is an example of decreasing returns to scale.

Increasing returns to scale is exhibited where an increase in input(s) (keeping the mix constant where there is more than one input) results in a greater than proportionate increase in output. Decreasing returns to scale exists where the result is a lesser than proportionate increase in output, as in the case examined in Section 4.7. Constant returns to scale, as assumed in earlier chapters, exists where the result is a proportionate increase in output. A formal definition of returns to scale is given by Banker [25].

Expressing this in simple graphical terms for a single output and a single input, constant returns to scale means that there is a straight line relationship between input and output, increasing returns to scale means that the relationship is expressed by a curve which increases more steeply than a straight line, and decreasing returns to scale means that the relationship is expressed by a curve which increases less steeply than a straight line.

Let us examine what this means in terms of measuring efficiency. Figure 5.1 reproduces the situation encountered in Figure 4.5. The curve indicated by a succession of crosses is an estimate of the relationship between *Total revenue* and *Revenue growth* obtained by regression analysis. Clearly, in

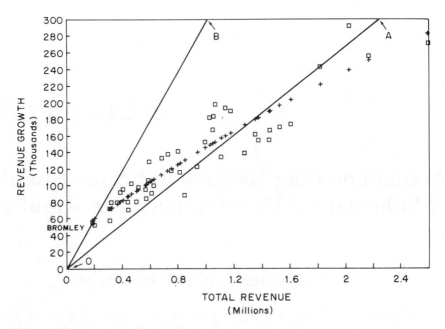

Figure 5.1 Introducing returns to scale

order to do this it is necessary to make an assumption about the form of the equation of the curve.

The line OA is the best estimate of the relationship, also obtained by regression, if constant returns to scale is assumed.

The line OB is the line against which we would measure efficiency using DEA under the assumption of constant returns to scale, as in the development in earlier chapters.

A popular misconception in arguments put forward against analyses which assume constant returns to scale is that, because the lines OA and OB diverge, it is unreasonable to project the line OB indefinitely—because, as the line is projected, measurement takes place against a boundary which becomes ever further from many of the observed values. However, it can be seen from Figure 5.2 that the measure is perfectly equitable provided the distribution of observed values remains equitable about the line OA.

In Figure 5.2, the point C on the line OA would have efficiency ID/IC and the point E on the line OA would have efficiency JF/JE. Elementary geometry establishes that the ratios ID/IC and JF/JE are equal. Hence as long as the data points are equitably distributed around the regression line, as would be the case when constant returns to scale exists, then the constant

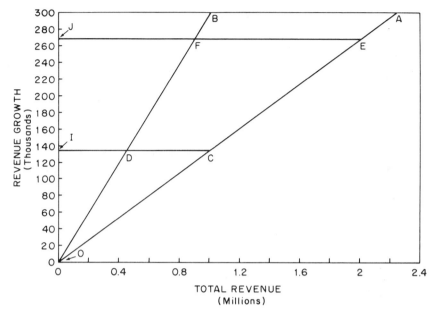

Figure 5.2 Efficiency: constant returns to scale

returns to scale DEA measure itself is equitable. In fact if decreasing returns to scale were assumed in such a case then a bias against the smaller shops would be introduced.

Hence it is important in general, before using a model which assumes decreasing returns to scale, to seek supporting evidence for the existence of decreasing returns to scale.

Figure 5.2 establishes that the validity of the assumption of constant returns to scale is effectively a question of how equitably the data points lie around the line OA. In Figure 5.1, it is clear that the distribution about OA is far from equitable, with the majority of data points for lower *Total revenue* values appearing above the line and the majority of data points for higher *Total revenue* values appearing below the line. Hence in this case we should be seeking to allow for decreasing returns to scale.

By way of comparison, if we refer back to Figure 2.1, where we first investigated the relationship between *Total cost* and *Total revenue*, the data points are quite evenly distributed about the regression line and the assumption of constant returns to scale would appear to be quite reasonable.

In deciding how to accommodate the effects of returns to scale, we will proceed along the lines of Chapter 2, that is by first establishing a graphical approach and developing this into a more general theory.

5.2   THE REVISED FRONTIER

Having established in Figure 5.1 that the constant returns to scale frontier, the line OB, does not provide an equitable base against which to measure efficiency, we must first establish an alternative frontier. Following the approach of Chapter 2, we can establish a frontier using best observed performance.

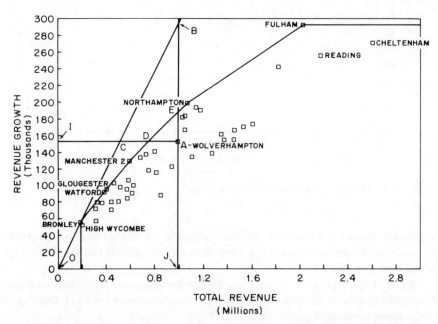

Figure 5.3   Efficiency assuming decreasing returns

Such an approach would give us the frontier containing the shops Bromley, Watford, Gloucester, Manchester 2, Northampton and Fulham, as shown in Figure 5.3. The shops identified on this frontier represent best performance in the sense that, for each shop on the frontier, there is no larger shop which has a higher ratio of *Revenue growth* to *Total revenue*. Also, for each of these shops with the exception of Bromley, there are smaller shops with higher ratios of *Revenue growth* to *Total revenue* but we are now attributing this to the effect of decreasing returns to scale. Once again, our assumption in constructing the frontier itself is that there is a trade-off between the actual achievements of the best performing shops. For example, in the case of Manchester 2 and Northampton, we assume that, because the points representing the performance of these two shops are demonstrably achievable, the performance represented by any point on the line joining them is achievable.

The difference between the trade-off in this analysis and that in the constant returns to scale analysis is that size is now part of the trade-off. In the constant returns to scale case, we had trade-off between outputs or trade-off between inputs, but the relationship between output and input was constant in that, if all input was doubled, all output would be doubled, as illustrated by the line OB in Figure 5.3. In the case of decreasing returns to scale, there is now an additional trade-off between output and input in that, if all input is doubled, the resultant output will be less than double, the amount being determined by trade-off between actual achieved performances.

Let us now turn our attention to shops not on the frontier. Taking the Wolverhampton shop as a typical example, we can see that it is not on the frontier because there is a smaller shop, Manchester 2, and a larger shop, Northampton, each of which has a higher ratio of *Revenue growth* to *Total revenue* than the Wolverhampton shop. Consequently there is a point on the trade-off line joining Manchester 2 and Northampton equal in size to the Wolverhampton shop but with a higher ratio of *Revenue growth* to *Total revenue*. This is the point E in Figure 5.3.

Let us now consider measurement of the efficiency of the Wolverhampton shop. For constant returns to scale, by analogy with our analysis of Figure 2.1, the efficiency measure would be the ratio JA/JB to maximize output given the input or IC/IA to minimize the input given the output. We established during the analysis of Figure 2.1 that these ratios were equal.

In the decreasing returns to scale case, we can proceed by analogy to establish an efficiency measure relative to our revised frontier. Our measure will therefore be the ratio JA/JE to maximize output given the input or the ratio ID/IA to minimize input given the output. Note that the equality of the two ratios (JA/JB and IC/IA) in the constant returns to scale case was a consequence of the frontier (OB) passing through the origin. For decreasing returns to scale this is no longer the case and the two ratios (JA/JE and ID/IA) are not equal. Hence, for decreasing returns to scale, the efficiency measure based on output maximization is not the same as the efficiency measure based on input minimization.

Considering again the constant returns to scale efficiency ratio IC/IA, we can manipulate this mathematically as follows:

$$\frac{IC}{IA} = \frac{ID}{IA} \times \frac{IC}{ID}$$

We have just established ID/IA as our efficiency measure under decreasing returns to scale. By analogy with our constant returns to scale analysis, the ratio IC/ID is equivalent to the efficiency measure of the point D under the assumption of constant returns to scale.

5.3   EFFICIENCY AND THE MOST PRODUCTIVE SCALE SIZE

Let us consider in greater depth what the latter measure means. If we retrace the very first steps of our efficiency analysis in Chapter 2, we established a single most productive shop, Reading, which had the highest ratio of output to input.

In Figure 2.1, we established the efficiency frontier as the straight line OC which contained all points equal in efficiency to Reading. Referring back to our definition of returns to scale at the beginning of the chapter, we can see that the assumption of constant returns to scale is inherent in this straight line projection. The assumption of constant returns to scale therefore determines that the performance of all shops is measured relative to the most productive shop.

In Figure 5.3, we have the identical situation where the assumption of constant returns to scale determines that the performance of all shops is measured relative to the most productive shop, Bromley, using the line OB. In establishing the existence of decreasing returns to scale, we do not refute that Bromley is the most productive shop, we merely accept that larger shops cannot be as productive as Bromley. In recognition of this fact, we can regard Bromley's scale of operation as the most productive scale size.

We observed that the ratio IC/ID above measured the efficiency of the point D under the assumption of constant returns to scale. We can now interpret this as measuring the inefficiency due to the divergence of the actual scale of operation at D from the most productive scale size.

Hence, we have established that our original constant returns to scale efficiency measure is the combination of productive inefficiency given the scale of operations (ID/IA) and inefficiency due to the divergence of the actual scale of operations from the most productive scale size (IC/ID).

The importance of this result in practice depends very much on the situation being analysed. In Figure 5.3, it is really only the ratio ID/IA which is of importance since it would be the ultimate in conflicting objectives for management to reduce the size of shops in order to increase their growth potential. In this case, management must accept that the proportional growth achievable becomes lower as shops become larger and the key criterion in judging a shop manager's performance is the proportional growth achieved compared with shops with a similar scale of operation.

On the other hand, both ratios would be of importance if decreasing returns to scale had been a feature of the analysis of *Total revenue* and *Total cost* in Figure 2.1. The ratio ID/IA would be important to senior management in assessing how efficiently a shop manager is running his shop given its scale of operation. The ratio IC/ID would be useful in making policy decisions as to what the scale of operations should be. For example, it may be that even if a shop manager is operating his shop as efficiently as possible, the marginal return of operating at a higher level of scale is not justified. The ratio IC/ID will provide the basis from which such an assessment can be made.

A feature of Figure 5.3 is that the most productive shop, Bromley, is the lowest point on the frontier and the frontier exhibits only decreasing returns to scale. In general this will not be the case. We can illustrate this using our original example of Figure 2.1.

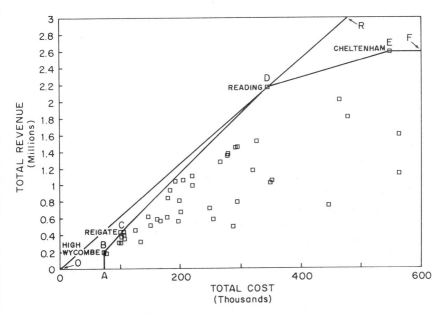

Figure 5.4   Returns to scale: revenue versus cost

Figure 5.4 shows the revised analysis in this case if we do not assume constant returns to scale. Here, as already established, the most productive shop is Reading. In this case, however, there are two smaller shops than Reading on the frontier. Hence the frontier exhibits increasing returns to scale up to the most productive scale size and decreasing returns to scale thereafter.

Hence our initial development has only referred specifically to decreasing returns to scale because of the nature of the problem being analysed, but the general problem may contain both increasing and decreasing returns to scale. The most convenient terminology for this is variable returns to scale.

5.4   EFFICIENCY BASED ON MINIMIZING INPUT

Having now derived a revised graphical approach to accommodate variable returns to scale, let us examine how this affects the mathematical formulation. We will again use notation similar to Chapter 3, for example $I(Wo)$ for Wolverhampton's inputs and $O(Wo)$ for its outputs.

First of all, it is worth noting that mathematics consistent with that developed in Chapter 3 for the constant returns to scale efficiency measure is established quite easily from Figure 5.3, in that:

$$IC = \frac{I(B)}{O(B)} \times O(Wo)$$

$$IA = I(Wo)$$

Hence

$$\frac{IC}{IA} = \frac{O(Wo)}{I(Wo)} \times \frac{I(B)}{O(B)} \tag{5.1}$$

which is the ratio of a weighted sum of Wolverhampton's outputs to a weighted sum of its inputs; and quite clearly if we substitute Bromley's outputs and inputs in place of Wolverhampton's, the ratio is 1. We can again constrain either the denominator or the numerator to 1, as was done in the earlier development.

Turning now to the variable returns to scale efficiency measure, we have produced a simplified diagram in Figure 5.5 which contains only those features of Figure 5.3 which are essential to this stage of the development. We will start with the efficiency measure based on minimizing input given the level of output which we defined above as the ratio ID/IA. [In practice we would use the minimum input approach only when the input is controllable. However this is a convenient example from which to generate the theory even though the input is uncontrollable.]

The equation of the line joining Manchester 2 and Northampton is

$$Y = 0.147\,X + 42.070$$

where 0.147 is the slope of the line and 42.070 is the value of the intercept on the Y-axis which defines the point P.

The point E has the same input value as Wolverhampton, $I(Wo)$, and therefore by virtue of also lying on the above line, has output value

$$0.147\,I(Wo) + 42.070$$

The point Q has the same output value as E.

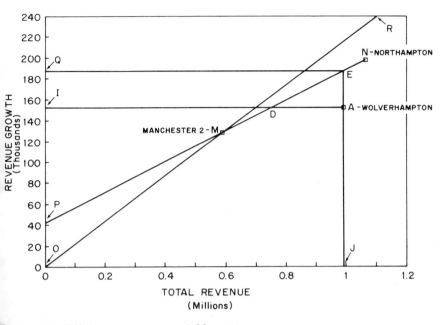

Figure 5.5 Efficiency measure: variable returns

Simple geometry establishes the following relationships in Figure 5.5:

$$\frac{ID}{IA} = \frac{PD}{PE} = \frac{PI}{PQ} = \frac{OI - OP}{OQ - OP} = \frac{O(Wo) - 42.070}{(0.147\, I(Wo) + 42.070) - 42.070}$$

$$= \frac{O(Wo) - 42.070}{0.147\, I(Wo)} \tag{5.2}$$

$$= 0.758$$

Since Manchester 2 and Northampton lie on the line itself, they satisfy

$$O(Ma) = 0.147\, I(Ma) + 42.070$$

$$O(Nh) = 0.147\, I(Nh) + 42.070$$

which rearranged give

$$\frac{O(Ma) - 42.070}{0.147\, I(Ma)} = 1$$

$$\frac{O(Nh) - 42.070}{0.147\, I(Nh)} = 1$$

Hence the variable returns to scale efficiency measure is similar in form to the constant returns to scale measure but has a constant term subtracted from the weighted output value in the numerator. As before, the shops defining the segment of the frontier to which measurement is made have a ratio of 1.

Also, as in the development in Section 3.1, the numerators and denominators of the ratios can be divided by the value of the denominator of equation 5.2 (= 145.62), to constrain the denominator of equation 5.2 to 1, giving the following revised ratio for Wolverhampton:

$$\frac{0.0687\ O(\text{Wo})\ -\ 0.2889}{0.0010\ I(\text{Wo})} \tag{5.2a}$$

and similar ratios for Manchester 2 and Northampton. Note that in so doing, the ratio of the input weight to the output weight would remain equal to the slope of the segment of the frontier to which measurement was made. Hence, as in the analysis in Section 3.1, the ratio of the weights gives us the value of the trade-off along the segment of the frontier to which measurement is made.

A similar argument to that used in Section 3.1 also establishes that the value of the ratio for Wolverhampton, 0.758, is the maximum value which can be obtained for a weighted ratio of this form subject to the same weighted ratio for other shops not exceeding 1.

The constant term in the ratio in equation 5.2 is the value of the intercept on the output axis (OP) of the projection of the segment of the frontier between Manchester 2 and Northampton (PMN). The line OMR shows the projection which would have existed if constant returns to scale had applied at M. By definition, a frontier exhibiting decreasing returns to scale is of lesser slope than the line representing constant returns to scale. Hence Figure 5.5 is typical of all cases of decreasing returns to scale, in that the actual frontier line segment MN is below the line representing constant returns to scale MR whilst the projections of these lines to the output axis are such that the projection of the frontier MP is above the projection of the constant returns to scale line MO, and hence, in particular, the projection of the frontier has a positive intercept on the output axis.

If increasing returns to scale had applied, the above situation would have been reversed, resulting in a negative intercept on the output axis. Finally, if constant returns to scale had applied, the frontier would be coincident with the line OMR resulting in a zero intercept on the output axis.

As the value of the intercept is subtracted from the numerator in the ratios above, then the general mathematical form of our measure has become

$$\frac{\text{Weighted sum of outputs} + \text{Constant}}{\text{Weighted sum of inputs}}$$

where the constant is

- negative for decreasing returns to scale,
- positive for increasing returns to scale, and
- zero for constant returns to scale (leaving the ratio as in equation 5.1).

Note that we could also develop the alternative view of efficiency as we did in Section 3.2. We will not do that in detail here since the mathematical steps are almost identical. The essential difference is that we no longer need a conversion of scale since the scale of our graph in Figure 5.5 is based on actual input and actual output as opposed to the output to input ratios of Figure 3.2. The mathematical steps required here are simply those of Section 3.2 with the substitution of I (input) in place of X (output 2/input) and O (output) in place of Y (output 1/input). However, in this instance, the mathematical process is complete following the identification of K_1 and K_2 since there are no output to input ratios to convert. Hence our final mathematical representation is identical to that of Section 3.2 but with L_1 and L_2 taking the values identified for K_1 and K_2. However, as $K_1 + K_2 = 1$ by definition, we have arrived at an identical mathematical representation but have imposed the additional constraint that $L_1 + L_2 = 1$. In other words, the dual weights must sum to one. This and other values derived in this section are confirmed by Tables 5.1 and 5.2 which show the complete set of results generated using the mathematics of Appendix A.

5.5   EFFICIENCY BASED ON MAXIMIZING OUTPUT

Let us now examine the efficiency measure based on maximizing output given the input which we defined as the ratio JA/JE. We pointed out in Section 3.4 that, although it is of no consequence in terms of measuring efficiency, the output maximization model should use a reciprocal formulation because of the effect on dual weights and slack values. We will therefore continue to adopt that procedure here and we confirm the need to do so in Appendix A. We therefore revise our efficiency measure to JE/JA. Using the values established above gives

$$\frac{JE}{JA} = \frac{OQ}{OI} = \frac{0.147\,I(Wo) + 42.070}{O(Wo)} \tag{5.3}$$

$$= 1.231 \text{ (reciprocal value} = 0.812)$$

Again, we can divide the ratio by the value of the denominator (=152.47) to constrain the denominator to 1. This gives the revised ratio

$$\frac{0.000963 \; I(\text{Wo}) \; + \; 0.2759}{0.00656 \; O(\text{Wo})} \tag{5.3a}$$

A similar argument to that used in Section 3.1 also establishes that the value of the ratio for Wolverhampton, 1.231, is the minimum value which can be obtained for a weighted ratio of this form subject to the same weighted ratio for other shops being at least 1. This ratio is similar to that in equation 5.2 but has the constant term associated with the input value rather than the output value and its sign is reversed; hence the conditions for the constant in this case are

- positive for decreasing returns to scale,
- negative for increasing returns to scale, and
- zero for constant returns to scale.

However, it is probably less confusing if we regard the constant here as being subtracted rather than added so that the mathematical form is

$$\frac{\text{Weighted sum of inputs} \; - \; \text{Constant}}{\text{Weighted sum of outputs}}$$

in which case the conditions for the constant are restored to

- negative for decreasing returns to scale,
- positive for increasing returns to scale, and
- zero for constant returns to scale.

as in the previous case.

Note that the two mathematical formulations provide further confirmation of an earlier observation that the measure based on input minimization is no longer equivalent to the measure based on output maximization unless constant returns to scale applies. In fact the mathematics allow us to extend this statement. For this purpose we revert to the original rather than the reciprocal ratio and proceed as follows:

$$\frac{O + C}{I} > \frac{O}{I - C'} \qquad \text{if } C > 0 \text{ and } C' > 0$$

$$\frac{O + C}{I} = \frac{O}{I - C'} \qquad \text{if } C = 0 \text{ and } C' = 0$$

$$\frac{O + C}{I} < \frac{O}{I - C'} \qquad \text{if } C < 0 \text{ and } C' < 0$$

In other words, the input minimization measure is higher if both measurements are made under increasing returns to scale, the measures are the same if both measurements are made under constant returns to scale, and the output maximization measure is higher if both measurements are made under decreasing returns to scale.

5.6 THE BOUNDARIES OF THE FRONTIER

So far, we have said nothing about the endpoints of the frontier. The development in this respect is similar to the development in Chapter 3 of the two output, one input case with constant returns to scale.

In Figure 5.3, the shop at the higher end of the frontier is Fulham. There are only two shops larger than Fulham in terms of *Total revenue* and these are Reading and Cheltenham. Fulham not only has a higher ratio of *Revenue growth* to *Total revenue* than either of these shops but actually has higher *Revenue growth* from a lower *Total revenue* base. In excluding Reading and Cheltenham from the frontier, we are asserting that, because they each have a larger *Total revenue* than Fulham, they should at least be capable of producing as much *Revenue growth* as Fulham. We are also discounting the possibility that they could produce more in the absence of demonstrable achievement in that respect. In other words we are accepting a reduction of returns to scale to zero but we do not accept that they can become negative. Hence in seeking to measure the efficiency of Reading or Cheltenham based on output maximization, we extend the frontier horizontally from Fulham.

We can apply a similar argument at the lower end of the frontier where we extend the frontier vertically below Bromley. Note, however, that this places a lower bound on the value to which input can be reduced and asserts infinite returns to scale between the lowest point on the frontier and the point vertically below on the input axis. Certainly this is less satisfactory in terms of direct practical interpretation than was the case for the higher end of the frontier, and many practitioners feel happier with a frontier which terminates at the origin rather than a point along the input axis. However, there is again the positive feature of being able to substantiate the measurement by demonstrable achieved performance.

The mathematical development above does, however, allow an alternative approach at the lower end of the frontier. This is best illustrated using Figure 5.4.

Our mathematical formulations in equations 5.2a and 5.3a apply to the frontier ABCDEF in Figure 5.4. We established that the constant term in the ratio was negative for decreasing returns to scale and so a negative constant will be obtained in evaluating each shop whose measurement is relative to a point on the segment DEF of the frontier. Similarly a positive constant will be obtained for each shop whose measurement is to a point on the segment ABCD of the frontier where increasing returns to scale applies.

Hence in order that measurement may be to any point of the frontier ABCDEF, our mathematics must assume that the constant can take any value positive or negative. We know from the constant returns to scale analysis (equation 5.1 above) that, if we were to restrict the constant to be zero, we would cause measurement to be with respect to the frontier ODR.

If therefore we restrict the constant to be less than or equal to zero, measurement with respect to the variable returns to scale frontier is now possible only where decreasing returns to scale applies. Where increasing returns to scale applies, measurement is enforced with respect to the constant returns to scale frontier. Hence our frontier under this restriction becomes ODEF. Our earlier discussion established that the point D represented the most productive scale size. The frontier ODEF therefore exhibits the features of constant returns to scale up to the most productive scale size and decreasing returns thereafter.

The use of this approach avoids the problems of interpretation at the lower end of the frontier referred to above. However, by overcoming the problem in this way, the ability to incorporate increasing returns to scale is sacrificed. It would be wrong to refer to either method of treating the lower end of the frontier as the recommended approach, each having the advantages and disadvantages discussed. The decision as to which to use in any particular case will usually be based on the importance of reflecting increasing returns to scale in the analysis.

A further alternative is to restrict the constant in the mathematical formulation to be greater than or equal to zero. This would lead to the measurement frontier becoming ABCDR which exhibits the features of increasing returns to scale up to the most productive scale size and constant returns to scale thereafter. However, as this method supports rather than avoids two of the most common practical objections raised, namely the lower end of the frontier terminating at a point other than the origin and the infinite linear projection of the upper end of the frontier, it is unlikely that this approach will find a great deal of use in practice.

The mathematics associated with the endpoints of the frontier also require separate discussion.

Figure 5.6 shows the lower end of the variable returns to scale frontier of Figure 5.3. The efficiency measure for High Wycombe based on input minimization is given by the ratio ID/IC. Using mathematical notation as above gives us

$$\frac{ID}{IC} = \frac{I(B)}{I(H)} = \frac{0 \times O(H) + I(B)}{I(H)} = 0.913 \qquad (5.4)$$

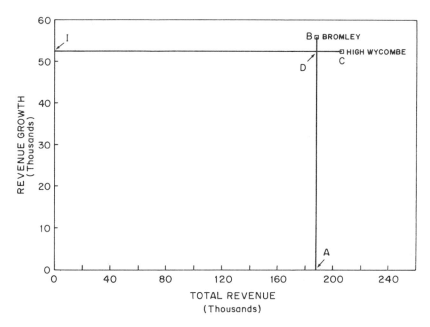

Figure 5.6 Lower end of variable returns frontier

Dividing this equation by the value of the denominator (205.44) to constrain the denominator to 1 gives

$$\frac{0 \times O(\text{H}) + 0.913}{0.00487\ I(\text{H})} \qquad (5.4a)$$

The ratio in equation 5.4 is similar in form to equation 5.2 but with an output weight of zero. The constant term is positive and therefore consistent with the results which established that a positive constant is obtained in equation 5.2 whenever measurement is to a segment of the frontier which exhibits increasing returns to scale.

A further observation is required here. Our efficiency measure asserts that, based on the performance of Bromley, input could be reduced to that of the point D with no loss of output but there is no demonstrable evidence that input can be reduced further. However, the performance of Bromley does provide evidence that performance at the point D could be improved through an increase in output by the amount BD without an associated increase in input. Such an increase can only be possible where the slope of the frontier is infinite as is the case for AB in Figure 5.6. The infinite slope also establishes the output weight of zero in the mathematical formulation.

Hence our efficiency measure, as defined, tells us the maximum decrease in input which can be made without an associated decrease in output based on demonstrable achieved performance, at which point there is an additional 'slack' value in output. The 'slack' value will always be obtained in conjunction with a zero output weight in the mathematical formulation. This result is wholly consistent with that established in the two output, one input, constant returns to scale analysis in Chapter 3.

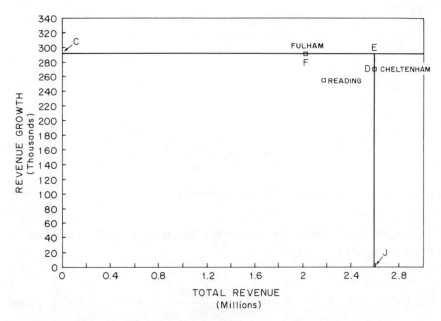

Figure 5.7 Upper end of variable returns frontier

A similar result applies at the other end of the frontier. Figure 5.7 shows the upper end of the variable returns to scale frontier of Figure 5.3. The efficiency measure for Cheltenham based on output maximization is given by the ratio JE/JD. Using mathematical notation as above gives us

$$\frac{JE}{JD} = \frac{O(\text{Fu})}{O(\text{Ch})} = \frac{0 \times I(\text{Ch}) + O(\text{Fu})}{O(\text{Ch})} = 1.076 \qquad (5.5)$$

Dividing this equation by the value of the denominator (=271.21) to constrain the denominator to 1 gives

$$\frac{0 \times I(\text{Ch}) + 1.076}{0.00369\, O(\text{Ch})} \qquad (5.5a)$$

The ratio in equation 5.5 is similar in form to equation 5.3 but with an input weight of zero. The constant term is positive and therefore consistent with the results which established that a positive constant in equation 5.3 is obtained whenever measurement is to a segment of the frontier which exhibits decreasing returns to scale.

A similar argument to that above establishes the existence of a 'slack' input value EF associated with the zero weight.

5.7 THE VARIABLE RETURNS TO SCALE MODEL APPLIED TO MARKET EFFICIENCY

As in the constant returns to scale case the results established in this chapter can be extended to any number of inputs and outputs and the mathematics associated with this is covered in Appendix A. We can employ a variable returns to scale model which uses the mathematics of Appendix A to re-analyse market efficiency as introduced in Chapter 4.

Tables 5.1–5.4 show a complete set of results in respect of the models developed above. Tables 5.1 and 5.2 show the results for the input minimization case whilst Tables 5.3 and 5.4 show the results for the output maximization case. The values obtained for the shops covered specifically above are confirmed by these tables.

It was pointed out during the development of the analysis that the efficiency scores obtained by the input minimization and output maximization methods are different. Figure 5.8 shows the relationship graphically. It can be seen that, although there is a well defined relationship between the two sets of scores, the output maximization scores are higher with the exception of High Wycombe. This is further confirmation of our earlier result that the output maximization scores are higher when both measures are made under decreasing returns to scale. By referring to Figure 5.3, it can be seen that only High Wycombe, Reading and Cheltenham involve measurements with respect to the endpoints of the frontier. It is noticeable that these shops have the largest differences between their input minimization and output maximization efficiency scores.

In terms of using the results to form the basis of a market efficiency model, only the output maximization results are relevant since the existing *Total revenue* base is an uncontrollable input—hence only the output, *Revenue growth*, can be changed. As in Chapter 4, the model is constructed using a stepwise approach in which a new factor is added at each step based on the correlation it exhibits with the efficiency measure derived at the previous step. Table 5.5 shows the efficiency scores at each step whilst Table 5.6 shows the correlations between efficiency scores and factors at each step.

Table 5.1 Variable returns to scale, input minimization efficiencies and reference shops

	Efficiency score	Reference shops		Dual weights
BIRMINGHAM 1	0.841	MANCHESTER 2	NORTHAMPTON	0.829 0.171
BIRMINGHAM 2	0.430	BROMLEY	WATFORD	0.102 0.898
BRADFORD	0.813	MANCHESTER 2	NORTHAMPTON	0.449 0.551
BRENT CROSS	0.622	BROMLEY	WATFORD	0.021 0.979
BRISTOL	0.913	MANCHESTER 2	NORTHAMPTON	0.939 0.061
BRIXTON	0.914	MANCHESTER 2	NORTHAMPTON	0.216 0.784
BROMLEY	1.000	BROMLEY		1.000
CHELTENHAM	0.697	FULHAM	NORTHAMPTON	0.780 0.220
CRAWLEY	0.991	BROMLEY	WATFORD	0.335 0.665
CROYDON	0.895	MANCHESTER 2	NORTHAMPTON	0.876 0.124
DUDLEY	0.569	MANCHESTER 2	NORTHAMPTON	0.918 0.082
EALING	0.638	MANCHESTER 2	WATFORD	0.650 0.350
FULHAM	1.000	FULHAM		1.000
GLOUCESTER	0.998	MANCHESTER 2	WATFORD	0.085 0.915
HAMMERSMITH	0.559	MANCHESTER 2	NORTHAMPTON	0.629 0.371
HARLOW	0.646	BROMLEY	WATFORD	0.310 0.690
HIGH WYCOMBE	0.913	BROMLEY		1.000
HOUNSLOW	0.791	MANCHESTER 2	WATFORD	0.390 0.610
ILFORD	0.703	MANCHESTER 2	WATFORD	0.695 0.305
KENSINGTON	0.529	MANCHESTER 2	NORTHAMPTON	0.629 0.371
LEAMINGTON SPA	0.891	BROMLEY	WATFORD	0.546 0.454
LEICESTER	0.954	MANCHESTER 2	WATFORD	0.279 0.721
MAIDENHEAD	0.866	BROMLEY	WATFORD	0.357 0.643
MANCHESTER 1	0.809	MANCHESTER 2	WATFORD	0.152 0.848
MANCHESTER 2	1.000	MANCHESTER 2		1.000

Table 5.1 (*cont.*)

	Efficiency score	Reference shops		Dual weights	
MILTON KEYNES	0.907	MANCHESTER 2	NORTHAMPTON	0.069	0.931
NEWCASTLE	0.835	FULHAM	NORTHAMPTON	0.474	0.526
NORTHAMPTON	1.000	NORTHAMPTON		1.000	
OXFORD ST	0.927	MANCHESTER 2	NORTHAMPTON	0.240	0.760
PLYMOUTH	0.857	MANCHESTER 2	NORTHAMPTON	0.117	0.883
READING	0.761	FULHAM	NORTHAMPTON	0.613	0.387
REDDITCH	0.592	MANCHESTER 2	WATFORD	0.828	0.172
REIGATE	0.609	BROMLEY	WATFORD	0.590	0.410
SLOUGH	0.603	MANCHESTER 2	NORTHAMPTON	0.530	0.470
SOLIHULL	0.599	BROMLEY	WATFORD	0.213	0.787
ST. ALBANS	0.683	MANCHESTER 2	WATFORD	0.203	0.797
SUTTON COLDFIELD	0.516	MANCHESTER 2	NORTHAMPTON	0.860	0.140
SWINDON	0.584	MANCHESTER 2	NORTHAMPTON	0.455	0.545
TONBRIDGE	0.735	BROMLEY	WATFORD	0.319	0.681
VICTORIA	0.558	MANCHESTER 2	NORTHAMPTON	0.354	0.646
WATFORD	1.000	WATFORD		1.000	
WINDSOR	0.633	BROMLEY	WATFORD	0.946	0.054
WOLVERHAMPTON	0.758	MANCHESTER 2	NORTHAMPTON	0.658	0.342
WOOD GREEN	0.574	MANCHESTER 2	NORTHAMPTON	0.397	0.603
YORK	0.709	MANCHESTER 2	WATFORD	0.086	0.914

Table 5.2 Variable returns to scale, input minimization weights and slacks

	Constant	Weights		Slacks	
		Revenue growth	Total revenue	Revenue growth	Total revenue
BIRMINGHAM 1	−0.3589	0.0085	0.0013	0.0000	0.0000
BIRMINGHAM 2	−0.1376	0.0064	0.0012	0.0000	0.0000
BRADFORD	−0.2738	0.0065	0.0010	0.0000	0.0000
BRENT CROSS	−0.1907	0.0089	0.0016	0.0000	0.0000
BRISTOL	−0.4221	0.0100	0.0015	0.0000	0.0000
BRIXTON	−0.2727	0.0065	0.0010	0.0000	0.0000
BROMLEY	0.0000	0.0179	0.0053	0.0000	0.0000
CHELTENHAM	−0.3679	0.0039	0.0004	0.0000	0.0000
CRAWLEY	−0.3625	0.0169	0.0031	0.0000	0.0000
CROYDON	−0.3951	0.0094	0.0014	0.0000	0.0000
DUDLEY	−0.2590	0.0062	0.0009	0.0000	0.0000
EALING	−0.1633	0.0069	0.0012	0.0000	0.0000
FULHAM	−0.4727	0.0050	0.0005	0.0000	0.0000
GLOUCESTER	−0.3290	0.0139	0.0025	0.0000	0.0000
HAMMERSMITH	−0.2093	0.0050	0.0007	0.0000	0.0000
HARLOW	−0.2328	0.0109	0.0020	0.0000	0.0000
HIGH WYCOMBE	0.9128	0.0000	0.0049	3.5184	0.0000
HOUNSLOW	−0.2255	0.0096	0.0017	0.0000	0.0000
ILFORD	−0.1767	0.0075	0.0013	0.0000	0.0000
KENSINGTON	−0.1978	0.0047	0.0007	0.0000	0.0000
LEAMINGTON SPA	−0.3748	0.0175	0.0032	0.0000	0.0000
LEICESTER	−0.2860	0.0121	0.0022	0.0000	0.0000
MAIDENHEAD	−0.3214	0.0150	0.0028	0.0000	0.0000
MANCHESTER 1	−0.2580	0.0109	0.0019	0.0000	0.0000
MANCHESTER 2	−0.2245	0.0095	0.0017	0.0000	0.0000
MILTON KEYNES	−0.2522	0.0060	0.0009	0.0000	0.0000
NEWCASTLE	−0.5256	0.0056	0.0006	0.0000	0.0000
NORTHAMPTON	−0.2696	0.0064	0.0009	0.0000	0.0000
OXFORD ST	−0.2798	0.0067	0.0010	0.0000	0.0000
PLYMOUTH	−0.2439	0.0058	0.0009	0.0000	0.0000
READING	−0.4405	0.0047	0.0005	0.0000	0.0000
REDDITCH	−0.1414	0.0060	0.0011	0.0000	0.0000
REIGATE	−0.2645	0.0123	0.0023	0.0000	0.0000
SLOUGH	−0.2126	0.0051	0.0007	0.0000	0.0000
SOLIHULL	−0.2040	0.0095	0.0018	0.0000	0.0000
ST. ALBANS	−0.2123	0.0090	0.0016	0.0000	0.0000
SUTTON COLDFIELD	−0.2250	0.0053	0.0008	0.0000	0.0000
SWINDON	−0.1972	0.0047	0.0007	0.0000	0.0000
TONBRIDGE	−0.2665	0.0124	0.0023	0.0000	0.0000
VICTORIA	−0.1787	0.0042	0.0006	0.0000	0.0000
WATFORD	−0.3032	0.0142	0.0026	0.0000	0.0000
WINDSOR	−0.3721	0.0174	0.0032	0.0000	0.0000
WOLVERHAMPTON	−0.2889	0.0069	0.0010	0.0000	0.0000
WOOD GREEN	−0.1879	0.0045	0.0007	0.0000	0.0000
YORK	−0.2336	0.0099	0.0018	0.0000	0.0000

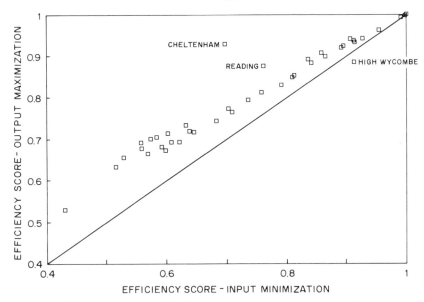

Figure 5.8   Efficiency: input minimization versus output maximization

In Section 4.7 we discussed the issues regarding the choice of factors to include in the constant returns to scale market efficiency model. That discussion is equally applicable here since, although the values of the correlations in Table 5.6 differ from those in Table 4.7, they indicate similar relationships. The only difference between the two model structures is that we are able to incorporate the breakdown of *Total revenue* into *Revenue Gp 1* and *Revenue Gp2+3* in the variable returns to scale model.

In comparing the results of the two approaches, it is immediately apparent that differences arise as a result of the fundamental concepts of the two approaches rather than just the ability to incorporate the revenue breakdown. The variable returns to scale approach requires many more shops from which to create a frontier. Hence despite the modest number of factors in the model, 31 out of the 45 shops lie on the efficiency frontier, leaving only 14 shops where improvement potential can be identified. Clearly, this allows us to derive little practical value from the approach in this instance and provides a further reason why care should be taken to establish the existence of variable returns to scale before taking the decision to construct such a model.

This does not mean that the approach should be discarded from further consideration. The number of shops on the frontier is related to dimensionality rather than sample size and it is unlikely that the above number would increase significantly if the sample size were 200. In such a case, the approach would be extremely valuable in allowing

Table 5.3 Variable returns to scale, output maximization efficiencies and reference shops

	Efficiency score	Reference shops		Dual weights	
BIRMINGHAM 1	1.132	MANCHESTER 2	NORTHAMPTON	0.560	0.440
BIRMINGHAM 2	1.883	MANCHESTER 2	NORTHAMPTON	0.456	0.544
BRADFORD	1.172	MANCHESTER 2	NORTHAMPTON	0.035	0.965
BRENT CROSS	1.444	MANCHESTER 2	NORTHAMPTON	0.956	0.044
BRISTOL	1.066	MANCHESTER 2	NORTHAMPTON	0.813	0.187
BRIXTON	1.072	MANCHESTER 2	NORTHAMPTON	0.026	0.974
BROMLEY	1.000	BROMLEY		1.000	
CHELTENHAM	1.076	FULHAM		1.000	
CRAWLEY	1.007	BROMLEY	WATFORD	0.319	0.681
CROYDON	1.082	MANCHESTER 2	NORTHAMPTON	0.715	0.285
DUDLEY	1.505	FULHAM	NORTHAMPTON	0.046	0.954
EALING	1.391	MANCHESTER 2	NORTHAMPTON	0.531	0.469
FULHAM	1.000	FULHAM		1.000	
GLOUCESTER	1.002	MANCHESTER 2	WATFORD	0.089	0.911
HAMMERSMITH	1.478	FULHAM	NORTHAMPTON	0.321	0.679
HARLOW	1.395	MANCHESTER 2	WATFORD	0.565	0.435
HIGH WYCOMBE	1.130	BROMLEY	WATFORD	0.909	0.091
HOUNSLOW	1.206	MANCHESTER 2	WATFORD	0.986	0.014
ILFORD	1.295	MANCHESTER 2	NORTHAMPTON	0.662	0.338
KENSINGTON	1.528	FULHAM	NORTHAMPTON	0.405	0.595
LEAMINGTON SPA	1.086	BROMLEY	WATFORD	0.373	0.627
LEICESTER	1.037	MANCHESTER 2	WATFORD	0.383	0.617
MAIDENHEAD	1.113	BROMLEY	WATFORD	0.110	0.890
MANCHESTER 1	1.179	MANCHESTER 2	WATFORD	0.627	0.373
MANCHESTER 2	1.000	MANCHESTER 2		1.000	
MILTON KEYNES	1.062	FULHAM	NORTHAMPTON	0.077	0.923

Table 5.3 (*cont.*)

	Efficiency score	Reference shops			Dual weights	
NEWCASTLE	1.121	FULHAM	NORTHAMPTON		0.787	0.213
NORTHAMPTON	1.000	NORTHAMPTON			1.000	
OXFORD ST	1.060	MANCHESTER 2	NORTHAMPTON		0.082	0.918
PLYMOUTH	1.101	FULHAM	NORTHAMPTON		0.117	0.883
READING	1.142	FULHAM			1.000	
REDDITCH	1.467	MANCHESTER 2	NORTHAMPTON		0.265	0.735
REIGATE	1.443	MANCHESTER 2	WATFORD		0.273	0.727
SLOUGH	1.402	FULHAM	NORTHAMPTON		0.299	0.701
SOLIHULL	1.486	MANCHESTER 2	WATFORD		0.908	0.092
ST. ALBANS	1.343	MANCHESTER 2	NORTHAMPTON		0.928	0.072
SUTTON COLDFIELD	1.580	FULHAM	NORTHAMPTON		0.221	0.779
SWINDON	1.419	FULHAM	NORTHAMPTON		0.409	0.591
TONBRIDGE	1.261	MANCHESTER 2	WATFORD		0.258	0.742
VICTORIA	1.448	FULHAM	NORTHAMPTON		0.567	0.433
WATFORD	1.000	WATFORD			1.000	
WINDSOR	1.366	BROMLEY	WATFORD		0.361	0.639
WOLVERHAMPTON	1.231	MANCHESTER 2	NORTHAMPTON		0.150	0.850
WOOD GREEN	1.427	FULHAM	NORTHAMPTON		0.484	0.516
YORK	1.309	MANCHESTER 2	WATFORD		0.888	0.112

Table 5.4 Variable returns to scale, output maximization weights and slacks

	Constant	Weights		Slacks	
		Revenue growth	Total revenue	Revenue growth	Total revenue
BIRMINGHAM 1	−0.2991	0.0071	0.0010	0.0000	0.0000
BIRMINGHAM 2	−0.4759	0.0113	0.0017	0.0000	0.0000
BRADFORD	−0.2520	0.0060	0.0009	0.0000	0.0000
BRENT CROSS	−0.4606	0.0109	0.0016	0.0000	0.0000
BRISTOL	−0.3163	0.0075	0.0011	0.0000	0.0000
BRIXTON	−0.2297	0.0055	0.0008	0.0000	0.0000
BROMLEY	0.0000	0.0179	0.0053	0.0000	0.0000
CHELTENHAM	−1.0761	0.0037	0.0000	0.0000	574.1631
CRAWLEY	−0.2679	0.0125	0.0023	0.0000	0.0000
CROYDON	−0.3063	0.0073	0.0011	0.0000	0.0000
DUDLEY	−0.6966	0.0074	0.0007	0.0000	0.0000
EALING	−0.3629	0.0086	0.0013	0.0000	0.0000
FULHAM	−0.3210	0.0034	0.0003	0.0000	0.0000
GLOUCESTER	−0.2480	0.0105	0.0019	0.0000	0.0000
HAMMERSMITH	−0.6065	0.0065	0.0006	0.0000	0.0000
HARLOW	−0.2919	0.0124	0.0022	0.0000	0.0000
HIGH WYCOMBE	−0.4090	0.0191	0.0035	0.0000	0.0000
HOUNSLOW	−0.2219	0.0094	0.0017	0.0000	0.0000
ILFORD	−0.3578	0.0085	0.0012	0.0000	0.0000
KENSINGTON	−0.6063	0.0065	0.0006	0.0000	0.0000
LEAMINGTON SPA	−0.2962	0.0138	0.0025	0.0000	0.0000
LEICESTER	−0.2307	0.0098	0.0017	0.0000	0.0000
MAIDENHEAD	−0.2707	0.0126	0.0023	0.0000	0.0000
MANCHESTER 1	−0.2417	0.0102	0.0018	0.0000	0.0000
MANCHESTER 2	−0.1833	0.0078	0.0014	0.0000	0.0000
MILTON KEYNES	−0.4846	0.0052	0.0005	0.0000	0.0000
NEWCASTLE	−0.3862	0.0041	0.0004	0.0000	0.0000
NORTHAMPTON	−0.2124	0.0050	0.0007	0.0000	0.0000
OXFORD ST	−0.2318	0.0055	0.0008	0.0000	0.0000
PLYMOUTH	−0.4932	0.0053	0.0005	0.0000	0.0000
READING	−1.1421	0.0039	0.0000	0.0000	147.2773
REDDITCH	−0.3435	0.0082	0.0012	0.0000	0.0000
REIGATE	−0.3337	0.0141	0.0025	0.0000	0.0000
SLOUGH	−0.5807	0.0062	0.0006	0.0000	0.0000
SOLIHULL	−0.2798	0.0119	0.0021	0.0000	0.0000
ST. ALBANS	−0.4226	0.0100	0.0015	0.0000	0.0000
SUTTON COLDFIELD	−0.6764	0.0072	0.0007	0.0000	0.0000
SWINDON	−0.5624	0.0060	0.0006	0.0000	0.0000
TONBRIDGE	−0.2931	0.0124	0.0022	0.0000	0.0000
VICTORIA	−0.5398	0.0058	0.0006	0.0000	0.0000
WATFORD	−0.2327	0.0109	0.0020	0.0000	0.0000
WINDSOR	−0.3703	0.0173	0.0032	0.0000	0.0000
WOLVERHAMPTON	−0.2759	0.0066	0.0010	0.0000	0.0000
WOOD GREEN	−0.5491	0.0059	0.0006	0.0000	0.0000
YORK	−0.2478	0.0105	0.0019	0.0000	0.0000

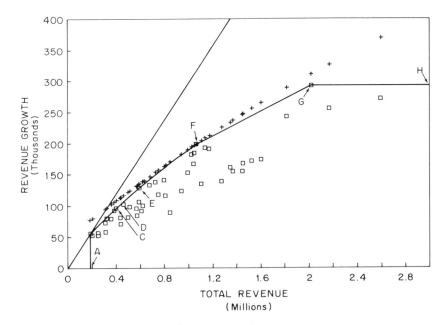

Figure 5.9 Comparison of efficiency frontiers

improvement potential to be identified for about 75% of the shops whilst ensuring that all important influences on performance had been accounted for. However, it is clear that the approach is only really useful for samples of this magnitude.

For our current sample of 45 shops, we would clearly prefer the degree of discrimination between the performance of shops allowed by the market efficiency model constructed in Chapter 4 which had 38 shops not on the frontier. Let us therefore consider further the merits of each approach.

The model developed in this chapter assumes variable returns to scale in all dimensions. By contrast, the model in Chapter 4 assumes constant returns to scale in all dimensions but incorporates the decreasing returns to scale relationship between *Revenue growth* and *Total revenue* by replacing *Total revenue* with *Expected growth*, the latter being determined by the regression curve shown in Figure 5.1.

At Step 1, the frontier for the Chapter 4 model is simply the regression curve of Figure 5.1 factored to pass through the shop with the best performance relative to the regression curve—Northampton. This is shown by crosses in Figure 5.9 alongside the Step 1 frontier (ABCDEFGH) for the variable returns to scale model. It can be seen that the difference at this stage of the analysis is not great and this is further confirmed by the similarity of the Step 1 results in Tables 4.9 and 5.5. However, comparing both of

Table 5.5 Steps in variable returns to scale market efficiency model

		Step 1	Step 2	Step 3	Step 4
OUTPUTS	Revenue growth	*	*	*	*
INPUTS	Total revenue	*			
	Revenue Gp1		*	*	*
	Revenue Gp2+3		*	*	*
	Competition			*	*
	Catchment population				*
	FULHAM	1.00	1.00	1.00	1.00
	MANCHESTER 2	1.00	1.00	1.00	1.00
	BROMLEY	1.00	1.00	1.00	1.00
	WATFORD	1.00	1.00	1.00	1.00
	NORTHAMPTON	1.00	1.00	1.00	1.00
	GLOUCESTER	1.00	1.00	1.00	1.00
	CRAWLEY	0.99	1.00	1.00	1.00
	OXFORD ST	0.94	1.00	1.00	1.00
	MILTON KEYNES	0.94	1.00	1.00	1.00
	CHELTENHAM	0.93	1.00	1.00	1.00
	READING	0.88	1.00	1.00	1.00
	SWINDON	0.70	1.00	1.00	1.00
	LEICESTER	0.96	0.97	1.00	1.00
	CROYDON	0.92	0.94	1.00	1.00
	NEWCASTLE	0.89	0.94	1.00	1.00
	BRISTOL	0.94	0.94	1.00	1.00
	BRIXTON	0.93	0.94	1.00	1.00
	PLYMOUTH	0.91	0.93	1.00	1.00
	YORK	0.76	0.93	1.00	1.00
	DUDLEY	0.66	0.88	1.00	1.00
	HAMMERSMITH	0.68	0.73	1.00	1.00
	VICTORIA	0.69	0.72	1.00	1.00
	KENSINGTON	0.65	0.69	1.00	1.00

Table 5.5 (cont.)

	Step 1	Step 2	Step 3	Step 4
HOUNSLOW	0.83	0.85	0.95	1.00
LEAMINGTON SPA	0.92	0.92	0.92	1.00
MAIDENHEAD	0.90	0.90	0.90	1.00
HIGH WYCOMBE	0.88	0.89	0.89	1.00
TONBRIDGE	0.79	0.79	0.79	1.00
WINDSOR	0.73	0.73	0.73	1.00
SUTTON COLDFIELD	0.63	0.63	0.72	1.00
REIGATE	0.69	0.72	0.72	1.00
BRADFORD	0.85	0.87	0.99	0.99
WOOD GREEN	0.70	0.96	0.96	0.96
BIRMINGHAM 1	0.88	0.90	0.94	0.94
WOLVERHAMPTON	0.81	0.82	0.93	0.94
ST. ALBANS	0.74	0.77	0.77	0.90
MANCHESTER 1	0.85	0.86	0.90	0.90
REDDITCH	0.68	0.69	0.69	0.85
EALING	0.72	0.73	0.80	0.80
ILFORD	0.77	0.78	0.79	0.79
HARLOW	0.72	0.72	0.74	0.79
SLOUGH	0.71	0.73	0.76	0.77
BRENT CROSS	0.69	0.71	0.76	0.76
SOLIHULL	0.67	0.68	0.72	0.75
BIRMINGHAM 2	0.53	0.54	0.64	0.64

Table 5.6 Correlations of factors with efficiency for variable returns

		Step 1	Step 2	Step 3	Step 4
OUTPUTS	Revenue growth	*	*	*	*
INPUTS	Total revenue	*	*	*	*
	Revenue Gp1		*	*	*
	Revenue Gp2+3		*	*	*
	Competition			*	*
	Catchment population				*
Age of shop (months)		−0.44859	−0.33612	−0.14026	−0.09740
Catchment population		−0.16124	−0.10589	0.30224	−0.06261
Central overheads		−0.10488	0.11030	0.29035	0.11846
Customer service		0.03521	−0.09965	−0.23688	−0.03952
Non-staff controllable cost		−0.01410	0.13293	0.38824	0.13909
Uncontrollable cost		−0.05096	−0.04688	0.08512	−0.12599
Pitch		−0.02181	−0.15765	−0.06550	−0.07055
Profit		−0.15448	0.05813	0.18313	0.12993
Revenue Gp1		0.24094	0.13446	0.22962	0.11000
Revenue Gp2		−0.15479	0.10581	0.25003	0.09901
Revenue Gp3		−0.18999	0.03304	0.31551	0.12396
Revenue growth		0.20572	0.35546	0.46654	0.24641
Revenue % growth		0.70163	0.48080	0.23667	0.30946
Staff cost		0.02021	0.20302	0.34545	0.15608
Competition		−0.36191	−0.16228	0.35365	0.13988
Non-staff cost		−0.04860	−0.02224	0.13737	−0.09338
Total revenue		−0.10488	0.11030	0.29035	0.11846
Total cost		−0.00957	0.12485	0.29551	0.05982
Controllable cost		0.01706	0.19895	0.35475	0.15664
Revenue Gp1 % of Total revenue		0.48542	0.15571	0.04214	0.05484
Revenue Gp2 % of Total revenue		−0.30259	−0.11522	−0.18150	−0.00874
Revenue Gp3 % of Total revenue		−0.14659	−0.02088	0.21085	−0.05321

these frontiers to the constant returns to scale frontier establishes that a much greater difference would be observed if no attempt had been made to represent the decreasing returns to scale relationship.

Discrepancies of the latter type emerge as the dimensionality is increased since the Chapter 4 model assumes constant returns to scale in other dimensions whilst the Chapter 5 model assumes variable returns to scale. Further, it is apparent from Table 5.5 that the Chapter 5 model requires six shops to determine its efficiency frontier at Step 1 whilst Table 4.9 shows that the Chapter 4 model requires only one shop to determine its efficiency frontier at Step 1. A similar requirement exists in each dimension with the consequence that in the final models a large difference exists between the number of shops on each of the frontiers.

A further difference between the two models is that it is straightforward in the variable returns to scale case to incorporate the breakdown of *Total revenue* into *Revenue Gp1* and *Revenue Gp2+3*. In the constant returns to scale case, it is necessary to select an appropriate mathematical form for the relationship between *Revenue growth* and the two revenue components. The difficulty of achieving this precluded the inclusion of such a breakdown in the Chapter 4 model.

In practical terms, therefore, consideration of the merits of the two approaches reduces to questioning the need for variable returns to scale in every dimension and the need to allow for revenue breakdown.

The decreasing returns to scale relationship between *Revenue growth* and *Total revenue* reflects the difficulty in continuing to achieve growth as the market becomes saturated. It is certainly not obvious that similar relationships should exist with *Catchment population*, *Competition* or *Pitch*. In fact, in the case of *Catchment population*, it seems reasonable to expect that twice the *Catchment population* should mean that everything happens on twice the scale. Further, although we have not reproduced the graphs, there is no obvious statistical evidence to support the existence of variable returns to scale relationships between *Revenue growth* and other factors as there is in the case of *Total revenue*.

In terms of the need to allow for revenue breakdown, we would want to establish whether lower proportions of *Revenue Gp1* were caused as a result *of* performance or whether they exerted a direct influence *on* performance. For example, if Group 1 is a recent product line which offers the best immediate opportunity for growth and lower proportions of *Revenue Gp1* occur through inefficient selling, there should be no allowance made for this in the efficiency assessment. Alternatively, if Group 1 is the type of product through which greater contact is maintained with the customer, thereby providing more frequent selling opportunities in other areas, then the existence of a lower Group 1 base need not be attributable to the current shop manager but will nevertheless make his

Table 5.7 Steps in decreasing returns to scale market efficiency model

		Step 1	Step 2	Step 3	Step 4
OUTPUTS	Revenue growth	*	*	*	*
INPUTS	Total revenue	*			
	Revenue Gp1		*	*	*
	Revenue Gp2+3		*	*	*
	Competition			*	*
	Catchment population				*
	FULHAM	1.000	1.000	1.000	1.000
	MANCHESTER 2	1.000	1.000	1.000	1.000
	BROMLEY	1.000	1.000	1.000	1.000
	WATFORD	1.000	1.000	1.000	1.000
	NORTHAMPTON	1.000	1.000	1.000	1.000
	GLOUCESTER	0.998	1.000	1.000	1.000
	CRAWLEY	0.993	1.000	1.000	1.000
	OXFORD ST	0.943	1.000	1.000	1.000
	MILTON KEYNES	0.941	1.000	1.000	1.000
	CHELTENHAM	0.929	1.000	1.000	1.000
	READING	0.876	1.000	1.000	1.000
	SWINDON	0.704	1.000	1.000	1.000
	LEICESTER	0.964	0.971	1.000	1.000
	CROYDON	0.925	0.943	1.000	1.000
	NEWCASTLE	0.892	0.941	1.000	1.000
	BRISTOL	0.939	0.940	1.000	1.000
	BRIXTON	0.933	0.935	1.000	1.000
	PLYMOUTH	0.908	0.933	1.000	1.000
	YORK	0.764	0.927	1.000	1.000
	VICTORIA	0.691	0.721	1.000	1.000

Table 5.7 (cont.)

	Step 1	Step 2	Step 3	Step 4
LEAMINGTON SPA	0.920	0.921	0.921	1.000
MAIDENHEAD	0.899	0.899	0.899	1.000
TONBRIDGE	0.793	0.794	0.794	1.000
REIGATE	0.693	0.716	0.716	1.000
BRADFORD	0.853	0.869	0.988	0.992
HAMMERSMITH	0.677	0.732	0.990	0.990
KENSINGTON	0.655	0.692	0.989	0.989
HOUNSLOW	0.829	0.846	0.935	0.967
DUDLEY	0.664	0.880	0.962	0.962
WOOD GREEN	0.701	0.956	0.956	0.956
BIRMINGHAM 1	0.883	0.905	0.937	0.939
WOLVERHAMPTON	0.812	0.820	0.934	0.938
HIGH WYCOMBE	0.885	0.886	0.886	0.912
ST. ALBANS	0.744	0.768	0.770	0.904
MANCHESTER 1	0.848	0.859	0.898	0.898
REDDITCH	0.681	0.688	0.688	0.847
WINDSOR	0.732	0.733	0.733	0.839
EALING	0.719	0.727	0.797	0.797
ILFORD	0.772	0.780	0.793	0.794
HARLOW	0.717	0.725	0.743	0.774
SLOUGH	0.713	0.735	0.759	0.769
SUTTON COLDFIELD	0.633	0.635	0.718	0.763
BRENT CROSS	0.693	0.713	0.758	0.758
SOLIHULL	0.673	0.681	0.716	0.741
BIRMINGHAM 2	0.531	0.539	0.643	0.643

Table 5.8 Correlation of factors with efficiency for decreasing returns

		Step 1	Step 2	Step 3	Step 4
OUTPUTS	Revenue growth	*	*	*	*
INPUTS	Total revenue	*			
	Revenue Gp1		*	*	*
	Revenue Gp2+3		*	*	*
	Competition			*	*
	Catchment population				*
Age of shop (months)		−0.44859	−0.33612	−0.15327	−0.20759
Catchment population		−0.16124	−0.10589	0.29753	0.04041
Central overheads		−0.10488	0.11030	0.28856	0.14609
Customer service		0.03521	−0.09965	−0.23411	−0.15141
Non-staff controllable cost		−0.01410	0.13293	0.38917	0.18577
Uncontrollable cost		−0.05096	−0.04688	0.08666	−0.06842
Pitch		−0.02181	−0.15765	−0.06357	−0.14113
Profit		−0.15448	0.05813	0.17829	0.12326
Revenue Gp1		0.24094	0.13446	0.23942	0.12773
Revenue Gp2		−0.15479	0.10581	0.24695	0.13267
Revenue Gp3		−0.18999	0.03304	0.30838	0.12110
Revenue growth		0.20572	0.35546	0.47084	0.31897
Revenue % growth		0.70163	0.48080	0.25016	0.32702
Staff cost		0.02021	0.20302	0.34775	0.19561
Competition		−0.36191	−0.16228	0.33509	0.15623
Non-staff cost		−0.04860	−0.02224	0.13891	−0.03373
Total revenue		−0.10488	0.11030	0.28856	0.14609
Total cost		−0.00957	0.12485	0.29778	0.11446
Controllable cost		0.01706	0.19895	0.35694	0.19746
Revenue Gp1 % of Total revenue		0.48542	0.15571	0.05771	0.04843
Revenue Gp2 % of Total revenue		−0.30259	−0.11522	−0.18922	−0.04960
Revenue Gp3 % of Total revenue		−0.14659	−0.02088	0.20330	0.01334

task more difficult and should be allowed for in an efficiency assessment of his performance.

Hence there are circumstances where the Chapter 4 model is a totally adequate model. Whatever the circumstances, the Chapter 5 model will often provide a safer option since managers will quite happily defend their performances using arguments of returns to scale whether they exist or not. The Chapter 5 model will always have the advantage of still being able to identify cases of inefficiency whilst taking these arguments on board, although in our current case this would apply to only 14 shops (see Table 5.5, Step 4).

We will end the chapter by briefly considering a third model. We illustrated earlier using Figure 5.4 that we could construct a model which assumes constant returns to scale up to the most productive scale size and decreasing returns to scale thereafter. Table 5.7 shows the results of constructing a market efficiency model of this type including the efficiency scores at each step of the analysis. Table 5.8 shows the correlations between efficiency scores and factors at each step.

It can be seen that this approach has the advantage of reducing the number of frontier points by eliminating the increasing returns to scale assumption in each dimension. It is now possible to identify performance improvements for 21 of the 45 shops whilst ensuring that decreasing returns to scale is accounted for. Further, as we introduced variable returns to scale into our model only to accommodate the decreasing returns to scale relationship between *Revenue growth* and *Total revenue*, it is reasonable to conclude that a decreasing returns to scale model is more appropriate than the complete variable returns to scale model. Note, however, that this conclusion is not general but is specific only to situations where the existence of increasing returns to scale can be discounted.

The purpose of this chapter has been to review the possible modelling approaches. We will conclude this review in Chapter 6 by looking critically at the most important issue of what they tell us about the shops themselves.

Chapter 6

The Case Study—Further Analysis and Interpretation

6.1 INTRODUCTION

The purpose of this chapter is to review the issues which were raised when we introduced the case study in Chapter 2 and to examine the extent to which our methodology has been able to resolve these issues.

We can be certain that the analytical issues have been fully addressed since our methodology was designed around these issues. However, we should consider, in addition, the extent to which alternative approaches could have addressed the same issues, and whether DEA replaces, complements or is complemented by other quantitative methods. In the early part of the chapter we will consider these further analytical issues and bring our analytical development to a conclusion. The remainder of the chapter will reconsider the management issues in the light of our analysis results. The conclusions drawn will form a basis for Chapter 7 in which we consider how DEA can be established as an integral part of the management process.

6.2 ANALYTICAL ISSUES—DEA IN RELATION TO OTHER QUANTITATIVE METHODS

In Chapter 2 we identified the company's current method of assessing performance which was on a shop profit basis. The problem identified with this method was that, although shop profit is a reliable measure of the current worth of a shop, it gives no indication in itself of whether low profitability for a particular shop is due to external factors, inadequate market penetration or inefficient use of resources. In particular, there is no indication of the potential for improvement.

We then examined the analysts' approach. Their problem was that, when additional factors were taken into account, many aspects to performance emerged, each of which could present a shop in a very different light. Further, the analysts not only found it difficult to present an overall picture whilst taking many factors into account, but had no clear indication of which factors these should be.

Our DEA approach has been able to address these issues. The stepwise model build-up allows us to identify the factors which influence performance. The DEA technique itself recognizes each aspect of performance but evaluates trade-offs between them to arrive at a single performance measure which allows an overall picture to be presented. So our approach addresses the issues, but the question remains—is DEA sufficient in itself or do we still need complementary information from other techniques? Indeed, do we need DEA at all or are there alternative techniques which would provide equivalent information?

The most common alternative techniques are unit costs and regression analysis. The unit cost approach attempts to apportion cost to each output from which a cost per unit output can be calculated. Hence in the context of our case study, if appropriate model outputs were the revenue from each product group it would be necessary to split the total cost into components attributable to each product group and then to calculate a cost to revenue ratio in each group. The lowest observed ratio in each group would then set the standard against which performance is measured.

Cost apportionment is straightforward for elements of cost such as product buying costs, but assumptions need to be made where costs such as those incurred for staff and premises are shared by the product groups. The quality of the results depends upon the accuracy of the assumptions. Large organizations using this approach need to ensure the consistency of assumptions within accounting systems throughout the organization.

Our cost efficiency model provides a good example of the limitations of the unit cost approach. Firstly, it is almost impossible to apportion costs to revenue growth. Secondly, there is no way to accommodate the breakdown of cost into controllable and uncontrollable elements. A further limitation is that apportionment is impossible when we use inputs which are not cost based, as in the case of population and competition in our market efficiency model.

Regression analysis can overcome problems of apportionment and the use of factors that are not cost based but still has limitations which would preclude some of the analyses that are possible using DEA. Regression analysis can determine a relationship between a single input and many outputs or a single output and many inputs. The restriction to either a single output or single input factor is its main limitation. Our cost efficiency model, for example, required both multiple outputs and multiple inputs.

A further feature of regression analysis is that it is a parametric technique. In other words there is a need to assume a mathematical form for the relationship which is derived. DEA on the other hand is non-parametric. A good example of this occurred in Figure 5.1 where we fitted a satisfactory curve to represent the relationship between *Revenue growth* and *Total revenue*. In fact, choosing the mathematical form of the curve was aided by the ability to see the relationship graphically. However, in seeking to break down *Total revenue* into *Revenue Gp1* and *Revenue Gp2+3*, we no longer had the advantage of a visible graphical relationship and to choose a mathematical form for the relationship would be much more of a trial and error process. The non-parametric nature of DEA avoids this problem.

When analysts choose regression in preference to DEA, it is often on the grounds that regression is more readily understood and accepted. This can be partly attributed to the fact that DEA is a relatively new technique. However, it is the authors' belief that a much greater part can be attributed to the way in which DEA has been traditionally presented. In terms of conceptual complexity, there could not be two more similar techniques in that:

(a)   both concern the calculation of a surface in many dimensions;
(b)   both require complex mathematics to calculate the surface;
(c)   in both cases, conceptual understanding relies on graphical illustration in two dimensions from which appropriate analogies can be drawn in many dimensions where physical representation is not possible.

The greater conceptual problem perceived with DEA in the authors' view stems from the fact that the analyst presenting regression analysis to management will present (c) with no more than a passing reference to the set of partial differential equations associated with (b). In fact, as a result of modern software, there are even many analysts using regression who are unaware of the underlying mathematics. On the other hand, the analyst presenting DEA to management tends to start with (b) which is equivalent to starting this book with the mathematics of Appendix A as the introduction. In doing so, the immediate relevance of DEA is never established. The authors feel most strongly that, in the management context, we should concentrate on (c) and the mathematics of DEA should never see the light of day.

Our overall conclusion on unit costs and regression as alternative techniques is that they are valid alternatives within their areas of applicability but DEA has wider applicability and requires fewer assumptions.

Let us now turn our attention to the extent to which other measures or techniques can complement DEA. We have already identified that a simple shop profit measure could not adequately address all of the management issues. On the other hand, we should bear in mind that profitability is still the critically important factor in managing the company and DEA does not in fact tell us whether a shop is profitable. We must still calculate shop profit in order to know this. The role we have established for DEA is to indicate cost and revenue improvement potential which can be incorporated into the profit calculation to establish profit improvement potential. Hence the existing shop profit calculation still has an important role but is complemented by DEA to provide information which the original method alone could not. We will be looking at examples of this in the context of specific shops in Section 6.5.

The analysts' ranking methods also have limitations in that each ranking evaluates only a single aspect of performance. However, we discovered in Section 4.4 that it was useful to know something about the individual aspects of performance as an aid to interpreting and confirming the DEA results. In theory, of course, since DEA delivers the same message as well as addressing the other important issues, there is no need for the ranking method. However, the nontechnical manager will often seek the additional reassurance of a similar message from a simpler technique when its area of applicability permits. Hence this is another way in which other techniques may complement DEA.

In Section 4.5 we made reference to a further aid to interpreting efficiency. We will now introduce this as the final stage of our analytical development.

6.3 ANALYTICAL ISSUES—AREAS OF EFFICIENCY REVISITED

Identifying Areas of Efficiency—A Simple Numerical Method

In Sections 4.3–4.5 we considered the shops which were identified as efficient by the cost efficiency model. The discussion was quite simple for shops which were identified as efficient in the early steps of the model construction but became complex for those identified in later steps. One factor which helped simplify the discussion of the earlier steps was the availability of simple graphical representations, in that we could see a spatial representation of a shop's performance and understand where it lay relative to other shops' performances. For example in Figure 4.1, we could see that Kensington had low *Controllable cost* relative to *Uncontrollable cost* and that Bradford had the reverse. Similarly, in Figure 2.3, we could see that Northampton's performance had a leaning towards *Revenue growth* which made it an appropriate comparator for Bromley which had a heavy leaning towards *Revenue growth*.

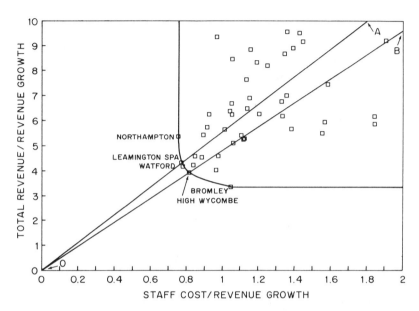

Figure 6.1   Areas of efficiency example

We can also see from the graphs the number of shops for which each shop on the frontier is a reference shop, and this allows us to gauge each reference shop's importance in setting the efficiency standard and the range over which it influences the standard. A good example of this is provided by Figure 3.5 which for convenience is reproduced as Figure 6.1. Our definition of a reference shop in Section 2.5 is sufficient to establish that Northampton is a reference shop for all shops to the left of the line OA, a range containing about half of the shops. Bromley, on the other hand, is a reference shop for all shops to the right of the line OB, a range containing only a few shops. It is not uncommon in practice to find an even more extreme example than Bromley such that although a shop is on the frontier it does not act as a reference shop for any other shop. With the aid of the graph such points become clear.

In many dimensions it is simply not possible to use graphs to achieve this level of interpretation. Instead, we must rely completely on numbers. We have seen that DEA allows us to evaluate efficiency scores and targets and to establish the identity of the comparators on which these are based, but we need still further information to achieve a level of interpretation similar to that available from graphs.

The number of shops for which a shop on the frontier acts as a reference shop is easily obtained by compiling this statistic within the computational process as the DEA results are produced. We will refer to this statistic as a reference shop's 'frequency'.

A shop's performance could clearly be expressed as a set of coordinates given by the shop's raw data values, but it is difficult to interpret a shop's overall relative position from this. Relative position is better gauged from normalized coordinates obtained by dividing each data value by the average for all shops. This approach helps interpret a shop's relative position in terms of both its scale of operation and its mix of inputs and outputs.

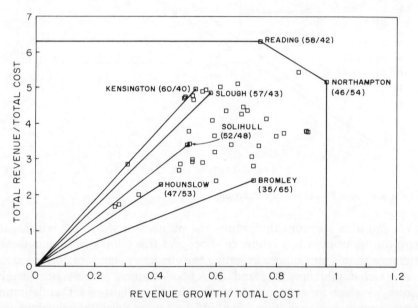

Figure 6.2 Balance percentages

Using normalized coordinates, the indication of input and output mix can be improved by converting the normalized quantities to percentages such that the sum of all normalized inputs is 100% and the sum of all normalized outputs is 100%. A shop's output mix, for example, can then be compared to a typical mix of (50,50) if there are two outputs or (33,33,33) if there are three outputs and so on. As these percentages describe the balance between inputs or between outputs, we will refer to them as 'balance percentages'. We will use Figure 2.3 which was Step 1 in constructing the cost efficiency model, to illustrate the concept. For convenience the figure is reproduced as Figure 6.2.

Graphically, each shop's output mix is represented by the direction from the origin of the point representing the shop. This is illustrated by the lines emanating from the origin in Figure 6.2. It can be seen that the direction is reflected by the balance percentages. For example, it is clear from the graph that Solihull has an average output mix and this is reflected by a balance percentage close to (50,50). Likewise, it is clear that Kensington (60,40) and Bromley (35,65) are at the opposite extremes in terms of mix. It is useful to record the extreme percentage values as an indicator of the extremity of other shops' performances.

The percentages can also be used to gauge the degree of similarity between a shop and its reference shops. For example, although Hounslow will have both Northampton and Reading as reference shops, its output mix is much closer to that of Northampton. Similarly, Slough has an output mix much closer to that of Reading. For a shop on the efficiency frontier, it is also of value to record the range of percentages across the shops which have the frontier shop as a reference shop. This then gives an indication of the area of efficiency of the frontier shop. For example, in Figure 6.2, we would record approximately (60,40) to (47,53) for Reading and (57,43) to (35,65) for Northampton. We could therefore have used the percentages rather than the graph to establish our initial observation from Figure 2.3 that Reading's efficiency is based primarily on its ability to economically maintain *Total revenue* whilst Northampton's efficiency is based primarily on the economical achievement of *Revenue growth*.

It should be noted that where there are three or more inputs or outputs, a shop's area of efficiency may not cover every possible combination of percentages within the ranges established and it would require an extremely complex procedure to establish the areas exactly. However, the area of efficiency does not extend outside of the range and this is usually sufficient information to provide an adequate level of interpretation.

Table 6.1 shows the result of calculating the above percentages and frequency statistics for the efficient shops in the final cost efficiency model. The table shows the frequency and three rows of percentages for each frontier shop. The percentage rows are:

Row 1 — The actual input and output balance for the frontier shop
Row 2 — The minimum percentage value for each input and output which exists across all shops for which the frontier shop is a reference shop
Row 3 — The maximum percentage value for each input and output which exists across all shops for which the frontier shop is a reference shop.

Table 6.1 Balance percentages for efficient shops

| | Frequency | Balance percentages | | | | Revenue growth | Revenue Gp1+3 | Revenue Gp2 |
		Staff cost	Control. cost	Uncont. cost				
Minimum all shops		10.93%	13.88%	10.28%		25.81%	14.17%	20.26%
Maximum all shops		52.12%	50.73%	75.19%		49.37%	46.43%	54.46%
BRADFORD	8	43.70%	46.02%	10.28%		36.33%	26.92%	36.74%
		34.05%	35.69%	10.28%		30.61%	26.09%	22.65%
		43.70%	50.73%	22.05%		49.37%	32.32%	41.58%
GLOUCESTER	4	38.82%	43.98%	17.20%		42.60%	34.92%	22.48%
		29.43%	35.28%	17.20%		32.01%	34.92%	20.59%
		38.82%	43.98%	35.30%		42.60%	43.36%	28.01%
HAMMERSMITH	6	29.45%	40.88%	29.67%		27.24%	38.78%	33.98%
		29.45%	35.69%	13.54%		26.02%	27.33%	33.20%
		42.26%	48.34%	29.67%		35.51%	38.78%	43.12%
KENSINGTON	26	22.45%	29.76%	47.79%		26.57%	36.78%	36.65%
		10.93%	13.88%	13.69%		26.36%	14.17%	20.26%
		43.29%	48.34%	75.19%		41.38%	46.43%	54.46%
LEAMINGTON SPA	4	23.64%	39.65%	36.71%		43.52%	30.21%	26.27%
		10.93%	13.88%	36.71%		33.86%	27.14%	26.27%
		24.33%	39.65%	75.19%		43.52%	33.89%	34.70%
LEICESTER	5	35.45%	47.60%	16.95%		40.32%	38.35%	21.33%
		33.05%	45.10%	13.54%		34.41%	30.85%	21.33%
		41.31%	48.34%	19.26%		40.32%	38.35%	33.27%

Table 6.1 (*cont.*)

	Frequency	Balance percentages					
		Staff cost	Control. cost	Uncont. cost	Revenue growth	Revenue Gp1+3	Revenue Gp2
MANCHESTER 2	6	32.12%	42.44%	25.43%	39.96%	38.81%	21.23%
		10.93%	13.88%	19.26%	33.86%	32.17%	21.23%
		36.58%	47.70%	75.19%	39.96%	38.81%	33.97%
NEWCASTLE	9	52.12%	20.87%	27.01%	31.00%	35.54%	33.46%
		23.91%	20.87%	26.15%	26.36%	32.86%	20.26%
		52.12%	35.36%	54.09%	35.17%	46.43%	37.99%
NORTHAMPTON	24	38.89%	34.44%	26.66%	40.26%	24.29%	35.45%
		10.93%	13.88%	11.99%	29.39%	18.64%	20.59%
		43.29%	50.73%	75.19%	49.37%	43.36%	44.68%
PLYMOUTH	1	44.89%	37.21%	17.89%	33.31%	42.05%	24.64%
		44.89%	37.21%	17.89%	33.31%	42.05%	24.64%
		44.89%	37.21%	17.89%	33.31%	42.05%	24.64%
READING	9	46.24%	30.36%	23.40%	30.70%	24.11%	45.18%
		31.53%	30.36%	13.69%	26.02%	14.17%	36.21%
		46.24%	43.01%	31.63%	33.36%	37.77%	54.46%
ST. ALBANS	1	50.52%	31.89%	17.59%	36.45%	26.36%	37.20%
		50.52%	31.89%	17.59%	36.45%	26.36%	37.20%
		50.52%	31.89%	17.59%	36.45%	26.36%	37.20%
SUTTON COLDFIELD	12	39.80%	38.87%	21.33%	25.81%	43.28%	30.91%
		29.43%	30.46%	13.54%	25.81%	27.82%	20.59%
		43.29%	45.14%	35.30%	37.40%	43.36%	41.58%

Table 6.2 Balance percentages for inefficient shops

Name	Efficiency	Staff cost	Control. cost	Uncont. cost	Revenue growth	Revenue Gp1+3	Revenue Gp2
WATFORD	0.964	35.19%	40.83%	23.97%	46.36%	21.94%	31.69%
CHELTENHAM	0.954	37.91%	30.46%	31.63%	26.44%	35.57%	37.99%
OXFORD ST	0.951	23.91%	27.16%	48.93%	35.13%	41.83%	23.04%
HIGH WYCOMBE	0.926	24.48%	46.97%	28.55%	48.27%	20.01%	31.72%
BIRMINGHAM 2	0.922	31.53%	41.80%	26.67%	26.02%	37.77%	36.21%
FULHAM	0.913	38.49%	35.36%	26.15%	32.70%	34.75%	32.55%
SLOUGH	0.892	35.53%	33.85%	30.62%	29.39%	32.86%	37.75%
WOOD GREEN	0.891	38.17%	36.56%	25.26%	31.37%	14.17%	54.46%
REIGATE	0.887	36.28%	48.34%	15.38%	35.51%	31.30%	33.20%
WOLVERHAMPTON	0.883	41.31%	45.14%	13.54%	34.41%	32.32%	33.27%
REDDITCH	0.874	41.45%	35.89%	22.66%	33.12%	22.21%	44.68%
CROYDON	0.858	29.43%	35.28%	35.30%	36.06%	43.36%	20.59%
BRIXTON	0.853	20.91%	25.36%	53.73%	38.15%	27.14%	34.70%
TONBRIDGE	0.852	34.26%	35.60%	30.14%	40.07%	23.91%	36.01%
DUDLEY	0.841	42.26%	35.69%	22.05%	30.61%	27.82%	41.58%
BRISTOL	0.838	33.05%	47.70%	19.26%	38.09%	37.71%	24.20%
MANCHESTER 1	0.832	36.58%	42.64%	20.77%	37.40%	38.06%	24.54%
ILFORD	0.820	10.93%	13.88%	75.19%	34.46%	33.89%	31.65%
BROMLEY	0.817	37.28%	50.73%	11.99%	49.37%	27.98%	22.65%
MAIDENHEAD	0.806	34.05%	49.97%	15.98%	43.23%	26.09%	30.67%
BRENT CROSS	0.806	24.33%	29.05%	46.62%	33.86%	32.17%	33.97%
SWINDON	0.806	41.82%	35.98%	22.20%	29.55%	27.33%	43.12%
CRAWLEY	0.780	26.26%	34.56%	39.18%	46.70%	23.76%	29.54%
SOLIHULL	0.771	32.44%	37.62%	29.94%	32.01%	39.98%	28.01%
BIRMINGHAM 1	0.745	32.83%	33.08%	34.09%	35.17%	41.18%	23.66%
EALING	0.743	43.29%	43.01%	13.69%	33.36%	30.20%	36.44%
VICTORIA	0.722	28.65%	25.28%	46.08%	26.36%	39.61%	34.03%
WINDSOR	0.715	32.47%	33.47%	34.06%	41.38%	18.64%	39.98%
MILTON KEYNES	0.708	32.11%	27.18%	40.71%	33.31%	46.43%	20.26%
HARLOW	0.616	24.16%	21.75%	54.09%	33.44%	41.37%	25.20%
YORK	0.548	38.58%	45.10%	16.32%	36.53%	30.85%	32.62%

Table 6.2 shows the input and output balance percentages for the inefficient shops and is referred to in later sections when discussing individual shops.

The Method Applied to Cost Efficiency

We can now use the results of Table 6.1 to comment on the areas of efficiency of the frontier shops and compare our conclusions with those of Sections 4.3–4.5 for the shops already discussed in those sections. We will consider the shops in the order identified in the stepwise build-up.

At Step 1, Reading was identified as efficient in terms of producing more revenue per unit cost than any other shop. If we compare Reading's output balance with the average, (33,33,33), we can see that Reading benefits from a high proportion of *Revenue Gp2* which we identified as 'cheap' revenue during the model construction. In terms of inputs, Reading benefits from a low proportion of *Uncontrollable cost*. The percentage ranges show that Reading acts as a reference shop for other shops with high proportions of *Revenue Gp2* and low proportions of *Uncontrollable cost* and that its area of efficiency is restricted to these features. Other shops, for example Kensington, appear less efficient at Step 1 prior to taking these factors into account.

At Step 2, Northampton was identified as efficient when *Revenue growth* was identified as being more 'expensive' than simply maintaining *Total revenue*. The balance percentages show that Northampton does have a high *Revenue growth* proportion although the ranges show its area of efficiency to be quite general with only a slight bias towards higher *Revenue growth*. The generality of Northampton's efficiency is reflected in its frequency count which shows that Northampton acts as a reference shop for 24 shops. The reason for Northampton's general efficiency begins to emerge in Figure 6.2 where it can be seen that not only does Northampton have the highest *Revenue growth* to *Total cost* ratio but it also has about the third best *Total revenue* to *Total cost* ratio.

At Step 3, we identified Kensington and Bradford as efficient and illustrated graphically that this was due to Kensington's low *Controllable cost* and Bradford's low *Uncontrollable cost*. For Kensington, the balance percentages confirm low proportional *Staff cost* and high proportional *Uncontrollable cost*. In terms of outputs, Kensington has a low proportional growth. However, Kensington's area of efficiency is general covering a large part of the overall range of input and output mix. Hence Kensington is generally efficient once its *Uncontrollable cost* is taken into account; this is further reflected by its frequency count which shows that Kensington is a reference shop for 26 shops. For Bradford, the balance percentages confirm that it has low proportional *Uncontrollable cost* and that its area of efficiency is restricted to shops which also exhibit this feature. Its area of efficiency is also biased towards higher *Revenue growth*.

At Step 4, four additional efficient shops were introduced—Gloucester, Leicester, Sutton Coldfield and Manchester 2. We referred to the analysts' ratio method in order to comment on these shops in Sections 4.3–4.5. Our conclusions were that all four shops had similar areas of efficiency with a leaning towards higher proportions of *Revenue Gp1+3* but were differentiated by slightly different leanings in other aspects.

The balance percentages confirm that each has a higher than average proportion of *Revenue Gp1+3* and an area of efficiency restricted to shops which are similar in that respect. Leicester's area of efficiency is further restricted to shops with very low proportions of *Uncontrollable cost* whilst Gloucester's area of efficiency is restricted to lower than average proportions of *Uncontrollable cost* but not as low as Leicester's. Manchester 2's area of efficiency covers the higher proportions of *Uncontrollable cost*. Gloucester, Leicester and Manchester 2 are all associated with higher than average proportions of *Revenue growth* and differ from Sutton Coldfield in this respect whose area of efficiency covers the bottom range of *Revenue growth* proportion.

Hence, although the discussions of Sections 4.3–4.5 were useful in terms of exploring the concept of efficiency and relating the work of the analysts to our final conclusions, it is possible to deliver the same message much more directly and coherently using Table 6.1.

We can now consider the five additional shops, not discussed in Chapter 4. These were introduced as efficient at Step 5 in constructing the cost efficiency model. They were—Hammersmith, Leamington Spa, Newcastle, Plymouth and St. Albans.

The key feature of the Hammersmith shop is the unusual combination of below average proportions for both *Staff cost* and *Uncontrollable cost*. Although Manchester 2 is similar in this respect, Hammersmith is associated with below average *Revenue growth* whilst Manchester 2 is associated with above average *Revenue growth*.

The key features of the Leamington Spa shop are high proportional *Revenue growth* and low proportional *Staff cost*.

The key feature of the Newcastle shop is that it has a low proportion of both *Non-staff controllable cost* and *Uncontrollable cost*, of which the former is particularly low.

It can be seen from the frequency count that the Plymouth and St. Albans shops differ from all other frontier shops in that they are not reference shops for any shop other than themselves. Their areas of efficiency are therefore also specific to themselves. Both are extreme in their cost mix with very low proportions of *Uncontrollable cost* allied to about average *Non-staff controllable cost*. This is not typical of other shops.

All of the features described for these five shops are concerned with *Staff cost* or *Non-staff controllable cost*. This is consistent with the shops being identified as efficient at Step 5 of the model construction when the breakdown of *Controllable cost* into these two elements was made. Similar consistencies are also observed for the other steps and confirm that the stepwise approach itself provides a further aid to interpretation.

As a final note on areas of efficiency, it is important to recognize the two types of efficiency which emerge. Firstly, there is general efficiency, of which Kensington and Northampton are the best examples, where a shop influences the efficiency standard across a wide range of input and output mix. Secondly there is specific efficiency, of which Plymouth and St. Albans are the best examples, where a shop influences the efficiency standard only within a narrow band of input and output mix. Often, this will be because this narrow band is not typical of the mixes exhibited by other shops. In such cases, although there is no evidence that the shop can do better given its mix of inputs and outputs, management must seriously consider whether possessing such a mix is in line with corporate objectives.

This is by no means the only instance in which it is necessary to combine a clear view of corporate objectives with the analytical capability which we have developed. Having now completed our analytical development we must turn our attention to management issues, and the interface between the analysis and corporate objectives is an appropriate starting point.

6.4 MANAGEMENT ISSUES—DEA AND CORPORATE OBJECTIVES

Our analytical development has established that DEA is a powerful analytical tool capable of evaluating relative performance defined in terms of many inputs and many outputs without the need to make assumptions regarding the mathematical form of relationships between outputs or inputs. In our experience, this has unfortunately raised the expectation in some quarters that the only requirement of a DEA investigation is to provide DEA software with data on many inputs and many outputs following which complete insight into the performance of management units throughout the organization will automatically ensue. This is not the case. The software will certainly produce efficiency ratings and targets for the units, but the extent to which these can be interpreted in a context which is relevant to managing the organization will be questionable.

We have already seen in developing our cost and market efficiency models that we can build a totally different model and present a totally different picture of the relative performance of organizational units depending on whether we are looking at the economical use of resources or the achievement of market potential. Even in the context of a single model, we could, for example, take a very different view of the performance of the Kensington shop according to whether or not we take separate account of its uncontrollable costs.

So are we concerned with the economical use of resources? Are we concerned with market potential? What constitutes controllable and uncontrollable cost? Each individual decision such as this has an analytical consequence but is also an important management issue. We have sought to build an approach which encompasses the resolution of these issues within the analytical process. However, in order to resolve the issues, we must understand the organization and its objectives and, more to the point, the organization must understand itself.

In introducing the case study in Section 2.1, we took as our starting point the fact that the management's primary objective was to increase profit. We also had a ready made list of possible cost and revenue breakdowns and environmental factors which might influence profitability. In practice, thorough reviews of corporate objectives need to be undertaken to get even to this stage, an aspect which we will not discuss in any greater depth here since it is the focus of Section 7.2 which discusses setting up a performance measuring system. However, even assuming this much, there were still instances during the construction of our models where significant management issues related to corporate objectives were raised.

For example, at Step 4 in constructing the cost efficiency model, we identified that *Revenue Gp2* could be achieved at a lower unit cost than other product group revenue. In allowing for this in the efficiency measure, we are not addressing the question of what the revenue mix should be but rather the efficiency of each shop in using resources to achieve the revenue mix which it generates.

However, this does raise questions regarding the corporate objectives in promoting and selling the Group 2 product line. If shops should be looking to achieve greater proportions of *Revenue Gp2* and if there is no good reason why some shops achieve lower proportions than others, then it would be correct not to include the revenue breakdown in our model. By not including the breakdown, we still acknowledge that low proportions of Group 2 revenue are a contributory cause of inefficiency, but we imply that shops which have the low proportions should rectify the situation in order to generate revenue more economically. Further, our estimate of cost improvement will include the element which would result from rectifying the revenue mix.

An alternative situation is that the Group 2 product line is a declining business and that the future of the company lies with other product lines. In this instance, the corporate objective will not be to rectify low proportions of *Revenue Gp2* but rather to accept it as a declining business and pursue sales in other product groups. It is now correct to incorporate the revenue breakdown into the model since the shops with lower proportions of *Revenue Gp2* cannot rectify the situation and it is unfair to expect them to operate as economically as those with the benefit of high *Revenue Gp2* proportions.

There is a further issue regarding the product groups. We identified at Step 2 in constructing the market efficiency model, that *Revenue growth* was higher where proportions of *Revenue Gp1* were greater. Again, we postulated two alternative situations which could lead to this result. Group 1 could be a recent product line offering the best immediate opportunity for growth, with the lower proportions of *Revenue Gp1* occurring through inefficient selling. In this case, no allowance should be made for revenue breakdown in the efficiency assessment. Alternatively, Group 1 could be the type of product through which greater contact is maintained with the customer thereby providing more frequent selling opportunities in other areas. In this case, the existence of lower *Revenue Gp1* base may not be attributable to the current shop manager but will nevertheless make his task more difficult and should be allowed for in an efficiency assessment of his performance.

These questions cannot be answered through mathematical and statistical analysis. They can only be answered through a clear understanding on the part of management as to why they sell these product ranges and what role each range has in their future strategy. For this reason, it is critical that corporate objectives are clear in the minds of both management and analysts and that model development takes place with the full cooperation of management rather than in isolation.

It is equally important to have a clear view of corporate objectives in deciding whether a particular expenditure breakdown should be taken into account. In our cost efficiency model, we took separate account of *Staff cost*, *Non-staff controllable cost* and *Uncontrollable cost*. In reviewing the results, we observed that Plymouth and St. Albans had atypical cost mixes although each was identified as efficient given its expenditure mix. However, as can be seen from the Step 4 results, if we do not take the breakdown between *Staff cost* and *Non-Staff cost* into account, then these shops would not be efficient, thus indicating that in terms of controllable cost as a whole the shops do less well than others. To be justified, therefore, in allowing for their unusual cost mix in our efficiency measure, we must be clear that it is necessary to operate with this unusual mix.

The features of the Plymouth and St. Albans cost mixes were: relatively high proportions of staff cost, low uncontrollable costs and about average non-staff controllable costs. A reason for this could be that these shops lack technology which forces them to operate with higher staff levels but keeps other costs low. If the manager had it at his disposal to introduce the necessary technology, then we should not take the breakdown into account. If alternatively the introduction of technology was part of a corporate programme in which these shops were seen as low priority, then it is reasonable to take the breakdown into account.

In concluding our discussion of corporate objectives, we contend that the ultimate choice of model structure depends on a clear statement of corporate objectives. In the case of cost efficiency, we will continue to use the model results of Table 4.2, but we accept that in some circumstances we would construct a model that did not use the full cost breakdown. In the case of market efficiency, we follow our preference stated earlier for the construction of a separate model (see Section 4.6) and we use the model results from Table 5.7 rather than Table 5.5 (see Section 5.7). Again, however, we accept that there is also the possibility that the results of Table 4.9 would be appropriate if corporate objectives dictate that allowance should not be made for revenue breakdown.

In Section 4.6 we chose *Revenue growth* as the sole model output for our market efficiency model with the specific objective of assessing the performance of the shop manager. We made the point that the shop manager can currently do nothing to control the historical decisions which have determined the shop's market penetration and for which a previous manager may have been responsible, but he can control current growth. However, it will often be relevant to assess the potential of the shop itself, particularly if potential closure is an issue. This does require an assessment of market penetration, and hence *Total revenue* as an output. This model can then be used to identify shop revenue potential whilst the market efficiency model is relevant in determining how well a manager is performing in moving towards that potential. Further, the cost efficiency model is relevant in determining how economically resources are being deployed in achieving the revenue potential.

It is to the issue of the shop potential and its achievement that we now turn our attention.

6.5 MANAGEMENT ISSUES—SHOP POTENTIAL AND ITS ACHIEVEMENT

The Shop Potential Model

The issue of shop potential and its achievement is perhaps the most critical issue of all. Although senior management will be grateful for the insights gained while constructing models, such as which factors influence performance, the key question will always be 'What does it tell us about our shops?'.

As pointed out above, an additional model is required to assess shop revenue potential. In a similar way to the case of the market efficiency model, we are seeking to build a model which is distinct from the cost efficiency model and it will therefore exclude resource related factors from consideration. The strongest relationship with *Total revenue* is exhibited by *Age of shop* (see Table 2.5) and there can be little doubt that this is a causal relationship since we expect shops to take time to build up their revenue bases. *Age of shop* was therefore included in the model at Step 1.

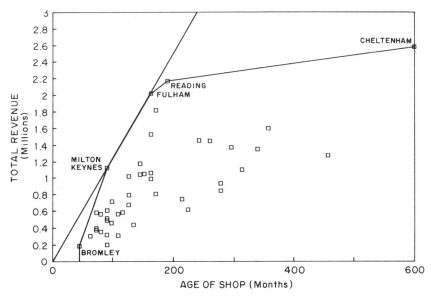

Figure 6.3 Shop revenue potential: Step 1

At Step 1, we experimented with variable, decreasing and constant returns to scale models and found the resultant efficiencies to be correlated with *Age of shop* (i.e. biased) in the constant and decreasing returns to scale cases. We have therefore used a complete variable returns to scale approach where the resultant efficiencies were found to be uncorrelated with *Age of shop*. In other words the relationship between *Total revenue* and *Age of shop* exhibits increasing returns to scale in the early years and decreasing returns to scale in the later years. The relationship is illustrated in Figure 6.3.

The subsequent correlation analysis during the construction of the model is shown in Table 6.3. The relationship between the Step 1 efficiency measure and *Customer service* is in the opposite direction to the expected causal relationship. We have therefore not included *Customer service* in the

Table 6.3 Shop revenue efficiency model—correlations

		Step 1	Step 2	Step 3
OUTPUTS	Total revenue	*	*	*
INPUTS	Age of shop	*	*	*
	Catchment population		*	*
	Pitch			*
Age of shop (months)		0.19566	0.07153	0.07558
Catchment population		0.27765	−0.14003	0.07227
Central overheads		0.68192	0.39802	0.28918
Customer service		−0.38289	−0.23894	−0.11545
Non-staff controllable cost		0.62842	0.25848	0.22815
Uncontrollable cost		0.23703	0.00810	0.07561
Pitch		−0.12844	−0.26246	0.51353
Profit		0.49088	0.35009	0.24717
Revenue Gp1		0.58494	0.34440	0.32800
Revenue Gp2		0.62289	0.38663	0.23913
Revenue Gp3		0.56280	0.23923	0.25398
Revenue growth		0.73115	0.40992	0.32139
Revenue % growth		−0.21085	−0.06308	−0.06193
Staff cost		0.71809	0.41049	0.26053
Competition		0.29530	−0.04105	0.03276
Non-staff cost		0.31279	0.04720	0.10404
Total revenue		0.68192	0.39802	0.28918
Total cost		0.62719	0.29613	0.22307
Controllable cost		0.71953	0.40123	0.26107

Table 6.4 Steps in constructing shop revenue efficiency model

		Step 1	Step 2	Step 3
OUTPUTS	Total revenue	*	*	*
INPUTS	Age of shop	*	*	*
	Catchment population		*	*
	Pitch			*
	BROMLEY	1.000	1.000	1.000
	CHELTENHAM	1.000	1.000	1.000
	FULHAM	1.000	1.000	1.000
	MILTON KEYNES	1.000	1.000	1.000
	READING	1.000	1.000	1.000
	LEAMINGTON SPA	0.557	1.000	1.000
	REIGATE	0.263	1.000	1.000

Table 6.4 *(cont.)*

	Step 1	Step 2	Step 3
TONBRIDGE	0.261	0.733	1.000
OXFORD ST	0.650	0.650	1.000
KENSINGTON	0.647	0.647	1.000
CROYDON	0.588	0.588	1.000
SUTTON COLDFIELD	0.522	0.565	1.000
NORTHAMPTON	0.527	0.560	1.000
HARLOW	0.441	0.488	1.000
FULHAM	0.939	1.000	1.000
BRIXTON	0.555	0.555	0.991
HAMMERSMITH	0.602	0.602	0.962
GLOUCESTER	0.527	0.527	0.948
MAIDENHEAD	0.390	0.908	0.908
NEWCASTLE	0.880	0.887	0.887
BIRMINGHAM 1	0.506	0.506	0.887
MANCHESTER 1	0.452	0.452	0.840
MANCHESTER 2	0.772	0.772	0.772
WOOD GREEN	0.756	0.766	0.766
EALING	0.394	0.394	0.724
WINDSOR	0.231	0.686	0.686
VICTORIA	0.685	0.685	0.685
PLYMOUTH	0.654	0.669	0.669
BIRMINGHAM 2	0.375	0.375	0.669
REDDITCH	0.415	0.658	0.658
SWINDON	0.654	0.654	0.654
YORK	0.610	0.610	0.610
BRADFORD	0.582	0.591	0.591
SLOUGH	0.581	0.581	0.581
HIGH WYCOMBE	0.181	0.268	0.560
ST. ALBANS	0.284	0.553	0.553
BRENT CROSS	0.538	0.538	0.538
WATFORD	0.503	0.529	0.529
WOLVERHAMPTON	0.492	0.509	0.509
DUDLEY	0.482	0.482	0.482
BRISTOL	0.431	0.431	0.431
SOLIHULL	0.421	0.425	0.425
HOUNSLOW	0.404	0.412	0.412
LEICESTER	0.376	0.376	0.376
CRAWLEY	0.283	0.365	0.365
ILFORD	0.342	0.342	0.342

model and we will discuss *Customer service* as a separate issue below. The relationship between the Step 1 efficiency measure and *Catchment population* is to be expected and again there can be little doubt that it is causal. *Catchment population* was therefore included in the model at Step 2.

On examination of the Step 3 correlations, it seems clear that *Pitch* should be included in the model since it is a factor which management feel is a strong influence on performance and it is supported by the correlation. The negative value of the correlation indicates the expected direction of the relationship, the higher value of *Pitch* (2) indicating an inferior siting for the shop which is detrimental to performance. We have already indicated in Section 4.7 that we would have preferred a more discriminating measure of *Pitch* and in practice would seek one. A more gradual measure would produce a more gradual compensation for *Pitch* in the model, whereas it is clear from the strong positive correlation which exists with *Pitch* after Step 3 that the sudden jump from one value to the other results in an overcompensation for the inferior sitings. However, we must accept this in the context of the case study. The efficiency scores at each step of the model construction are shown in Table 6.4.

Detailed Analysis of an Individual Shop—Milton Keynes

Having now constructed a complete set of models, we can address the question of what the models tell us about the potential of individual shops. Let us start by considering the Milton Keynes shop which was mentioned specifically in Section 2.2 in connection with the analysts' rankings. The Milton Keynes manager claimed the best revenue growth record in the company and he mentioned that his high costs were essential to the achievement of this, although some of the cost is attributable to high building costs beyond his control.

Milton Keynes provides the best example of historical growth, a fact established initially by the analysts' rankings (Table 2.2) and confirmed by Table 6.4 and Figure 6.3. Further, the results from the market efficiency model shown in Table 5.7 establish that there is no better example than Milton Keynes' growth record within the last year, given its revenue mix, population and competition characteristics. However, it is important to emphasize the qualification 'given its characteristics' since it can be seen from Table 6.2 that Milton Keynes' growth as a percentage of *Total revenue* is now only about average. Hence there are shops currently achieving similar and higher proportions of *Revenue growth* with which Milton Keynes can be compared in cost terms. It is this type of comparison on which the cost efficiency model results in Table 4.2 are based. The results show a cost efficiency rating for Milton Keynes of only 0.71. In other words, based on comparison with other shops of similar characteristics at the present time, Milton Keynes could operate at 71% of its current controllable costs.

Note that we are not implying that Milton Keynes could have achieved its excellent historical growth record at 71% of its controllable costs ever since its inception. In fact, we cannot comment on this since we do not know what its costs in earlier years were. Our finding is based purely on

Milton Keynes' current position and our conclusion is that, having arrived in that position, its costs are now too high.

We must therefore refute the manager's claim that his high costs are essential but we must not overlook his further claim that some of the high cost is beyond his control. In fact, we have already taken this into account in the cost efficiency model by taking separate account of the *Uncontrollable cost* and the 71% to which we refer above is purely in terms of the controllable costs. However, for the reader who has followed the theoretical development in depth, the analysis does identify a slack value of £44 000 for Milton Keynes in respect of *Uncontrollable cost*. This supports the manager's claim to the extent that, relative to other shops, there is an additional £44 000 of *Uncontrollable cost* from which Milton Keynes gets no return.

One point we have stressed throughout our analytical development is that the DEA efficiency scores are based on comparison with actual achieved performance. The reference shops on which the cost efficiency assessment of the Milton Keynes shop were based will be of interest to the shop manager. These shops were Kensington and Newcastle. One of the most effective methods of presentation to illustrate the difference in performance between Milton Keynes and its reference shops is simply to show the input and output data values in bar chart form but with each data value expressed as a percentage of the Milton Keynes value. Figure 6.4 shows such a chart comparing Milton Keynes and Kensington. It can be seen very clearly that Kensington's costs are 70% or below those of Milton Keynes whilst Kensington's outputs are 80% of or higher than those at Milton Keynes. It would be possible to place an upper bound of 0.875 (=70/80) on Milton Keynes' efficiency based on these figures but the DEA efficiency score of 0.71 cannot be deduced directly from the chart. What DEA is providing is a more accurate assessment which takes into account the fact that the percentages for some inputs are well below 70% and for some outputs are well above 80%. However, the graphs will make a bigger impression on the shop manager than the theory of DEA itself.

Figure 6.5 shows a similar comparison between Milton Keynes and Newcastle. Here one of Newcastle's costs is 107% of the corresponding Milton Keynes cost whilst one of the outputs is only 103% of the corresponding Milton Keynes output; but nevertheless the overall picture of generally higher output in return for generally lower input again emerges strongly.

We do not have the data available to be able to comment on the historical build-up to Milton Keynes' current high costs. However, there are two courses of action which the shop manager might have taken which would be likely causes. He could have set too ambitious a growth plan through failure to recognize that growth would decline as a proportion of the revenue

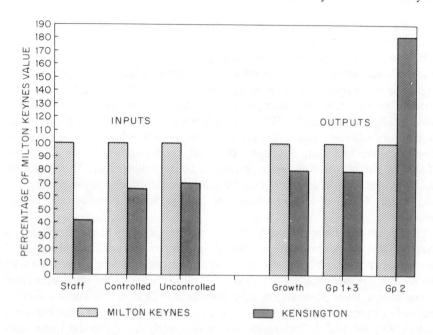

Figure 6.4 Milton Keynes and Kensington comparison

base as the latter increased over time. Alternatively he could have over-budgeted his costs through failure to recognize that they should decrease in proportion to *Total revenue* as the *Revenue growth* proportion becomes smaller.

Whatever the cause, the net result was that the shop showed a loss over the past year in terms of the company profit measure despite its excellent growth record. However, the potential controllable cost savings identified by the cost efficiency model amount to £117 531. Hence it should be within the manager's capability to convert his £93 850 loss to a profit of £23 681. In addition, we have estimated that a further potential £44 000 of profit was eroded by high costs beyond the manager's control. Although the latter costs are beyond the shop manager's control, they are not necessarily irrevocable and it may be possible to reduce them through decisions at a higher management level, possibly to the extent of resiting the shop!

The corporate objectives issue regarding revenue mix, discussed in Section 6.3, is extremely relevant in the case of Milton Keynes which has an exceptionally low proportion of *Revenue Gp2*, attracting lower costs and an exceptionally high proportion of *Revenue Gp1+3* which attracts higher costs. It is important to confirm that this mix aligns with corporate objectives if it is to persist.

It is critical at all times—but particularly when senior management are

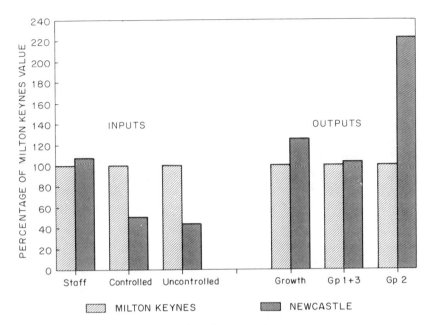

Figure 6.5 Milton Keynes and Newcastle comparison

making key decisions such as whether or not to close a shop—that the performance of each shop is fully understood in all of the above aspects; it may have considerable potential to improve. On the basis of last year's performance, Milton Keynes' loss would make it a prime target if potential closure decisions were taken on the basis of current profitability alone. However, when assessed on its potential, it is at least a viable proposition.

A further point is that improvement potential exists not only through the potential for improved management but through the potential for additional growth over time. Hence it is also important to know something about the profitability of Milton Keynes in say five years' time. Since our model of shop revenue potential contains the time based input *Age of shop*, we can also use our models as predictive tools to aid this decision. First of all we can revise the value of *Age of shop* for Milton Keynes from 90 to 150 months in the model of shop revenue potential. On this basis, Milton Keynes would have an efficiency rating of 0.741, indicating that in five years' time its *Total revenue* should increase from its current £1 135 640 to £1 533 520 in current-year prices. We can then repeat this process using the market efficiency model to estimate a value of *Revenue growth* based on the projected *Total revenue*. Finally, we can use the cost efficiency model in the same manner to estimate the controllable costs which should apply for the revised levels of *Total revenue* and *Revenue growth*.

Where necessary within this process, we assume that the proportional breakdown of *Total cost* and *Total revenue* remains unchanged. For example, where the market efficiency model requires separate projections of *Revenue Gp1* and *Revenue Gp2+3* we split the projected revenue into the same proportions which apply currently. A further point to note is that our projections must not influence the efficiency frontier. This can be avoided by assuming an initial value for the quantity which we are seeking to estimate. A small value in the case of an output or a large value in the case of an input will ensure that the model does not place the shop on the frontier. The correct estimate can then be determined from the resultant efficiency score as in the case of the revenue projection above.

If we further assume that uncontrollable and centrally apportioned costs change in proportion to *Total revenue*, we can forecast Milton Keynes' profitability as follows:

	Current year (actual)		Current year (if efficient)		Five years' time (if efficient)	
Total revenue	1 135 640			1 135 640		1 533 520
Staff cost		356 290	252 134			340 470
Non-staff controllable		45 720	32 354			43 690
Uncontrollable cost		160 530	160 530			216 778
Central overheads		666 940	666 940			900 609
Total cost	1 229 480			1 111 959		1 501 547
Profit	(93 840)			23 681		31 973

The final figure of £31 973 is a 35% increase beyond the current potential of £23 681 if the shop were run efficiently. However, the figure is still relatively small in comparison with most shops, and it can be concluded that the shop will not make significant profits in the foreseeable future unless other issues regarding revenue mix and uncontrollable costs can be resolved.

Note that it is not essential to the above forecasting procedure to assume that revenue and cost proportions remain unchanged, but if a mix is to be changed, there must be a replacement assumption as to what the revised proportions will be.

As a final observation on the Milton Keynes shop, it is important to recognize that identifying its potential does not guarantee its achievement, since, for example, management and administrative procedures may have to be significantly revised at Milton Keynes. A close scrutiny to compare the current procedures at Milton Keynes with those at Kensington and Newcastle is likely to aid this process.

Issues Concerning the Potential of Other Shops

The Reigate shop was also mentioned in Section 2.2 in connection with the analysts' rankings. Here the manager's claim was that he had achieved miracles given his low *Catchment population*. We will not consider this in great depth since the situation is similar to Milton Keynes. The Reigate shop is efficient both in terms of its *Revenue growth* and *Total revenue*. However there is scope for cost improvement, its cost efficiency rating being 0.89. Note that Reigate will achieve higher profits than Milton Keynes for as long as it has the benefit a much lower proportion of *Uncontrollable cost* and a higher proportion of *Revenue Gp2*.

The Milton Keynes shop produced a loss in terms of the company profitability measure but has considerable improvement potential. In general, shops making small profits do not necessarily have improvement potential and improvement potential is not necessarily restricted to shops with small profits. The Leamington Spa shop is an example of a low-profit shop which is assessed as efficient by all three models. Its potential is limited by the fact that it has only been in operation for a relatively short time and has a small *Catchment population*. On the other hand, the Slough shop is the eighth best shop in terms of profitability (see Table 2.2) but is given relatively low efficiency scores by all three models, and hence has considerable improvement potential. We can calculate Slough's potential profitability by following the procedure adopted when projecting future profitability for Milton Keynes. In Slough's case, we make no projection but we can use its revenue potential efficiency score to calculate its potential *Total revenue* and then derive *Revenue growth* and costs from potential *Total revenue* as in the Milton Keynes case. The potential profitability figure arrived at by this means is £524 449 compared with its current profit of £278 330. Note that the possibility exists to repeat this calculation for each shop and aggregate the results to estimate the profit potential of the company.

There are many combinations of cost efficiency, market efficiency and revenue potential efficiency which shops can exhibit. In Figure 6.6, these combinations have been shown graphically for some shops by plotting market efficiency against cost efficiency and then labelling the points on the graph with the revenue potential efficiency. For clarity, we have labelled only the extreme shops.

The graph tells us a lot about the shops themselves. For example, St. Albans and Sutton Coldfield are inhibiting their growth through lack of resources. Both, by virtue of their cost efficiency, have made maximum use of the resources at their disposal but neither has achieved their potential *Revenue growth* in the last year. In the case of Sutton Coldfield, this can only have been a recent occurrence—Sutton Coldfield is efficient in terms of its historical growth achievement. In the case of St. Albans, however, this situation may well have persisted for many years since only half of the shop's revenue potential has been realized.

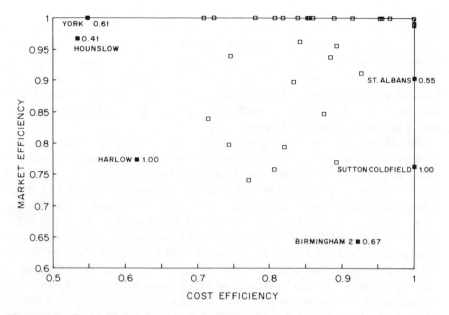

Figure 6.6 Cost, market and revenue efficiency

The Birmingham 2 shop has some scope to improve its cost efficiency but the scope is insufficient to allow its growth potential to be achieved, and hence this shop is also inhibiting its growth through lack of resources.

Harlow has sufficient resources to achieve its *Revenue growth* potential but has not done so. However growth has not been a problem historically since Harlow is efficient in terms of its historical growth achievement.

York has fulfilled its *Revenue growth* potential in the current year but has committed excessive resources in doing so. York's historical growth has been insufficient to achieve its revenue potential and its over-commitment of resources may have resulted from an over-ambitious growth plan in the current year in an attempt to compensate. Hounslow is similar to York but was a little way from achieving its *Revenue growth* potential even in the current year.

Whilst considering shop potential, we must return to an issue raised in Section 4.2. We observed that following the model construction, a correlation existed between cost efficiency and the component part percentages of cost despite the fact that these component parts had been accounted for in the model. We attributed this to a group of shops with particularly high values of *Uncontrollable cost* to *Total revenue* which also had high values of *Controllable cost* to *Total revenue*. We observed that this was consistent with trying to put too large a shop in these locations relative to the market potential. The graph in Figure 6.7 examines this issue further. The graph shows the value of *Uncontrollable cost* to *Total revenue* plotted against *Age of shop*. The points in the graph representing shops with the higher values of *Uncontrollable cost* to *Total revenue* are labelled with the shop's cost efficiency measure. These shops tend to be newer shops and the labels confirm that in general their cost efficiency scores are low. As the cost efficiency measure takes the uncontrollable element of cost into account, this confirms the above statement that the controllable element of cost for these shops is also high. Hence there is a problem of frequently over-committing resources to shops in their earlier years.

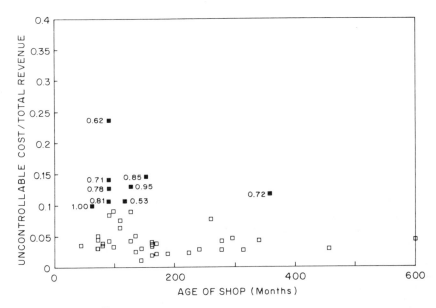

Figure 6.7   Cost efficiency

A possible cause of this problem would be if the business levels targeted in the earlier years were beyond the bounds of potential achievement. Figure 6.8 shows a graph similar to Figure 6.7 but with the label now indicating the revenue potential efficiency measure. It can be seen from this that about half of the problem shops do not even achieve their revenue potential. Hence whilst over-ambitious targeting remains a possible cause in about half of the cases, the problem as a whole is a more general one encompassing the control of newer shops as well as their planning.

Management and Customer Service

Let us now consider the statement made in Section 2.2 that the managers

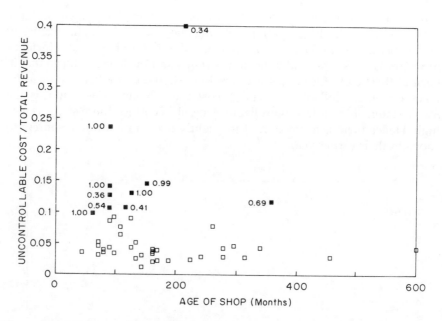

Figure 6.8 Revenue potential efficiency

of the more profitable shops argue that their achievements are based on customer service and good management. We will begin by considering good management. Our cost efficiency and market efficiency models are in fact measures of good management in that they each measure achievement in terms of factors under the manager's control. We can plot each of these measures against profit. Figure 6.9 shows cost efficiency against profit whilst Figure 6.10 shows market efficiency against profit. Figure 6.9 shows that the general standard of cost management is higher in more profitable shops but nevertheless some less profitable shops are well managed in cost terms. Figure 6.10 shows that the shops with very high profits also tend to be well managed in growth terms, but below this threshold, growth management can be good or bad. Overall, it is clear from the graphs that good management does contribute to the profitability of shops but some low-profit shops are equally well managed and there are shops at all levels of profitability with scope for improved management.

Let us now consider customer service. The *Customer service* measure included in our data is based on questionnaires returned by customers in which they are requested to rate specific aspects of shop service on a pre-specified scale. We observed at Step 1 in the construction of the model of shop revenue potential that a negative correlation was observed between efficiency and *Customer service* which is the opposite direction to

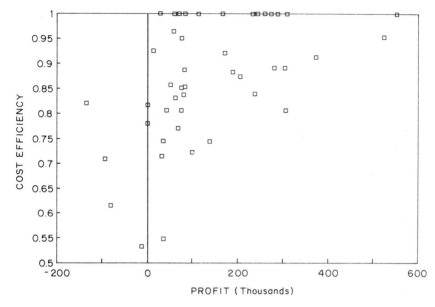

Figure 6.9   Cost management

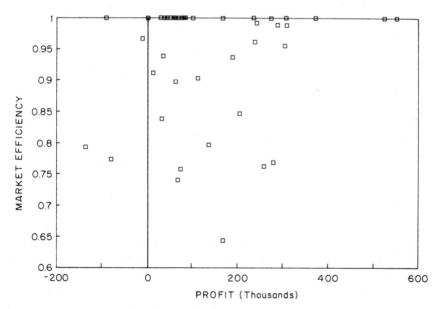

Figure 6.10   Growth management

that which would be expected if a causal relationship existed. If the negative relationship is causal it means that a shop's business grows less quickly if they provide a better customer service. This would be a possibility if customer service counted for nothing and the provision of a higher level of customer service caused a drain on staff time which could have been better used in generating new business.

There is, however, another strong possibility. If customer service is to be measured, then service as perceived by the customer must be reflected in the measure but it is possible that customer perception might vary according to the shop environment. Table 2.5 shows that *Customer service* is negatively correlated not only with a shop's level of *Competition* but also with factors which are generally related to the size of a shop, such as *Total cost* and *Total revenue*. *Competition* and size are themselves related because bigger shops are associated with areas of higher revenue potential and competitors are more likely to have shops in these areas. Hence it might be that customers simply perceive smaller shops as being more friendly.

Alternatively, it might be that customers are less critical where there is less competition with which to compare a shop. The former case is not something which senior management would wish to be represented in the *Customer service* measure since their primary objective is to grow. The latter case would mean that the *Customer service* measure was biased in favour of shops with low *Competition*. In order to fully investigate these possibilities, the senior management should use the questionnaires to determine what aspects of service their customers perceive are important and then to appoint an independent arbiter to give consistent ratings to these aspects in each shop. In the absence of such an investigation, it would be dangerous to come to any firm conclusion on the effects of customer service.

The way in which *Customer service* should be treated in a DEA model is heavily dependent on such an investigation. If the effect of *Customer service* is truly negative but it is a management objective to provide it, then *Customer service* should be an output in the models since it either consumes additional resources or detracts from gaining business. If *Customer service* has no effect on the business then it has no role in the models. If *Customer service* has a positive effect on business then much depends on whether or not it consumes resources. If there is no evidence that it consumes resources, then it should be regarded as a factor which explains efficiency but not one for which allowance should be made in the models, otherwise we would condone lower business levels where a lower level of *Customer service* is provided. If there is evidence of resource consumption then *Customer service* must be allowed for in the cost efficiency model but, again, not in the other models otherwise lesser performance would be condoned.

Shop Potential—Conclusions on the Modelling Approach

In this section we have been able to comment in great detail on the potential of individual shops and the degree to which that potential has been achieved. We have also been able to identify future potential. Fundamental to this analysis has been the ability to combine the functions of three separate models which identify in a logical manner:

(a)   the historical achievement of shop potential;
(b)   the influence of this and environmental factors on current *Revenue growth*;
(c)   the influence of current *Revenue growth* and historical growth (i.e. *Total revenue*) on cost.

Had we instead attempted to use the combined model constructed in Section 4.7, not only would it become impossible to isolate these effects but in many cases we would not be able to identify any improvement potential. For example, in the case of Milton Keynes, our analysis above indicated that it had considerable profit improvement potential. However, the combined model would identify no potential improvement since Milton Keynes was efficient in this model.

In Section 4.7, we indicated that the inclusion of two aspects of performance in the same DEA model should imply that a trade-off exists between them. In this sense, the combined model would imply that higher cost is necessary where the market is smaller. We also showed in Section 4.7 that, if this is not actually the case, then the combined model will underestimate true performance potential. The cost efficiency model indicates that Milton Keynes's costs are excessive for its level of *Revenue growth* and *Total revenue*. It is therefore the additional factors in the combined model (*Catchment population* and *Competition*) which are providing the justification for these costs. In other words, the model is saying that Milton Keynes needs these costs to justify its level of *Revenue growth* and *Total revenue in its particular market which is small*. The correlations did not support this view and, logically, whilst a small market will restrict the potential for growth, there is no obvious reason for additional cost to be associated with the growth which is achievable. Hence overall, we feel that the separate models:

(a)   give the true representation of potential;
(b)   offer advantages with interpretation (see previous paragraph);
(c)   correctly reflect management accountability (see Section 4.7).

Having identified potential, it is fundamental to its achievement that realistic targets are set and that sufficient but not superfluous resources are allocated. It is the issue of targeting and budgeting to which we now turn our attention.

6.6 MANAGEMENT ISSUES—TARGETS AND RESOURCE ALLOCATION

We discussed the company's current method of targeting when introducing the case study in Section 2.1. Shops are targeted to achieve a uniform percentage profit increase in line with the overall company target, but *ad hoc* adjustments are frequently made in the case of low-profit shops where senior management feel that the percentage target is too lenient. Newer shops will inevitably fall into this low-profit category and it is likely that the associated adjustments are a contributory cause of the control problem with newer shops to which reference was made in Section 6.5.

A more general problem with targeting purely on a profit basis is that it fails to provide sufficient direction for the underlying objectives of increasing *Total revenue* and containing *Total cost*. It is clear from the results of our analysis (see Figure 6.6) that some shops have grown well but have not contained costs whilst others have contained costs but ignored growth. It is therefore important, even though the ultimate objective is a profit target, to identify separate cost and revenue targets in order to clearly direct the means by which each profit target should be achieved and to ensure, in particular, that each shop target is correctly aligned with the stage of growth which the shop has currently reached.

In Section 2.5, we showed how a DEA model calculates a target for a shop by identifying a point on the efficiency frontier which has the same input mix and the same output mix as the shop itself. The mathematical derivation of such targets is described in Appendix A. Figure 6.11 shows the market efficiency model revenue growth targets expressed as percentages of their associated shop *Total revenue* and plotted against similar percentages calculated for achieved growth. The target percentages are not uniform but vary between 10% and 30%. The symbols on the graph differentiate older shops (over 140 months) and newer shops (under 140 months) and it can be seen from this that, in general, the newer shops are set higher targets. This is because older shops are at more advanced stages of growth and have less opportunity for further growth. However, the overlap between the two age groups indicates that other factors (*Total revenue*, *Catchment population* and *Competition*) have been taken into account.

For a number of shops, this method would set targets substantially higher than the growth levels actually achieved. For example, it might appear reasonable that Sutton Coldfield achieved a lower growth than Reading since the former is an older shop with only a slightly smaller *Catchment*

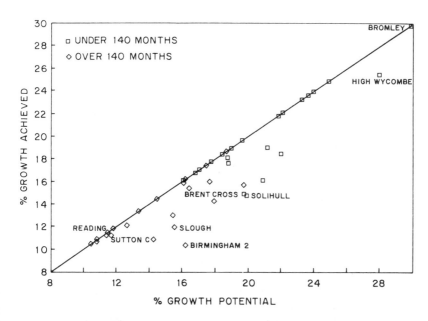

Figure 6.11 Targeting growth

population and about the same level of *Competition*. However, the DEA model takes historical growth into account and Sutton Coldfield, by virtue of its much lower revenue base, is actually at a less advanced stage of growth than Reading and is therefore targeted for higher growth. A similar argument applies in the cases of Slough and Birmingham 2. Brent Cross and Solihull are newer shops whose current growth is at a similar level to the older shops. High Wycombe had the second highest achieved percentage growth rate but is still targeted at a higher level since, although it has been in existence twice as long as Bromley, it has reached only a similar stage of growth and has therefore been targeted accordingly.

Our method therefore sets targets on the basis of potential and seeks to rectify under-achievement. It is important that the targets compensate in this way when a shop has not reached an adequate stage of growth for its age, otherwise the lost opportunity would remain lost. This further emphasizes the importance of the decision in Section 4.7 not to include *Age of shop* as factor in the market efficiency model which, if included, would have the effect of reducing targets for older shops even where they had not reached an adequate stage of growth.

A common criticism of the DEA approach, or indeed any method of comparative assessment, is that there is no way in which we can set improvement targets for 'the best'. The use of growth as an output demonstrates that this is not strictly true since 'the best' are targeted to continue growing, albeit at a rate which they have established for themselves. The argument would be well grounded, however, in the case of cost efficiency in that we would need to make assumptions outside of the DEA model if we wanted efficient units to make even further increases in output relative to cost.

A further feature of the use of growth as an output is that it measures a single year's achievement and we can therefore be confident that targets set on this basis are achievable within a year. This would not be so if targets had been derived from the shop potential model where the output, *Total revenue*, has built up over many years. Here, there are shops where the difference between actual revenue and potential revenue is well beyond the bounds of a single year's growth. This problem is avoided by the growth based model, although general adjustments may still be required in exceptional circumstances. For example, a uniform factor may have to be applied to all growth targets in the face of severe economic downturn.

Costs are also accumulated over a single year and therefore cost budgets derived from the cost efficiency model should be achievable in the following year. The *Total revenue* values, from which the cost budgets are determined, should be adjusted to include the *Revenue growth* targeted by the market efficiency model. We have already provided an example of this process in Section 6.5 when assessing the future profit potential of Milton Keynes. Where a shop has costs which are considerably in excess of the desired budget, the shop should be the subject of a scrutiny, possibly in conjunction with its reference shops, to determine the cause of the excessive expenditure and an appropriate timescale for its rectification. If the timescale is longer than a year, the budgets can be amended in accordance with the findings of the scrutiny.

There are other contexts in which management may wish to adjust DEA targets. For example, Building Society finance requires a delicate balance between lending and investment. A balance must therefore be maintained between mortgage accounts and investment accounts across the society as a whole. Whilst DEA targets would generally maintain this balance within each branch, this does not guarantee that the aggregate target maintains the balance for the Society. Adjustments may therefore have to be made to individual branch balances in order to rectify the balance for the Society. However, it is important that the adjustments are made with reference to the DEA efficiency frontier to ensure that targets are maintained within achievable bounds. Hence DEA has a role in the targeting system even where adjustments to the targets are necessary.

Our analytical development was designed to address the issues faced by company management. As a result, a targeting system has emerged that:

- is aligned with corporate objectives;
- gives due direction to the achievement of growth and the control of costs;
- takes account of the critical factors which influence performance; and
- can be substantiated by demonstrable achieved performance.

This should enable senior management not only to set targets but also to communicate the underlying reasoning and to establish the fairness of the targets as they move towards a system where remuneration is linked to achievement of targets.

Throughout Chapters 2 to 6 we have covered many topics that are essential to addressing the management issues raised at the outset of the case study. In Chapter 7 we summarize these topics in the wider context of organizations in general and present a framework essential to establishing a successful performance measuring system which incorporates DEA.

Chapter 7

Using DEA—The Management of Complexity

7.1 SETTING UP A PERFORMANCE MEASURING SYSTEM

The art of management can be summarized by the two words 'Decision' and 'Control'. Leadership, pastoral care, planning—all these and the other managerial attributes—can all be subsumed by these two overriding demands. For both, information is vital, and a major part of that information relates to judgements of performance—of people and processes. Very rarely are these judgements easy for they concern the relationships between many, often conflicting, factors.

Few decisions can be made in isolation, since any part of the organization necessarily reacts with many other parts. In other words the organization is an interconnecting system that requires integrated checks and controls. It is a complex system that needs sophisticated tools to manage it, at both the strategic and day-to-day levels. In turn, these tools involve the collection and analysis of data to provide relevant and concise information to aid the decision makers.

Managing complex operations is itself a complex operation that relies on the provision of information for its decision and control processes. In certain situations, where the performance of a group of units needs to be assessed, Data Envelopment Analysis can play a part. The value of its contribution will depend on how well the analysis is planned and how well the results are integrated with other elements of management information. We have set out to describe and demonstrate the technique of DEA and, just as importantly, to show how an organization should develop its use within the decision making framework.

In this chapter we build on the analysis and exploration of management issues described in Chapter 6 and look at the complete process of introducing DEA into a management information life-cycle. This is shown diagrammatically in Figure 7.1.

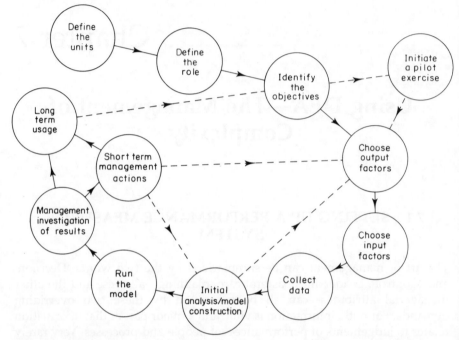

Figure 7.1 Performance measuring system

Throughout the whole exercise it is essential, in making the work relevant and useful, to keep in mind:

- the roles and objectives of the organization;
- the roles and objectives of the units;
- the objectives of the performance assessment exercise.

It is also important to prevent the analysis becoming a backroom or theoretical exercise. To this end, local management should be involved in all stages of the work from the definition of factors to the interpretation of results. This will also ensure that the results are relevant to the units themselves as well as to central management.

Some of the major benefits from introducing performance measures are that management gains:

- a better understanding of the process carried out within the units of the organization;

- a means for better control;
- a knowledge of where and when management action is needed to improve performance.

DEA, together with the actual process of introducing this analytical approach into the organization's management information structure, provides an ideal means of realizing these benefits. It also provides an additional tool to aid the evaluation of the quality of managerial control and decision making at a local level.

7.2 DEFINING THE ROLE AND OBJECTIVES OF UNITS

Managements routinely acknowledge the need to 'improve performance' but they often founder on the next step, which is deciding how to find a way of *measuring* performance improvement. Clearly, there must be a baseline of current performance standards against which improvements can be assessed, but this is easier said than done. In this chapter we set out a step by step guide to setting up a performance measurement system that will cover the general principles of such a system together with the specific role of DEA.

Before embarking on a performance measurement exercise it is essential that management is clear about why it is doing it, since this will, to a large extent, determine the approach to be adopted. Reasons would include:

- increasing sales;
- reducing costs;
- improving effectiveness;
- identifying high performers;
- identifying poor performers;
- investigating organizational structures;
- rationalization;
- rewarding performance.

This theme was taken up in the chapters on the case study (notably in Section 6.4) where the importance of choosing the right model, from a range of alternatives, was emphasized. In particular, it was shown that the model for investigating *shop* performance will be different from that for investigating *shop manager* performance (see Section 6.5). Care must also be taken to avoid undertaking what could be a lengthy, and costly, exercise which results in conclusions that cannot (or will not) be acted upon. Otherwise the work will not only be a waste of time but will also have the effect of raising expectations only to confound them.

DEA produces measures of *comparative* efficiency and is relevant in situations that contain a number of comparable units, such as:

- bank/building society branches;
- retail outlets (as part of a chain);
- secondary schools;
- hospitals;
- rating offices;
- public utility undertakings.

The first step then is to

DEFINE THE UNITS

and this will require the identification of:

- where authority lies (and its limits);
- where responsibility lies (and its limits);
- what resources (staff and other) are part of the units.

Note that this again raises the question of whether it is the performance of the shop or the manager that is to be analysed.

The boundaries will now be delineated and the next step is to

DEFINE THE ROLE OF THE UNITS

The role must be determined in the context of the role of the whole organization or service; this will commonly be set out in a Mission Statement. At both levels we will be answering the questions:

- why was this organization/unit set up?
- what does it do?
- whom does it serve?

The definition of the role of the unit, within the organization, leads in turn to the identification of a range of objectives that must be achieved. Thus, the final step in the preliminary stages is to

IDENTIFY THE UNIT OBJECTIVES

In our case study, the organization is a national retail organization and the units will be the 45 shops. The role of the shops could be stated as:

To provide a full range of goods for sale to the public at a profit for the organization.

This is a necessarily simplified version of a Mission Statement since we make no reference, in this context, to quality of goods, working environment etc. All these would be legitimate factors to consider (see the next section) but, for consistency with the worked example in the previous chapters, we have not included them.

The units' objectives, in the first instance, derive directly from their role, namely:

- provide a full range of goods;
- make a profit for the organization.

The 'bottom line' is to make a profit, but we have already seen (Chapter 2) that it can be difficult, if not impossible, to attribute profit at a unit (shop) level. We therefore have to dig a little deeper to identify objectives that are more closely related to the units under consideration.

These two levels can be termed 'primary objectives' and 'secondary objectives'. In a retail shop the management could decide that the way to improve profits lay in:

- collecting more revenue by a variety of methods;
- making more transactions;
- increasing the number of shop credit cards in circulation.

A similar process must be gone through when working in the public sector, where again the primary objectives are too intangible for direct inclusion in the analysis. Examples, which serve to illustrate, could include:

Health Service (District Health Authorities)

Primary Objective | Increase in the general level of health in the District.
Secondary Objectives: | To prevent disease;
 | To cure sickness;
 | To care for the infirm.

Education Service (Local Education Authorities—or Schools)

Primary Objective: | Improvements in literacy, numeracy, and social skills.
Secondary Objectives: | To achieve high educational standards;
 | To produce graduates who will be good citizens.

Naturally, these objectives have to be refined further before they become tangible, measurable objectives. This is examined later.

7.3 CONDUCTING A PILOT EXERCISE

All organizations have management information systems, albeit crude in some cases, and the comparative performance measurement produced by DEA has to be fitted in so that it becomes an integral part of the process. It may not be immediately obvious how this can be achieved, and most organizations prefer to carry out a pilot exercise to investigate both the DEA approach (and technique) and how the results can be applied. Where the organization covers the whole or a substantial part of the country it is customary for geographical regions, themselves, to be high level management units. It is logical, therefore, to conduct the exercise in one of these regions.

Several factors affect the choice of pilot region, amongst them:

- commited/cooperative management;
- units which in management's opinion cover the range from poor performers to good performers;
- sufficient units to render the analysis comprehensive.

This last point requires some explanation. In the case study we saw that as we increased the number of factors we ran into the problem of generating a high proportion of units that were diagnosed as relatively efficient, thereby robbing the analysis of the opportunity to provide the rich variety of information that is possible with DEA (cf. Table 5.5). Our experience is that the minimum number of units that should be considered is 20, even though some reported studies have used fewer. In fact, 20 is barely sufficient, especially if it is felt necessary to include many factors in the analysis.

In this and the previous section we have described the preliminary stages of the performance measuring system, as shown in Figure 7.2.

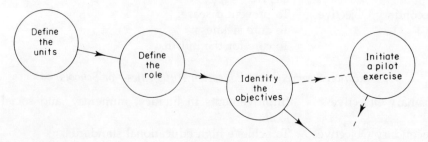

Figure 7.2 Preliminary stages in setting up a performance measuring system

7.4 CHOOSING THE FACTORS—OUTPUTS

By this stage, the units whose performance is to be measured will have been chosen. Their role and objectives will be defined, but more tangible factors have to be found before hard analysis can be undertaken.

We begin the task of choosing factors by first defining the outputs—outcomes that reflect and support the unit objectives. They will be measurable quantities that refer to aspects of achievement; examples, from a variety of organizations and services, would include:

- throughput;
- accuracy;
- number of new accounts opened;
- revenue from investments;
- (reduction in) numbers of complaints;
- number of acute patients treated;
- academic results;
- number of jobs filled.

Whatever the type of organization, the golden rule is to choose factors that cover the whole gamut of work that the units undertake. Sometimes this can be quite difficult and it is recommended that the *customers* of the units are identified first. These will be people outside the unit—bank customers, group management, patients, students (and parents), unemployed people in the area—whom the units are serving. The questions to answer, then, are:

- who receives the products/services of the units?
- how can these products/services be measured?

In our case study there are two types of customer—the public, who will be expecting the 'full range of goods', and the senior management who will be looking for a profit. For the purposes of this book we have concentrated on the latter since, ultimately, the viability of the organization is dependent on it continuing to make a profit. We could have looked at the service angle as a special study, but this would have been too narrow, and we used the Customer Service measure as a proxy for shop popularity.

In some cases it is important to consider certain outputs as satisfying *group* objectives even though they might not directly benefit an individual unit. Examples will include:

- cashing a cheque for a customer whose account is held at a different branch of the bank;

- exchanging goods bought at another shop in the chain.

Here the main customer—senior management—is 'benefiting' from the undertaking of these tasks.

Outputs, then, are tangible manifestations of the work the units carry out. In addition to the straightforward quantitative measures it is often necessary, in order to obtain a full picture, to include some qualitative factors. These usually relate to customer satisfaction in one form or another, which could be measured by means of carefully constructed surveys, but sometimes the issues are more difficult.

A good example of a difficult issue is the assessment of the non-academic development of children in a secondary school. Some teachers stated, during one of our studies, that the objective of secondary education is to help children 'to become good and useful citizens', and there is strong resistance in the teaching profession to basing the performance assessment of a school solely on its academic record. We agreed with this sentiment but we also insisted that a way has to be found to measure how successfully the school has been in achieving these non-academic objectives. This provoked intense debate, and continues to do so during courses and seminars on performance measures. In the end we obtained agreement that 'idealistic' objectives, such as good citizenship, could be made more accessible by describing specific attributes that reflect the principles of the objective. In this case we looked for non-academic achievements, in sport and the arts, together with the student profiling assessments that were being trialled throughout the country at the time of our study.

7.5 CHOOSING THE FACTORS—INPUTS

Outputs are measurable statements about what the units are achieving. We now need to look at the other side of the coin—the inputs—and included here are factors that are internal to the unit (process factors) and also external or 'environmental'. The aim is to account for everything that aids or hinders the production of the outputs, and the factors will normally involve financial investment in staff, equipment and facilities.

For both profit making and service organizations it is reasonably straightforward to choose numerical staffing factors but harder to account for experience and ability. It is often sufficient to split staff into 'managerial' and 'other', but in some cases (education for example) staff ability can be a crucial influence. Here, use can be made of appraisal markings—or it might be necessary to take a proxy for ability in the form of length of service or qualifications.

Some units actually take an input, process it, and send it out again.

This time the state of that input on arrival will affect the quality of the final output. Factors are required which measure this state. Some examples would be:

- academic ability of children entering school;
- quality of manuscripts submitted to a typing pool;
- state of health of a patient entering hospital.

Finally, there are the environmental factors that have a great bearing on how a unit performs. Examples include:

- socio-economic background of customers/scholars/patients;
- location of a store/bank branch;
- unemployment rate in the area;
- competition.

During the choosing of all these factors it is very important to involve as many people as possible. First of all, this will help to ensure that no aspects are missed and that, in particular, the influencing/environmental factors are adequately covered. Secondly, the more that people are 'involved' the more likely they are to support and assist the work. It is natural that staff will feel threatened by a 'closed' assessment tool, but by giving them an active

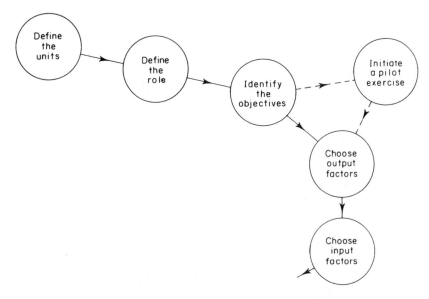

Figure 7.3 Choosing the factors for a performance measuring model

part in deciding what factors to include they will be more ready to accept the results of the exercise.

At the end of this stage it is not uncommon to end up with a list of factors that is impractically long. It might be possible to review the list and to eliminate obvious duplications or irrelevancies, but it is often tactful to leave factors on the list until a later stage (see the next two sections).

Figure 7.3 illustrates the progress we have made in this section.

7.6 COLLECTING THE DATA

The choice of factors described in the previous section reflects the beliefs, or impressions, that people have of issues that are important to the operation of the organization. This can be an illuminating and important exercise for both management and the staff involved in the performance study. Now comes the first major snag: It will nearly always be the case, certainly in the authors' experience, that there will be a number of chosen factors for which no (or little) data exists. In addition, although some data will be held centrally, many factors will only be recorded locally, and then not always in a consistent manner across the organization. The alternatives available when this situation arises are:

- cull the list of factors;
- initiate data gathering exercises;
- a mixture of the two.

The first step is to check through the list again to see if there are two or more factors that cover the same aspect, so that the factor or factors for which it is difficult to obtain data can be dropped. Examples of these overlaps are:

- 'number of people entering the shop' and 'number of individual purchases' (both reflect the width of popularity/attractiveness/convenience of the shop);
- 'number of children from a socially deprived background' and 'number of children entitled to free school meals'. (The latter is a proxy for the former.)

Next, it might be necessary to take factors off the list where it would be too inconvenient or expensive (or, even, too 'obscure') to expend resources on collecting data. Even after this 'rationalization' the list will probably still be long, and a full data collection exercise has to be undertaken. This is where the goodwill, created by accommodating the opinions of the wide number of people, repays the effort put in during the earlier stages; people are much more willing to put themselves out to collect the data if they feel it will help their ideas to be included.

It is often an eye opener to management to find that information that they consider to be important is either not available at all, or is distinctly unreliable. In fact, one of the immediate outcomes of a DEA exercise is often the introduction of systems to collect and store information in a more comprehensive and reliable fashion.

7.7 INITIAL ANALYSIS OF THE DATA

Once the data have been collected and brought together in a composite file, often on some form of computer based spreadsheet, some initial analysis will be undertaken to check for consistency and integrity before passing the information through to the DEA model. There will, inevitably, be factors for which the data are incomplete and one or more factors where the data relate to a different timescale or period from the other factors. If there are factors where there are large gaps in the data it will probably be necessary to drop the factor from the exercise, at least until such time as a data collection system is in place. Where different timescales or periods are concerned there is usually a fairly straightforward way of recalculating the data on a common basis.

It is important, when setting up a DEA model, to clearly delineate which factors are inputs and which are outputs. This may seem obvious, but it is not always so, particularly in the service sector. An example is truancy at a school. Is there truancy because of factors relating to the school or are the values of these factors affected by the level of truancy? This sort of question can be argued endlessly but, for the purpose of DEA performance analysis, answers can be found by examining the objectives of both the organization and the analysis. (In the case study, *Total revenue* was an output in the cost efficiency model—Table 4.2 and an input in the market efficiency model—Table 5.7). The aim is to ensure that any change in the value of an input is reflected in either no change in each output or, if there is a change, one in the 'right' direction. Hence, it would be an unhelpful model that allowed an 'increase in investment' to be reflected in a 'decrease in performance'. If this was in reality the case, the causal relationships between factors would need to be re-examined and a new model constructed.

The correlations between each factor (input and output) and all other factors (inputs and outputs) are calculated. An additional result of this is the ability to identify input factors that are closely correlated to other input factors, and similarly for outputs. This gives a further opportunity to reduce the numbers of factors, though care must be taken not to assume, without enquiry, that a *mathematical* correlation automatically implies a *logical* or *causal* correlation.

Having completed these last two stages (Figure 7.4) the data are ready to be entered into the model.

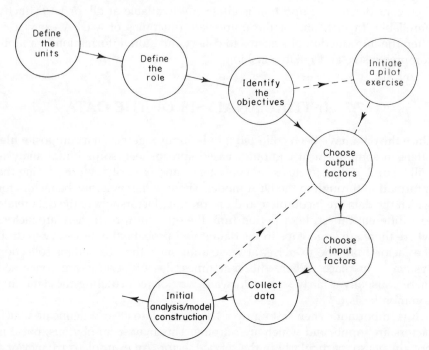

Figure 7.4 Data collection and analysis

7.8 RUNNING THE MODEL

Building a DEA model and interpreting the results are covered by Chapters 4 and 6. However, it is worth mentioning again the role that management has to play during this stage. Model building, which includes factor choice and initial data analysis, is an iterative process. Firstly, those involved with creating the initial list of factors should be consulted when data problems, or correlation analysis, indicate that certain factors should be dropped. In some cases, alternative factors may be suggested, or if that is not possible at least goodwill is maintained by keeping people involved.

Similarly, when the first DEA analysis has been run and the results interpreted, detailed examination will usually throw up questions about the model construction. This will involve the building of alternative models, changing the numbers and mix of factors, until there is reasonable agreement that the analysis provides a comprehensive and fair performance evaluation. The discussion in Section 4.7 on whether or not to include the factor *Age of shop* in the market efficiency model exemplifies the need to consult widely.

7.9 MANAGEMENT INVESTIGATION OF THE RESULTS

It is important to present the results in such a way that they become genuine building blocks of management information that provide insight into the operations of the organization. The immediate, and most straightforward, output is a list of units in descending order of relative efficiency. Those with a relative efficiency score of 1.0 are differentiated by computing the number of times they appear in the reference sets for relatively inefficient units. Thus, there is a single list with, crudely, the 'best' units at the top and the 'worst' units at the bottom.

The efficiency list splits into four main groupings:

(a) *The robustly efficient units.* These will appear on many reference sets and are likely to remain efficient unless there were major shifts in their fortunes.

(b) *The marginally efficient units.* These will appear on only one or two reference sets (including their own) and would be likely to drop to below 1.0 if there was even a small drop in the value of an output variable (or a small increase in the value of an input variable).

(c) *The marginally inefficient units.* These will have an efficiency rating in excess of, say, 0.9 (but less than 1.0) and could soon raise their score towards 1.0.

(d) *The distinctly inefficient units.* With an efficiency score of less than 0.9, these units would have difficulty in making themselves efficient in the short term. Those with scores of less than, say, 0.75 would remain inefficient until there was a major change in circumstances.

Some analysts combine the middle two groupings on the grounds that they are separated by only small changes in data values. On the other hand, we feel that it is helpful to separate out those units that actually achieve a relatively efficient score.

Units in group (a) can be held up as exemplars of good practice. They will be managing their resources, in the environment in which they operate, to great effect. Those in group (d) are clearly not succeeding in this area and, provided care has been taken to equalize any effects not covered by the chosen factors, questions must be asked about the management of the units.

A unit in group (b) appearing on no reference set other than its own is likely to have an unusual data set and is clearly different from the other units in the analysis. In such a case, a close look at the unit is called for, to establish whether or not there are certain characteristics that mark it out as too different from the other units to be properly compared with them. It might also be the case that the unit is working to different priorities and, as such, should be investigated.

Management will be particularly keen to know if the DEA results are consistent with those from other performance analyses. In few instances, however, will it be possible to make direct comparisons since DEA is probably the only analytical tool in use that attempts to assess performance 'in the round'. Most traditional techniques, such as Performance Indicators (see Chapter 1), are concerned with measuring one particular aspect of the operation and can be put alongside DEA only to a limited extent, as was done with the analysts' rankings in Sections 4.3–4.5. Such a comparison can be carried out by looking at some key indicators and making a judgement as to how well a unit is doing 'on the whole', but a more effective approach is to compare inefficient units with units on their reference sets.

This caveat also applies to the comparison of results from DEA and regression analysis. The latter is an established technique that derives a relationship between a single output (input) factor and several input (output) factors. The analysis then highlights those units which perform better or worse than average. It is possible, where the DEA model is constructed with only one input or output variable, to compare the two sets of results, but it must be borne in mind that regression evaluates against the *average* whilst DEA evaluates against the *best* performance. Further discussion on regression analysis can be found in Section 6.2.

Although direct *comparison* between DEA and other techniques cannot be made, it is useful to use a mixture of techniques, in concert, to further extend the range of management information. For example, an organization may use a traditional performance measure as its main evaluation tool for its units. This and the DEA output can then be plotted, as in Figure 7.5 which is a generalized version of Figures 6.9 and 6.10, where *Profit* was the traditional performance measure.

In this example, the results from six units, A–F, are highlighted. Interesting points may be made for each:

Unit A: This is quite a high scorer on the traditional measure but it is not (relatively) efficient—group (c) above. Probably no immediate action need be taken.

Unit B: As for Unit A except that its DEA score of 1.0 places it in group (b).

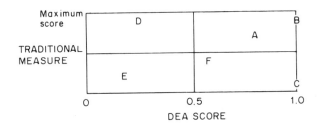

Figure 7.5 Plot of traditional and DEA performance scores

Unit C: This is an interesting case that also highlights one of the strengths of DEA. The unit has traditionally been characterized as a poor performer, whereas it is shown to be efficient when the assessment is more comprehensive. An actual example of this (see Section 8.4) is a school that has poor examination results but, when environmental factors are taken into account, is shown to be performing better than most.

Unit D: An opposite case to Unit C. Traditionally considered to be a high performer, it nevertheless is not making best use of its resources and environment. A typical example is a building society branch in an affluent area producing high savings returns. Closer inspection shows that it is resting on its laurels and could, by increasing the efficiency of its operation, contribute much more.

Unit E: This unit has nowhere to hide. It has probably used 'other factors' as an excuse for its poor rating on the traditional measure; but DEA takes account of these 'other factors' and the unit still scores poorly. Units that fall into this category clearly need to be scrutinized by management.

Unit F: This is an interesting case because management has several options. It can ask it to improve performance either on the traditional measure or by raising overall efficiency—or by a combination of both. Figure 7.6 shows this.

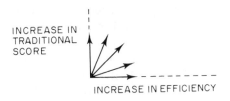

Figure 7.6 Alternative improvement paths

7.10   SHORT TERM MANAGEMENT ACTIONS

The first task of management and the study team, after the DEA results have been interpreted, is to ensure that the messages that emerge are accepted throughout the organization with a view to getting the approach accepted. One of the most effective ways is to undertake, with the management and staff concerned, a detailed scrutiny of a unit that has been deemed relatively inefficient by the DEA analysis. A unit from group (d)—'distinctly inefficient'—would offer the best opportunity. The survey should cover:

- (DEA) highlighted reasons for the good and bad aspects of the unit's performance—factors that contributed to, and detracted from, its efficiency rating;
- a unit's reference set—a detailed qualitative comparison with the reference units;
- a unit's management style—have the staff been set performance criteria implicit within the DEA analysis (and, if so, are these at odds with senior management's criteria)?
- 'special factors' that have not been incorporated into the DEA model.

This can be an extremely useful exercise in the context of both the DEA analysis and organizational management as a whole. It can, of course, be made broader by extending the survey to all the units in a region, but time constraints will probably limit it to one unit.

There are various steps that need to be taken once the results of the initial, or pilot, DEA exercise have been accepted—at least to the extent that the work is authorized to continue. Firstly, a decision has to be made as to whether to continue as a pilot study or to extend the analysis to the whole organization. If the latter course is chosen, it is likely that new systems will need to be set up to collect the data required on a consistent basis across the organization. This will be more effective if it can be combined with existing procedures.

One of the most powerful pieces of information that is output by the DEA analysis is the set of target factor values for those units assessed as inefficient. If the model has been set up for 'output maximization' there will be target output values that the inefficient units would need to achieve to reach a score of 1.0. Clearly, as was discussed in Section 6.6, there must be 'manual' management intervention here because it might be impractical, if not impossible, for some targets to be met in the next evaluation period. Bearing in mind that the output targets were set (by the analysis) in the light of the current levels for input factors, there may be some scope for lowering these latter values to ease the problem. Naturally, the same argument applies in reverse to 'input minimization' models.

During the review of the pilot exercise the model itself will come under scrutiny and alternative formulations will be suggested. Where the data are already available, further analysis can be undertaken whilst the review is proceeding and a view formed as to whether an alternative model should be adopted. If new data gathering is required, the testing of the alternative model(s) will have to take place during the next phase and a decision delayed until after the ensuing complete analysis.

Finally, and of the utmost importance, conclusions have to be drawn concerning the role DEA might play in the context of an integrated management information system. DEA is just one technique that provides management with the background information upon which to base decisions. It may supplant some (partial) performance assessment techniques but it will remain complementary to others. The question as to which part of the 'total picture' each technique provides information for has to be addressed so that management is not presented with conflicting or blurred advice. Steps need to be taken during the next evaluation period to assimilate DEA into the mainstream of management information so that, when the analysis is carried out, the results are not considered as 'experimental' but are absorbed into the management process.

7.11 LONG TERM USAGE OF DEA

Once the DEA system is up and running as part of a general management information system, further work can be undertaken to elicit additional insights into the running of the organization. The immediate outcome of having more than one set of results is that the technique can be tested for consistency. There will naturally be changes in efficiency scores from one period to the next but any violent swings should be investigated. It has not been the authors' experience that DEA results have exhibited marked changes from period to period; in fact, in all the studies we have undertaken where data from more than one period were available the results have shown a remarkable stability, with only a few units rising or falling dramatically in efficiency scoring.

Another aspect that can be investigated concerns the increase or decrease in the general level of efficiency. This can be checked by plotting efficiency scores for two years (where one might be a 'base' year) using a combined data set as reported in Section 8.2 (Figure 8.3).

A joint efficiency score of 1.0 (i.e. a point at the top right corner of Figure 8.3) indicates a consistent level of efficiency from one period to the next, and an examination of the regression line through the plotted points and the line joining the origin to the top right hand corner will indicate whether or not the general level of performance of the relatively inefficient units is rising.

One of the short term actions described in the previous section was the setting of targets for inefficient units. The results for the subsequent period(s) should be checked to see if progress has been made and to examine new targets that are indicated by the analysis. If this monitoring is continued over time a coherent strategy can be adopted and control procedures put in place to ensure that targets set by management, as opposed to those resulting directly from the DEA results, are practical and consistent.

As regards the model structure itself, it will clearly be necessary to monitor this continually to ensure that the DEA results are truly reflecting an assessment of performance that remains consistent with the changing circumstances in which the organization is operating. This will also entail re-analysis of the relationships between each of the model factors, particularly between key output variables and the causal (input) factors. However, even though the model may change over time, it is helpful to retain the original model to use for analytical purposes, such as period to period monitoring.

A side benefit of introducing DEA as an analytical assessment tool is that the procedures described in this chapter can lead to considerations of the efficacy of the organizational structure of the units being analysed. The identification of the major input and output factors will have indicated the processes that use those inputs and produce those outputs. This, in turn, will have highlighted where management responsibility should lie. If it is suspected that there is a mismatch of processes and organizational structure, it can be helpful to break down the processes into sub-processes so that work can be tracked through from input to output. Figure 7.7 shows an outline schematic process structure.

The DEA model can also be used in a limited predictive role by deriving an estimate for an input or output factor, based on previous DEA results. An example of this was given in Section 6.5 in deriving a profit for a particular shop five years into the future. A further example would be the prediction of likely sales levels at a proposed new store. The normal practice in a retail organization is for the New Business Department to identify a promising site and to estimate the potential sales revenue that would be generated. However, the estimates can be unduly optimistic, particularly if the Finance Department has laid down a rate of return that has to be achieved before money will be released, or raised, for the development, and the New Business Department 'engineered' their prediction to satisfy this criterion.

The method is to assemble all the data that can be predicted with some accuracy. This will usually refer only to input factors, though some outputs

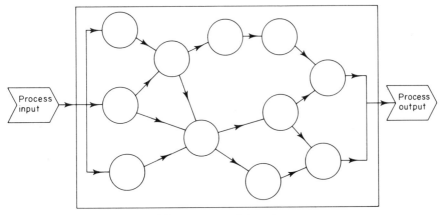

Sub-processes and dependencies

Figure 7.7 Schematic process structure

might be inferred. Next, an efficiency rating is allocated to the new store, based on experience from similar sites, and the emerging profile of the store is compared with the profiles for all the existing stores. A pattern of values for inputs and outputs will be built up and the level of sales (or any other chosen output variable) will be indicated. The method of calculation is similar to that set out in Section 6.5.

These types of test can be extended to areas such as return on investment and required funding levels, the latter being particularly important for public services. Other examples include predictions of:

- crime clear-up rates;
- job placements;
- patients attended;
- academic results;
- insurance policies sold.

The final stages of the performance monitoring system have now been described, and so Figure 7.1 is completed.

Chapter 8

Further Case Studies

8.1 INTRODUCTION

The case study that has been used throughout the book to illustrate the technique and attributes of DEA was put together to give the technical theory some focus and to highlight aspects of the various stages in the development of a practical DEA system. In Chapter 7 we brought together the processes involved in carrying out the case study and combined them into an integrated procedure for carrying out DEA exercises. In this chapter we describe some real studies undertaken by the authors, not only to show how the approach can be relevant to a range of organizations but also to comment critically on the conduct of the studies. This latter point is very important because it is the authors' conviction that the success of a DEA project has as much to do with *how* the work is carried out as with the mathematical success of the models. Crucial to this is the extent of the involvement of the people working in the units being assessed.

We will report on seven projects in the public and private sector but give full descriptions, in Sections 8.2 and 8.8, of two—one from each sector—which contain all the elements, good and bad, that are found in such studies. The reports follow the pattern of development described in Chapter 7, in each case preceded by a brief outline of the sponsoring organization. The aim is not to give a blow by blow account of the conduct of each study but, rather, to identify characteristics that will enable the reader to identify with the situations—and to draw encouragement from the way that the work led to positive outcomes.

8.2   HEALTH SERVICE

The Organization

In England and Wales, the Secretary of State for Health, who heads a central government Department, is responsible for the efficient discharge of health services. The operational side is delegated to various bodies, and the organization of responsibilities in this area underwent important changes of emphasis during the period of the studies that make up the project described in this section. At the outset of the project there were two strands of administration:

- Regional Health Authorities (RHAs) who allocated funds to District Health Authorities (DHAs), who in turn allocated funds to hospitals, community care units etc. These reported to a Management Board;
- Family Practitioner Committees (FPCs) who administered the local doctor/clinic practices. These reported directly to the Department of Health.

The essential change that was made to this arrangement was the introduction of the concept of health service providers and health service purchasers. The split between policy and operational management was also made more explicit by the setting up of two distinct Boards, with the Secretary of State heading the Policy Board and the Chief Executive of the National Health Service (NHS) heading the Management Executive. After the changes the RHAs allocate funds to:

- DHAs who enter into contracts for services from hospitals directly administered by the DHA, hospitals administered by other DHAs, hospitals who manage their own affairs (NHS Trust Units), and hospitals in the private sector;
- General Practitioner Fund Holders—local doctor groupings that are self managed and who 'purchase' services in the same way as DHAs.

General Practitioners who do not hold funds liaise with their DHA who purchase services on their behalf. However, Family Health Service Authorities monitor the performance of all GPs and are accountable to RHAs.

There are some 190 DHAs in England with a further nine in Wales. Some service provisions, such as the Ambulance and Blood Transfusion Services, cross District boundaries and are administered either independently or by some Districts on behalf of all.

At the time of writing, work on the project has been conducted in three phases or studies, with the respective foci being:

(1) the feasibility of using DEA in the health services;
(2) presentation and production of results in a meaningful and useful way for management;
(3) revamping the models to reflect the new NHS responsibilities.

Background to the Studies

There is a responsibility within the Department of Health to achieve the most beneficial application of available funds, and over the years a number of systems and procedures had been put in place to allocate, monitor and control expenditure and service delivery. However, none of these fully addressed the question of overall efficiency within a management unit, such as a DHA or hospital unit. This was of specific concern to the team of analysts, drawn from Statistics, Economics and Operational Research, which is responsible for the monitoring and evaluation of the annual and long term plans drawn up by regional managements. The team has the title of Central Appraisal of Regional Performance—CARP!

There were currently a number of performance measures used in the Health Service, among the most prominent being a centrally evaluated set of Performance Indicators (PIs) and Cost Weighted Activity Indices. Several hundred PIs were available, covering both the provision of services and the cost of resources, for DHAs to compare specific aspects of performance against national or regional averages, or to compare changes in performance through time. Each PI can be viewed either as a measure in its own right or as a link in a logical chain of investigation. A computer system allows the District Health Authorities to study the PIs for their own and all other Districts. This allows them to identify problems and to compare their own performance with similar Districts. In order to make these comparisons meaningful, many PIs are computed from 'standardized' data, i.e. account has been taken of such factors as age, sex, diagnostic and case mixes. An attempt has been made to make the system more comprehensive by disaggregating these factors. The PIs are also analysed as a preliminary to the annual regional performance reviews. Here the aim is to identify extreme values for a set of key PIs.

In an experimental analysis the key PIs were ranked nationally and a District assigned a score of +1 or −1 depending on whether the score was considered 'good' (e.g. low numbers of child in-patients in an adult ward) or 'possibly indicating poor performance' (e.g. high length of stay for a patient with a fractured femur) compared with the average. The District net scores (i.e. the sum of all the +1, 0, −1's) were then computed and plotted on a two-dimensional graph. Districts with exceptionally high scores (either positive or negative) were identified and became subject to investigation. This cluster analysis of the PIs was, by the nature of the assigned values

(1 = good, −1 = possibly not good), fairly crude and elementary, but it was a good starting point for further investigations. Questions that could be addressed included:

- If a District has a low net score in one area of treatment, is there a compensating high score in another area?
- Are low net scores related to low (or high) levels of spending?

An example of the plotting of high and low PI scores is given in Figure 8.1. Each cell shows the number of Districts nationally having the combination of high (+1) and low (−1) performance scores indicated by the scales of the axes. For example, if a District has five PI scores in the top 10% and four scores in the bottom 10% then it would be plotted on the grid at coordinates (4,5). The Districts marked * have performed well overall and those marked ** have performed not so well overall—for those PIs chosen for the analysis.

		0	1	2	3	4	5	6	7
	6	2*	4*	2					
	5	1*	2*	2	4	2			
DISTRICT	4	3	12	10	1	5			
SCORE FOR	3	9	6	7	5	7	2	1	
HIGH	2	9	16	15	8	1	1	1**	
PEFORMANCE	1	8	5	11	5	7	1	1**	1**
	0	5	6	4	4				

DISTRICT SCORE FOR LOW PERFORMANCE

Figure 8.1 Plot of high and low PI scores

Cost Weighted Activity Indices have also been used within the planning processes of the Health Service. In particular, they underpin the calculation and assessment of the extent of non-cash releasing Cost Improvement Schemes. The indices can be computed as follows:

Aggregate intermediate output

= National unit cost for an activity × Local level of the activity

where the national unit costs are the averages for the whole country, and examples of activity are discharges and deaths, out-patient attendances and day cases. The groupings of activity and the disaggregations of costs (for example, into treatment and hotel components) may change, but the basic principle remains the same.

Various comparative measures can then be derived, such as:

- output per head of managed population;
- ratios of outputs to expenditure (i.e. 'expected' versus 'actual').

However, all these measures are based on the expected levels of spending as indicated by historical national average unit costs. They do not help in assessing how efficiently these funds have been used in a particular District. Their main benefit lies in highlighting Regions (or Districts) that appear to require excessive funds to generate a given level of activity. Thus, as with Performance Indicators, they can act as stimuli to discussion and investigation.

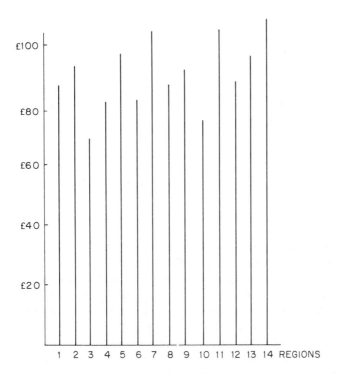

Figure 8.2 Aggregate intermediate outputs per head

In the example shown in Figure 8.2, intermediate outputs are hospital activities, such as discharges and deaths, and out-patient attendances, and day cases. Aggregate intermediate output for a Region's hospitals is defined as a cost weighted index of intermediate output. The cost weights are derived from national estimates of the amount of resources used by different hospital activities.

Neither of the above approaches was considered to provide a satisfactory method of gauging the all-round performance of managerial groupings within the Health Service. The analysts in CARP, together with those in the Operational Research Group, began casting about for a more holistic technique and their attention was brought to DEA, then under evaluation by one or two other central government Departments. Consequently, a feasibility study was commissioned to investigate DEA and to assess its potential for use within the Health Service. Subsequent studies, in which the work was taken further to investigate the possible role of DEA in the management assessment and review processes, are described later in this section.

The Feasibility Study

Of its nature, the feasibility study was exploratory and a great deal of the time was spent in research. At that time, DEA was relatively new in the United Kingdom and only one or two commercial companies were investigating the technique. Even amongst Government Department Operational Research Groups, often in the forefront of such research, little work had been carried out although two were seriously examining its potential. Consequently, the first steps in the study, alongside gaining expertise in the technique itself, were to examine and review the current state of knowledge and the success of any applications. A parallel exercise looked into existing methods of performance assessment in the Health Service, the major approaches of which are outlined above.

It was clear that any progress in applying DEA elsewhere in central government had been, at best, tentative and in the main had concentrated on examining the mathematical and technical intricacies of the technique. Attempts had been made to use DEA to assess some public service units (rent offices, police authorities and prisons, housing associations) and there had been at least one application in the private sector (retail warehousing), but in no cases had the studies led to a system of continuing assessment. Each had, to a large extent, been a 'one-off' project. This first Department of Health study was of a different ilk since it was assumed at the outset that if DEA 'worked' it would be adopted on a regular basis, and to give it more of a chance of leading to a useful conclusion discussions were held with officials throughout the organization to present the approach and ensure that comments and suggestions from those experienced in the management of the Health Service were taken into account when drawing up models and interpreting the results.

There was almost universal acceptance that a measure (or measures) needed to be found to assess efficiency on a broad scale, but concern was also voiced that any such measure should be relevant to 'real life' managerial situations. This latter point was very much to the fore during the course of the study and at each stage it was felt important to keep in mind any eventual use for the work.

The objectives of this study can be summarized as:

- undertake research into DEA;
- develop a broad measure of efficiency;
- make the evaluation technique *and results* relevant to real life;
- ensure management involvement.

Choosing the Factors

The question of final health outcomes and the impracticality of finding appropriate factors to measure these outcomes in the Health Service was alluded to in Chapter 7. The task, then, was to find suitable variables to represent outputs. In the final analysis, the Health Service apparatus and organization is there to prevent illness and to improve mental and physical health; in practice this means treating—caring for and curing—people. It was therefore decided to use 'activity' as a common unit of output. It was also decided that, for this feasibility study, the appropriate administrative units to be assessed would be District Health Authorities since they had money allocated to them to deliver the service. (Other groupings, including those at major acute hospital level, were to be investigated in subsequent studies—see later.)

Accepted definitions of activity were taken and, first, the following categories of hospital patient were used:

Non-psychiatric in-patients (discharges and deaths)
Psychiatric in-patients (average occupied bed–days)
Day patients (total attendances)
Day cases (regular day cases)
Out-patients (total attendances)

The available data on non-psychiatric in-patients made no distinction between 'successful' and 'unsuccessful' patient care, nor were there any measures of the state of health of the patient on entry. Hence, no qualitative measure of the quality of the care or treatment could be used. 'Day patients' are those who attend special day care centres. They would not be undergoing medical treatment during these visits. 'Day cases' refer to patients who receive some form of medical treatment, but do not occupy a bed overnight. Finally, data were not available to distinguish multiple attendances (of patients undergoing a course of treatment on an out-patient basis) from the single attendances (such as accidents and emergencies).

Community outputs, on the other hand, were more difficult to define, and statistics more difficult to obtain. In the end it was decided to use 'number of people seen', by care programme, as the activity measure.

An omission was any measure of preventative work, the third 'arm' of the Health Service. Unfortunately, no statistical measures could be found in this area.

These then were the output factors chosen for the study. The basic input to the Health Service, indeed to any service, is money. The various levels of aggregation chosen were as follows:

- DHA headquarters administration

- Hospital services, incorporating

  Patient care: Medical and dental staff services (direct treatment)
  Nursing staff services (direct treatment)
  Remainder (diagnostic departments)
  Medical and paramedical supporting services
  General services: Administration (less direct credits)
  Ancillary
  Estate and miscellaneous

- Community health services, incorporating

  Patient care: Staff services
  Remainder + medical and paramedical

- Community health general services + other services + community health council

Model Building and Computer Runs

For the purposes of the feasibility study it was agreed that the model would use the following level of aggregation for its input factors:

- Headquarters administration
- (All) Hospital services
- (All) Community health services.

This had the virtue of simplicity and helped to avoid undue attention being focused on any relatively minor aspect of financial sub-accounting. Also, data for the Welsh DHAs were included in the trials—yielding a total of 200 units (DMUs). The runs were carried out on a micro-computer, using a spreadsheet package for data manipulation and model formatting together with a proprietory Linear Programming package. Some scaling of variables to avoid rounding errors in the LP calculation was required to ensure that there were no serious imbalances in the scale values of different factors.

During the model building process it was suggested that some account should be taken of capital expenditure; this could include monies spent on building works, maintenance and equipment. The inclusion of such factors was rejected on two counts:

(a) Total capital employed—the total assets accumulated over all time—*is* important, but no data were available. On the other hand, capital expenditure—the annual spend, for which data were available—is not necessarily related to the efficiency with which an Authority uses its current resources to deliver care to its clients and its inclusion would also unfairly penalize a DHA that just happened to face a construction bill in that particular year.

(b) Maintenance charges would need to be tempered by an allowance for the state of the building fabric—difficult to assess, and certainly no data were available for this study.

Results of the Feasibility Study

The first two objectives of the study—undertaking research into DEA and developing a broad measure of efficiency—were manifestly achieved, with the nine input and output variables ensuring a satisfactory level of discrimination between DHAs. There was a spread of efficiencies ranging from 0.62 to 1.0 and approximately 40 DHAs with a score of 1.0.

In order to provide a focus for the analysis and to ensure management commitment, three Regions were chosen for special attention. Discussions were held with officials in those Regions to discuss the findings and to choose one DHA from each for detailed scrutiny. In addition to these, CARP analysts chose three further DHAs for investigation. The scrutiny revealed the following:

• *Examples of Districts that achieved DEA results that accorded with their Performance Indicator (PI) analyses.* For example, one DHA which was 'generally considered' to be inefficient, and with PI results supporting this view, showed an efficiency score of 0.87. The highlighted target areas were day patients (40% low) and day cases (71% low). These, again, accorded with PI analyses.

It is important to point out that DEA and the Health Service PI analysis cannot be considered as equivalent evaluation techniques since DEA adopts an holistic approach whereas PI analysis is directed at particular aspects of performance. For this reason there will necessarily be instances where the results will be different, thus providing a different insight into the unit under investigation.

• *Examples of Districts where special characteristics pertained*. For example, one of the 'efficient' Districts in a particular Region was found to have a peculiar activity mix. It achieved an efficiency of 1.0 with its own set of weights but scored lowly on the weights for all other Districts, and the remaining DHAs all scored lowly on its weights. During the Regional discussions it was discovered that the District in question was without a major acute hospital.

• *Good examples of the similarity between 'inefficient' Districts and their comparators on their reference sets*. For example, one District had neither an obstetric unit nor provision for psychiatric patients. The DEA analysis selected reference set Districts that did not appear in any other reference set and which had attributes similar to the chosen District—very low mental health provision and no provision for the mentally handicapped. This outcome is, in the experience of the authors, typical of DEA studies and serves to strengthen confidence in the technique, especially amongst senior management.

In another Region, the range of District efficiencies was 0.88 to 1.0 (again with three DHAs having a score of 1.0). The DHA chosen for detailed analysis had a score of 0.93, and together with this 7% reduction in overall funding, a further target reduction of £750 000 in DHA administration costs was identified. However, only one output (the number of day cases) was identified as being out of step with its peers—and by only $2\frac{1}{2}$%.

• *Additional factors that might affect the performance analysis but had not been included in the scope of the model*. This was particularly the case in the third Region which had widely acknowledged problems and where the DEA analysis showed a range of DHA efficiencies from 0.63 to 0.83. This put all nine Districts in the bottom quartile of the efficiency table and indicated that considerably more money was spent per unit of activity in that Region. It was suggested that demographical and geographical factors made this Region atypical. However, note that in the second phase of the project (see later) an examination of efficiency by area type did not support this claim. For the individual DHA identified for analysis, the number of out-patients was highlighted as being 'too low'—but this is a good example of a case where extreme caution has to be exercised before translating DEA results into direct management targets. The reason for an apparent shortfall in out-patients could be because:

(a)   the demand for out-patient services was low, or
(b)   it would be difficult for more people to make the journey to an out-patient clinic, or
(c)   some out-patients were treated in another District.

In another Region, an Inner London District was responsible for a number of teaching hospitals. In the feasibility runs no provision had been taken to account for either the problems of the generally higher costs of working in Inner London Districts or for teaching responsibilities. General opinion was that these factors detracted from patient 'throughput'. The fact that the District achieved a score of 0.97 was felt to be a tribute to the local management.

Conclusion of the Feasibility Study

An important phase in the study was the series of presentations to the three Regions. The planning functions within each Regional Health Authority continually monitor the work of the Districts and a degree of 'performance analysis' is undertaken as a matter of course. Following the formal presentations, which concentrated on the DEA approach and a general outline of the results for a particular Region, detailed discussions were held to identify points of agreement and divergence between local and DEA results. This often took the form of asking Regional officials to rank their Districts in order of perceived efficiency or productivity *before* they saw the DEA results, and then debating any differences with them.

In many cases the DEA analysis confirmed local opinion/analysis, but in some instances the differences appeared significant. The latter often arose out of different interpretations of what was meant by efficiency (and, indeed, by the terms efficiency and effectiveness). When these were straightened out the divergence between local perceptions and DEA analysis was lessened or removed.

The results of the feasibility study were then presented to senior management in participating Regions together with interested parties in the Health Service economics, statistical and operational research communities. There was a positive response to the outcome of the study but it was felt that further work was required, especially to address the issues raised concerning:

- demographical and geographical factors;
- location (rural/city etc.);

- case mixes;
- the difficult problems of presenting the results for ready understanding at management level.

It was also felt that the opportunity should be taken to analyse a more recent year's data and compare the results with those from the feasibility study, in order to test the stability of the approach.

Second Phase

In 1988 economic pressures on the National Health Service meant that performance became a major issue. In addition, the recommendations of a review of data requirements in the Service were about to be implemented, thus offering the prospect of more focused data availability. Consequently, this was the time chosen to carry the DEA project forward. As well as the objectives described at the end of the previous sub-section, the second phase of the project was also to:

- build a computer system so that results could be generated on a regular basis;
- provide further model structures to reflect accountability at different management levels.

The first step was to revisit all the data sources to extract information about the Districts for a more recent year which would be in the same format

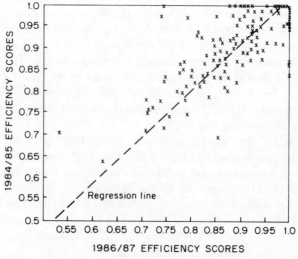

Figure 8.3 Plot of two years' results with regression line

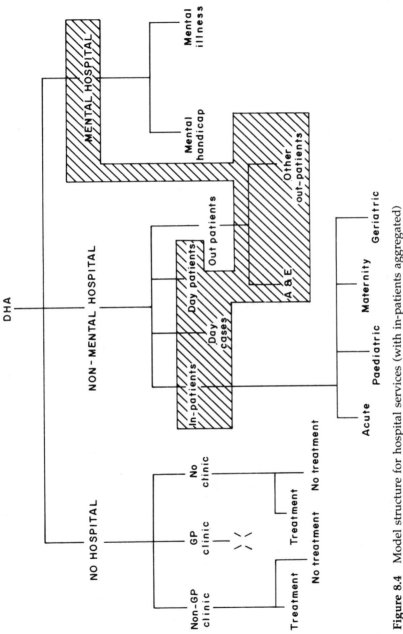

Figure 8.4 Model structure for hospital services (with in-patients aggregated)

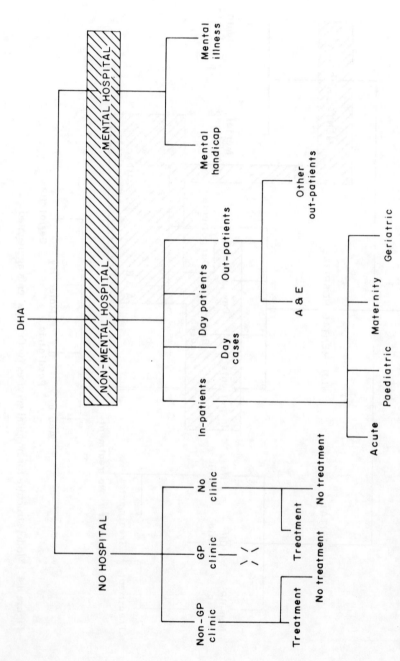

Figure 8.5 Model structure for two output variables—psychiatric and non-psychiatric patients

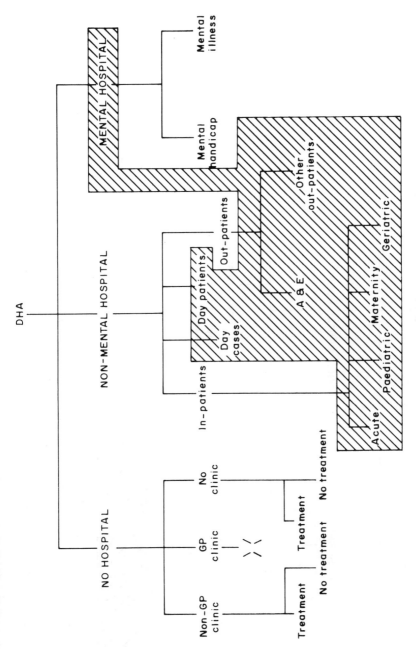

Figure 8.6 Model structures for Hospital Services (with in-patients disaggregated)

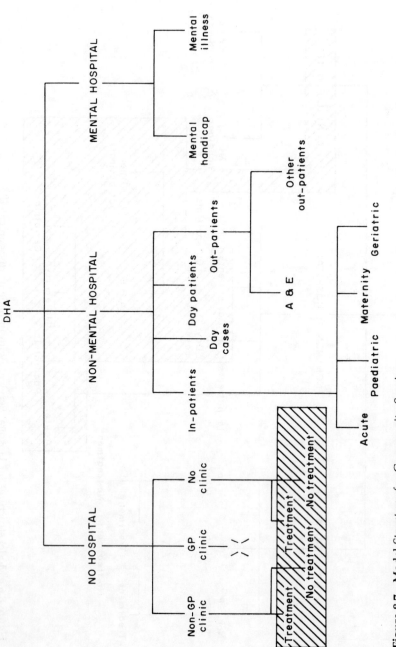

Figure 8.7 Model Structure for Community Services

(and with the same interpretation) as that used in the feasibility study. The DEA runs were carried out on a combined data set and the results for each year were then plotted, together with a regression line (of new results on old) and the leading diagonal (Figure 8.3). It can be seen that the results were generally consistent, with a large overlap of the sets of efficient Districts. The slight tilting of the regression line in an anticlockwise direction from the diagonal indicates a general improvement amongst the less efficient Districts—a point of some comfort to Health Service Management!

Work then proceeded to update the DEA model with more recent data and to carry out research to establish methods of allowing for London weighting, teaching and case mix within the DEA analysis. One method used was to establish factors that would convert the data so that the DEA analyses were undertaken on an equivalent basis to that used in determining Performance Indicators (PIs). Another method was to account for case mix by using a more detailed breakdown of in-patients within the DEA model. This done, further alternative model structures were built to reflect accountability at different management levels. The proposed structures are set out in Figures 8.4–8.7 and it can be seen that they allowed for aggregations at different levels of management so that monitoring and planning could be appropriately targeted. A further data gathering exercise (from centrally held records) was undertaken for new sets of units—hospitals, for example.

Results of the Second Phase

During the work on this phase, results were made available to special studies—run at senior management level—of Regional performance, which also addressed important issues relating to the changing needs of the NHS. The main results were:

- the distribution of efficiency scores of the 190 English DHAs;
- a comparison of efficiency scores for Districts, broken down by inner city/outer city/rural and by those with/those without teaching hospitals;
- an estimate for potential reduction in financial outlay for the NHS, broken down by Region, if the potential identified productivity improvements could be realized.

The latter point was, of course, of great interest to senior managers. The national estimate accorded with their perceptions of the scale of reductions that could be made but the regional breakdowns were questioned; however, these latter were substantiated by reference to raw data and to graphs (similar to Figures 6.4 and 6.5) showing comparisons of data for inefficient

Districts with those for their reference set Districts. This experience served to emphasize the importance that should be accorded to the presentation of results; in particular, care taken over illustrating the underlying messages that can be extracted from the analysis will be rewarded by a much greater chance of acceptance of the results (and the technique) by the targeted audience. This all helped to raise the profile of DEA within the NHS and it was decided to carry the research to grass roots level by examining, in depth, a specific case where the DEA results did not accord with the traditional view of that District's performance. Several lines of enquiry were pursued:

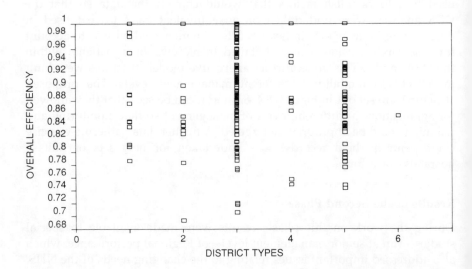

Figure 8.8 Health service efficiency scores by district type: (1) inner-city non-teaching, (2) inner-city teaching, (3) outer-city non-teaching, (4)outer-city teaching, (5) rural non-teaching, (6) rural teaching.

- Data for the District's hospitals were compared with similar data for hospitals in two of its reference set Districts, and similar differences in performance were observed.
- It was objected that some of the DEA reference set Districts were located in area types that were dissimilar to that of the District under investigation—but an examination of national data showed that, beyond the allowances made for London Districts, there was no evidence that area type had any impact on efficiency (see Figure 8.8, for example).

- It was claimed that the District's generally small hospitals could not properly be compared with larger hospitals in other Districts—but an examination of national data showed no relevant evidence of economies of scale.
- It was argued that the District concentrated on *quality* of care—but there was no evidence that the results showing cost savings were unduly biased towards 'direct treatment'.

Third Phase

In January 1989 a Government White Paper [26] was issued which made recommendations on changes to the role of DHAs in which they would become 'purchasers' of services from:

- their own directly managed hospitals;
- local hospitals who opted for direct running of their own affairs;
- hospitals in other DHA areas;
- hospitals in private sector health organizations.

The commissioning role of the DHA will therefore be to meet the health needs of their resident populations and to secure value for money from contracts. The main responsibility for *providing* an efficient service will lie with hospitals themselves. Overall responsibility for directly managed hospitals lies with the DHA.

At the time of writing, work has commenced on re-examining the model structures in the light of these revised roles.

Comment

In the United Kingdom, Government Departments have some of the strongest operational research, statistics and economics groups. It is not surprising then that some of these have taken the lead in looking at Data Envelopment Analysis. Some impressive technical investigations have been carried out and a number of feasibility studies undertaken, this by the Department of Health being the most extensive. However, these studies have been largely experimental and have been instigated only occasionally by senior management saying, 'We have a problem, please can you think of a (new/better) way to solve it'. What has usually happened is that a scientific branch has carried out, or commissioned, a technical study of the technique using some readily available data and then tried to interest the relevant management in adopting it as part of their management information system.

Although we experienced difficulty in explaining the underlying technique to senior managers, there were a number of positive factors that enabled the work reported here to reach a more practical conclusion:

- The Health Service was undergoing a period of political pressure and change, resulting in greater emphasis being placed on operational efficiency.
- The project had the backing of the senior official with responsibility for productivity and efficiency in the Health Service.
- The study was undertaken under the auspices of a unit that had a specific remit to analyse performance within the Regions—rather than a more general unit.
- Senior management in Regions and Districts expressed interest in the results and were prepared to commit the time to discuss them in detail.

Despite these advantages, the progress of the work was not rapid and examination of the timetable is instructive:

Project start	March 1986
Completion of feasibility study	November 1986
Commencement of second phase	February 1988
Completion of second phase	February 1989
Commencement of third phase	December 1989

A significant aspect of the success of the work was the increasing ease with which the computations were carried out as the studies progressed. A micro-computer with mathematical co-processor was used, together with a proprietory spreadsheet package. The choice of a linear programming (LP) package exercises many an analysis department and this was certainly true during the early part of this project. For the feasibility study the LP package used necessitated exporting the data from the spreadsheet and importing it to the LP, and then running a BASIC program to translate the results ready for transfer back to the spreadsheet for analysis and presentation. This was not particularly convenient when 200 LP runs had to be carried out, and so an LP package was found that runs as an (integral) 'add-on' to the spreadsheet package. This simplified matters considerably since a spreadsheet program ('macro') could be set up to carry out the full series of LP runs without operator intervention.

Other advantages of using the micro-computer, with the spreadsheet, were that it fitted with Department of Health standards, and hence a great deal of the data were already available in this form. It was then a simple matter to transfer the data set and handle it in its natural spreadsheet environment.

There has been continuing development of the software capability throughout the project, from basic spreadsheet data input and output handling allied to an LP package to a more sophisticated system that automatically:

- takes the data and feeds it into the LP package in the appropriate form;
- translates the LP output into suitable spreadsheet format;
- performs analyses on the basic results and presents management information in several levels of detail.

As this and other studies progress, the software becomes more sophisticated and 'user friendly' to both analysts and management.

The success of the project can be gauged by the involvement of the management and the fact that DEA results were used in special studies at senior level. However, it is clear from the timetable that it took time to achieve this level of acceptance. This is certainly not uncommon and we hope that others working in this field will take heart!

8.3   PUBLIC UTILITY—WATER COMPANIES

Background

At the time of the study in 1987/88 water extraction and supply, sewage disposal and treatment and storm relief services were the responsibility of public bodies known as Water Authorities. There were 10 of these, each covering a specific geographical region. Approximately 25% of water extraction, purification and supply was, however, carried out by independent Water Companies who were 'Statutory Bodies', which meant that they had a duty to supply water, of the required standard, to homes and businesses in their defined areas whilst making charges sufficient to cover their running and investment costs but not to operate for profit.

The Government was preparing legislation which would sell off the Water Authorities to the private sector. This would have a knock-on effect on the Water Companies who were offered the opportunity to change their status to become private companies. This was expected to lead, in time, to a series of mergers and takeovers. However, the companies were proud of their independence and were keen to show the Government that they provided an economic and efficient service to the public. The Water Companies' Association, which represents the 28 Companies, were already producing an annual series of Performance

Ratios, but these did not take into account the geographical, economic and demographical environments in which each Company worked. Consequently, the Association was interested in what, if anything, Data Envelopment Analysis might offer.

A map showing the areas serviced by the Water Companies is given in Figure 8.9.

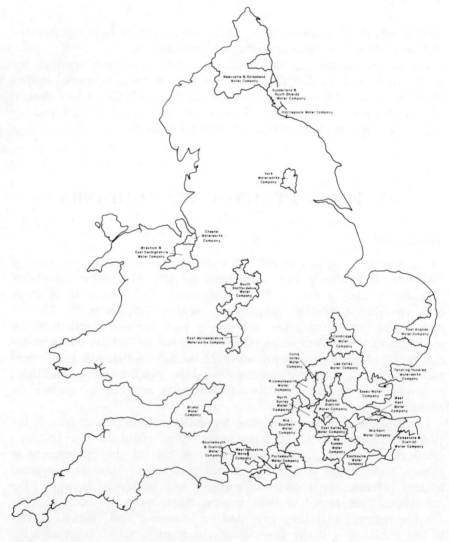

Figure 8.9 Map of Water Company areas

The Study

One of the Companies stored and analysed data on behalf of all Companies in the Association and it was determined that only available data would be used. However, the Association was keen that, as far as possible, the study should comprehensively examine the issues of 'objectives', 'environmental factors' etc.

It was difficult to translate the stated aim of Water Companies, that is

'To supply water, at least possible cost to customers within given standards of quality, continuity and pressure'

into quantifiable objectives that were common across all Companies and could be measured consistently and accurately. Also, the Companies could not be expected to increase output (since customers received all the water they wanted), so the emphasis would have to be on assessing efficiency in the light of providing the existing output. After much discussion and analysis the following model structure was used:

- Inputs: Manpower costs
              Power costs
              Chemical costs
              Remaining costs (including an allowance for capital renewal)

- Outputs: Total potable water supplied
              Total properties supplied (to account for service density)
              Average pumping head (to account for variations in power required)
              Length of mains piping (to account for service dispersion)
              Average peak—a factor to account for the amount of contingency storage that had to be maintained.

The efficiency scores resulting from the Data Envelopment Analysis are shown in Table 8.1. Company E, with a score of 0.85, was chosen for special analysis and an examination of the values of the input and output factors of this company alongside those for its reference set—Companies J,S,Y and AB—is interesting. Reference set companies are 'chosen' by DEA, not because they are similar in size or 'look the same', but because they have the same *pattern* of factor values as the analysed company. This can be seen clearly in Figures 8.10 and 8.11.

In comparison with the other Companies, the analysis identified that Company E should be looking for an annual saving in cost up to £1 225 000.

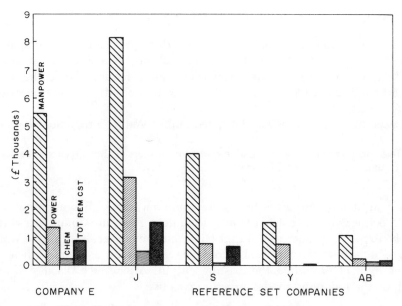

Figure 8.10 Water Company reference set patterns—inputs

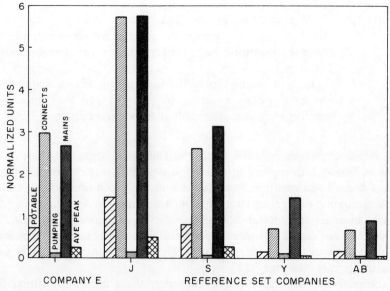

Figure 8.11 Water Company reference set patterns—outputs

Table 8.1 DEA results for Water Companies

Company	DEA efficiency score	Company	DEA efficiency score
A	1.00	O	1.00
B	0.78	P	0.88
C	1.00	Q	0.96
D	0.96	R	1.00
E	0.85	S	1.00
F	0.97	T	1.00
G	0.68	U	0.90
H	0.84	V	1.00
I	1.00	W	0.95
J	1.00	X	1.00
K	1.00	Y	1.00
L	1.00	Z	1.00
M	0.97	AA	1.00
N	0.81	AB	1.00

Comment

The study proved instructive to the Companies and helped to inform their debates on the restructuring of the industry. In particular, it helped to inform their discussions on establishing common quantifiable objectives. In this area it was clear that they needed to define measures of *service quality*, since their output *quantities* were by and large fixed, before the model could be used as a reliable test of efficiency.

8.4 EDUCATION—CENTRAL GOVERNMENT DEPARTMENT

Background

The administration of schools within England and Wales is the responsibility of Local Education Authorities (LEAs). However, in a similar fashion to the Health Service (Section 8.2), general policy and advice is provided by a central government department, in this case the Department of Education and Science.

Several research studies into efficiency and effectiveness in schools had been carried out by a variety of public finance groups and academic institutions. What was lacking, however, was a means of measuring how efficiently an LEA (and its schools) used the resources available, within the local environment and socio-economic context, to produce a set of educational outcomes, both academic and non-academic. The Department was interested in Data Envelopment Analysis and commissioned a research study to determine the feasibility of using DEA to assess efficiency in secondary schools (ages 11–16).

The Study

Since this was to be a methodological study, it was decided not to devote time and resources to the gathering of new data but, instead, with the agreement and assistance of the Inner London Education Authority (ILEA), to use a large bank of information which they had already amassed concerning the 132 secondary schools within their jurisdiction.

Little information on non-academic achievements is generally held consistently across all schools in an area. Inner London was no exception and the choice of output factors was restricted to academic results achieved at age 16, although it was also possible to derive the numbers of pupils continuing their education after that age—as a measure of the 'success' of a school in promoting educational goals.

Considerable research had been carried out by ILEA into the effects of social deprivation on educational progress and some of the basic data were used in this study. Similarly, data were also available that gave some measure of the academic standard of pupils on entry to the schools at age 11. The final list of factors used was:

- Inputs: (I_1) Non-teaching staff costs per pupil
  (I_2) % of age group from top two socio-economic groups
  (I_3) Teacher/pupil ratio
  (I_4) % of age group who had been in the top verbal reasoning band on entry at age 11

- Outputs: (O_1) % of age group obtaining at least one graded A-level
  (O_2) % of age group obtaining 5 or more grades
  (O_3) % of age group obtaining at least 1 graded 'O-level' or CSE equivalent
  (O_4) % of age group staying on at age 16

Seven model structures were used, as shown in Table 8.2.

The range of model structures was used to examine how the technique itself behaved and to test which schools showed up consistently well or not so well. It is in the nature of the technique that the greater the number of variables, the higher the proportion of units (schools) that achieve a relative efficiency score of 1.0. In this study, the increase was from one school in structure 1, to 27 in structure 7. There was a measure of consistency

Table 8.2 Model structures for education study

Structure	Inputs $I_1,$	$I_2,$	$I_3,$	I_4	Outputs $O_1,$	$O_2,$	$O_3,$	O_4
1		*					*	
2		*				*	*	
3		*		*			*	
4		*		*		*	*	
5		*	*	*	*	*	*	
6	*	*	*	*	*	*		*
7	*	*	*	*	*	*	*	*

in efficiency ranking across the models, with the only efficient school in structure 1 retaining that score across all structures.

The Research and Statistics Branch of ILEA regularly carried out regression analyses and it was possible to compare some results from the two techniques. In this experiment a direct comparison was made between the results from regression analysis and those from the DEA model structure 3. The top ten schools in the regression analysis overlapped with six of the top DEA scorers. The comparisons were useful in establishing the credibility of DEA, although the techniques attempt to answer different questions, with DEA evaluating efficiency/productivity in the round, and regression concentrating on assessing the influence of individual factors.

Comment

The study was strictly a research project, with no involvement of the schools themselves. However, representatives of the Schools Inspectorate were consulted throughout the study and they took a critical look at the results, particularly the identification of reference sets. Their report was encouraging and it was acknowledged that DEA could help by providing additional input to their own schools' assessment.

One particularly pleasing aspect of the study was the fact that the school which proved to be most robustly efficient, in DEA terms (across all model structures), had been at the bottom of league tables based solely on academic results. The way in which DEA takes account of multiple input factors was of benefit to this school which is situated in a very poor neighbourhood.

8.5   EDUCATION—LOCAL EDUCATION AUTHORITY

Background

During 1987 the (UK) Secretary of State for Education issued a paper on financial delegation to schools. Part of this declared that comparisons would be carried out to evaluate a school's actual expenditure against original plans. This information, together with that required of governors relating to the achievement of the national curriculum, would provide a basis on which parents could evaluate whether best use had been made of the resources available to the governors.

Considerable interest was being generated into performance evaluation techniques, and one Local Education Authority was keen to investigate the potential of Data Envelopment Analysis in assessing secondary schools.

The Study

Unlike the project for the Department of Education and Science (Section 8.4) this study was very much participative in nature. One of the first steps was to take representatives of the schools away from the classrooms for a two-day residential workshop to explore how the study might proceed and to give the teachers the opportunity to suggest and discuss factors that might be included in the DEA model. In the event, it proved quite difficult to establish quantifiable objectives. It was a time of considerable unrest within the teaching profession who were resisting attempts to introduce staff appraisals and the establishment of performance standards.

Although the teachers were unanimous that academic results should not be the sole 'output' criterion, there was little agreement on what other measures should be introduced. Eventually, a list of some 55 factors, both input and output, was drawn up and subjected to scrutiny on both statistical and practical grounds. A data collection exercise was undertaken, although this was somewhat restricted by the situation pertaining in the schools. The final model structure was:

- Inputs: Running costs
  Proportion of children for whom English was their first language (in some schools a significant proportion of pupils were from immigrant homes where the lingua franca was not English)
  Proportion of children who had not been referred for social counselling support

Proportion of children achieving higher than average (deemed to be greater than 68%) scores in aptitude tests

- Outputs: Examination results, with weightings supplied by the schools to match grades from differing types of examination Proportion of children who went on to higher education or definite employment

Further models were designed to take account of additional factors such as sporting and artistic achievements.

The results were presented to head teachers and, as was to be expected in the political climate of the time, they received a mixed reception. However, there was some informed discussion and officials within the Local Education Authority were sufficiently encouraged to commission a second study, this time of primary schools.

Comment

The study was one of a number of initiatives taking place in the education service in general and in this Authority in particular. Also, there was disruption in the schools, with teachers providing no cooperation outside their classroom duties. Nevertheless, the Authority found the DEA results instructive and the considerable amount of extra information provided, particularly in the areas of data storage and availability, proved to be a welcome bonus.

To some extent the application of DEA was premature, since the schools needed a period of stability after a rationalization programme to take account of falling student rolls. But the models and analytical tools provided to the Authority have proved useful in subsequent assessments.

8.6 FINANCIAL INSTITUTION (1)

Background

The client this time was one of the five major ('high street') retail banks in the UK which was undergoing a review of its branch operations. In common with the other traditional retail banking organizations it was coming into intense competition with building societies (see Section 8.8) and other specialist financial companies.

The Management Sciences Department (MSD) had built up a good relationship and reputation with the Operations Division and the latter commissioned a DEA feasibility study through MSD.

The Study

A regional pilot project was initiated, but opinion on which factors to include in the model were sought from senior staff at head office as well as from the region. In this first stage, emphasis was placed on clarifying the objectives of the branch network and on establishing how these could be translated into quantified factors. Research was also conducted into possible data sources, and into the reliance that could be placed on the data. This caution was introduced after discovering discrepancies in the recording of data concerning time spent on different work activities in the branches. The final model structure was:

- Inputs: Number of personal account holders (split into two factors according to the socio-economic groupings of the catchment population)
  Number of business account holders
  Number of senior staff
  Number of junior staff
  Equipment purchase cost—as a proxy for degree of automation
  Number of competitive branches in the neighbourhood

- Outputs: Key product sales in the time period
  Number of teller transactions
  Contribution to profit (pre-bad debt)

The question of whether competition is a positive influence (as indicative of the potential of the area) or a negative influence (because it reduces business opportunities) generated considerable debate which was only resolved when the correlation analyses were carried out, and it was found that there was a positive relationship between competition and each of the output factors. This was because competition is essentially a proxy for such factors as population, pedestrian traffic flow and pitch. (See Section 4.2 for a further discussion on this topic.)

A significant finding concerned staff turnover—an issue that branch and area managers thought to be influential in restricting productivity. In the event the correlation analysis showed no such relationship to exist.

The DEA scores were presented in efficiency bands, as in Figure 8.12. Particular attention was paid to reference sets since regional management were attracted by the idea of being able to present the manager of an inefficient branch with proven evidence of better performance. The traditional measure of branch performance was 'contribution to profit (per account base)' and a plot of this against the DEA scores, as shown in Figure 8.13, was instructive. The 50% and 25% lines progressively identify those branches that require particular attention.

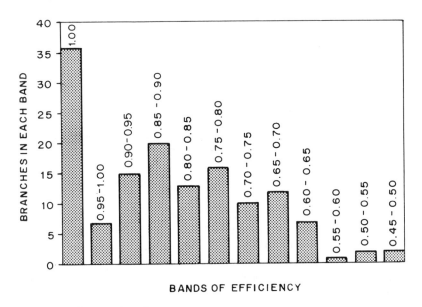

Figure 8.12 Efficiency bands

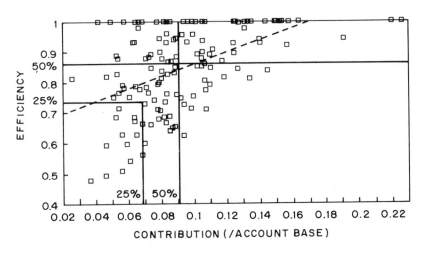

Figure 8.13 Plot of DEA efficiency scores versus profit measure

Comment

Retail banking was undergoing great change with increasing emphasis being placed on improving service to the customer whilst reducing operating costs. This was manifest in the provision of more automatic cash dispensing, and other, equipment and in the redesign of branches to make them more 'user friendly'. In this context, officials of the bank concluded that:

- the DEA process was a useful means of focusing on objectives;
- the technique requires a numerate user (available through their Management Sciences Department);
- the DEA results were useful in addressing complex issues.

A non-technical banker, with practical experience of running a branch operation, was seconded to the study team. This helped the team not only to ask the right questions but also to interpret and screen the data before using them in the model. This commitment to carrying out a practical pilot study, rather than a research project, was instrumental in getting the results of the exercise accepted.

8.7 GOVERNMENT DEPARTMENT—PROPERTY VALUATION SERVICE

Background

The UK Valuation Office offers, through its network of local offices, a professional service to local and central government departments on all matters relating to the valuation of property. In order to be able to carry out these duties each office has a mixture of professional and administrative staff who carry out clearly defined duties. A register is kept of all property in the area and the staff need to be fully aware of the current state, and trends, in the market at any one time.

When a request for a valuation comes in, a case is opened which remains open until either the valuation has been accepted or the case is closed for any other reason. A productivity index had been in use for some time, based on the number of cases of different types completed. The cases were weighted according to work study findings of the average time each type of case was expected to take, and an aggregate score of the sum of all weighted cases compiled which served as a target. Adjustments were made to this target each year to encourage offices to increase productivity. However, there was some dissatisfaction at this index and management were interested in testing out whether DEA could offer an alternative approach taking account of factors that influence the amount of work that can be carried out.

The Study

The initial impetus for the study came from the Operational Research Department of the Inland Revenue, the 'mother' Department of the Valuation Office. The first step was to undertake a short research project to demonstrate to the management of the Valuation Office what DEA could contribute. Data were taken from centrally held computer files and advice was taken from senior officers in head office, most of whom had worked in local offices, as to which factors should be included in the model.

After the usual correlation analyses had been completed, the following model structure was agreed for the pilot exercise:

- Inputs: Number of professional valuation staff
  Number of junior valuation officers
  Number of administrative officers
  Non-staff office costs

- Outputs: Number of cases completed, split into subsets of Revenue, Compensation and Rating cases

The range of efficiency scores was 0.63 to 1.0, with approximately 50% achieving the highest score.

The next step was to get feedback on the pilot study and to get suggestions for factors from staff in the local offices. A day's workshop was arranged in one of the eight regions, with the senior valuation professional (who was also Office Manager) and their Chief Clerk from each of the nine offices in the region. The central part of the workshop was taken up with syndicate work, with analysts acting as facilitators, to elicit input and output factors.

A significant proportion of senior officers' time is taken up with management matters and some of the officers wished to have 'staff reports' as an output factor. This generated discussion on the *objectives* of a local office—why it was 'in business'—and the suggestion was dropped. Another candidate put forward as an output factor was the time taken to maintain and update their property registers. This, however, is an example of an intermediate activity undertaken in support of the final output which consists of the actual caseload.

The officers had been unhappy that, with the existing productivity index, there was an implicit assumption that the time taken to complete cases in a particular category could always be averaged out. The point was made that one case could take a few days whilst another, for example a motorway compensation case, could take several months. It was discovered that when an officer completed a case, some classification of the complexity was registered. This provided a possible weighting factor.

There was a considerable overlap in the factors put forward by the different syndicate groups and a revised model structure was drawn up, under the constraint that, since the DEA analysis would cover the offices for all the country, no data gathering exercise could be undertaken.

Comment

The Operational Research Group were using the study in the Valuation Office as a testbed for DEA within the Inland Revenue. The Valuation Office were initially happy to be merely providers of data but the involvement of their regional and district officers in the exercise engendered a more proactive interest. At that stage the study took on a higher profile.

8.8 FINANCIAL INSTITUTION (2)

The Organization

The client for this study was one of the larger Building Societies in the United Kingdom. It provides a range of financial services, principally to personal customers, through a network of high street retailing outlets. These branches were grouped geographically into six Areas, each having a number of sub-areas (or Regions). Each level—branch, region and area—has its own management structure, reporting ultimately to the General Manager (Operations). The remainder of the senior management responsibilities at the time of the study were split along functional lines:

- Finance
- Corporate Planning
- Marketing
- Personnel
- Information Technology,

together with a number of specialist account functions.

The Society covers the UK but with a bias towards the East and South East. The branch network was supplemented by agents, but the number of these was being reduced.

Background to the Study

Building Societies began life as 'Friendly Societies', set up to provide the working man who wanted to buy a house with a secure means of saving for it. In time, the Societies provided additional funds by way of mortgage loans and, in order to source these loans, they were permitted to offer a savings service to people who were looking for steady interest, again secure, but who would not necessarily be using the money to purchase a house. Eventually, a Society was permitted to provide loans to people who were not savers with that Society, though only for house purchase (or for extensions/renovations).

By the late 1970s the major UK banks entered the home loan (mortgage) market and, initially, took a significant corner of that market. The Building Societies felt threatened and campaigned for changes to the law to allow them to take on the banks on a wider financial front. Successive changes to the legal framework eased the restrictions on the Societies and many now offer a range of personal banking services equivalent to those of the banks, although retaining a primary interest in savings and loans for house purchase.

In 1960 there were over 200 Building Societies of all shapes and sizes—with branch networks consisting of 1–500 outlets. Many Societies began to merge with others to create sufficient critical mass to survive in the new competitive climate. One such merger brought together two Societies which formed the client for this case study. These two Societies had contrasting cultures and organizations and, although their main catchment areas were different, there were many overlaps in coverage.

The new management had to look at their merged organization and evolve a new culture and set of working practices. One area that needed urgent attention was the branch network; some way had to be found to evaluate the performance of the individual branches so that objective decisions could be made on how to rationalize the network where there were overlaps—in some cases where two branches, previously rivals, were within a few yards of each other. There were no accepted measures of performance but officers in Corporate Planning were interested to explore the potential of, what was then, the newly discovered technique of Data Envelopment Analysis.

The Society approached consultancies who offered DEA, but most of these concentrated their services on:

- advising on the appropriate model;
- carrying out the analysis on data collected by the Society;
- interpreting and presenting the results.

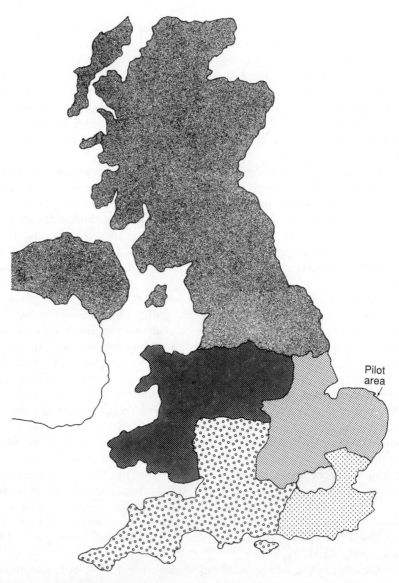

Figure 8.14 Map of Building Society Branch Areas

This approach had the advantage of being relatively inexpensive but the Society would end up with no expertise in the topic and, therefore, no basis for continued work. The Society wanted a joint study, with full involvement throughout, ownership of the models, and the ability to carry out further analyses.

A number of other initiatives were under way at the same time, most notably a study to determine the most effective 'delivery channel' mix for the range of products. Although a number of radical proposals were expected from this latter study it was clear that the high street branch was going to remain one of the most important locations of these 'delivery channels'—such as:

- general over-the-counter transactions;
- individual 'advice-and-sale';
- most of the automatic teller machines which a customer could use, 24 hours a day, without needing to speak to a member of the staff (although, strictly speaking, these constitute a distinct delivery channel of their own).

Considerable effort was expended by both the study sponsors and the project team to obtain support from senior managers across the Society. This initial phase was taken very seriously since it was recognized that, regardless of any intrinsic merits that DEA might have, the study would languish under the 'backroom research' label unless management commitment was obtained up front.

It was decided to undertake a pilot study in one of the geographical Areas, in which there were 60 branches. However, a series of interviews was carried out with all senior head office managers and a number of other Area managers to elicit their ideas on what should be taken into account when assessing branch performance. The country-wide coverage, together with the chosen area, are shown in Figure 8.14.

The Factors

The first important step in the pilot study was to interview representatives from all levels of management within the Area including:

- The Area Manager;
- The six Regional Managers;
- Central Area Business Managers.

Finally, two group discussions were held with selections of Branch Managers, taking care to include a balance between those from each of the Societies that merged to form the client organization.

The objective of these meetings was to learn as much about the business as possible and to derive factors that could be incorporated into the model(s). Inevitably, there was much discussion about the problems that merger had brought—particularly with respect to using two incompatible computer systems. However, a 'long list' of both output and input factors was drawn up and the initial stage of the analysis concentrated on sifting through them.

When considering output variables, the following classifications were mooted:

ASPECT—What is the factor being used to measure?

- Management control
- Existing business
- New business
- Quality of business
- Service quality
- Workload
- Cross-selling (marketing) capability

PRODUCT—With which product is the factor associated?

- Cheque account
- Investment
- Mortgage lending
- Other lending
- Commission on related services

The factors that had been identified were then sorted, using these classifications. The result is shown in Table 8.3.

When building a DEA model it is important to be clear about which factors actually refer to the objectives of the business and which factors refer to activities that are undertaken to support the production of those outputs—see the discussion below on 'workload'. Usually, when faced with a long list of factors, it is useful to place them in the following categories:

- Final output (FINAL)—a direct measure of the degree of achievement of an objective. For example, if an objective is to sell mortgages, the value of mortgage completions is a final output.
- Intermediate output (INTERMEDIATE)—an indirect measure of the degree of achievement of an objective—used as a substitute when a final output is not available, either through inability to measure or lack of data. For example, if cheque accounts are sold as a platform for future cross-selling, it will not be possible to measure the cross-selling benefit, but the number of cheque accounts sold serves as an intermediate measure. Similarly, if an objective is to provide a high

quality customer service we have no direct measure of that service, but we can quantify customers' perceptions of the service.
- Means to achieving an output (INFLUENCING)—not a measure of the degree of achievement of an objective but a measure of a quality which may aid the achievement of an objective. For example, ability to cross-sell should aid the sale of investment accounts to existing cheque account customers. Note that this ability is already reflected in the output measurement 'Number of new investment accounts opened' and that to include both would be double counting. The interest in variables of this type is usually to test if possession of the quality being measured does have the desired influence on achievement.

Table 8.3 Classification of output variables

Aspect	Product area	Variable
CONTROL	Cheque account	Amounts of overdraft
		No. accounts over limit
EXISTING	Cheque account	Balances +
		Balances −
		No. live accounts
	Investment	Net receipts (destination)
		Net receipts (source)
		No. live accounts
	Mortgages	No. live accounts
NEW	Commission	Endowment
		Other
		Travel
	Cheque account	No. new accounts opened
	Investment	No. new accounts opened
	Mortgage	Applications
		Approvals
		Completions
	Other lending	No. further advances
		No. secured advances
		No. unsecured advances
		Value unsecured advances
QUALITY	Mortgages	No. above 2.5 times salary etc.
		No. above 95% advance
SERVICE	General	Market survey results
		Complaints
		Interviews
	Mortgages	Drop outs (application to approval)
WORKLOAD	General	No. transactions
	Investment	Withdrawal ratio
	Mortgages	Arrears
X-SELL	General	Increase in multiple relationships

As a general guide we should include in the DEA model all final outputs subject to elimination of double counting, e.g. variables expected to be highly correlated such as 'Number of unsecured loans' and 'Value of unsecured loans'. We should also include in the model intermediate outputs where no final output exists for the objective being measured, subject again to the elimination of double counting. We should not include means to achieving outputs but should test the correlation of each of these variables with the resulting DEA efficiency score to test its effect on achievement.

Applying this logic to the identified aspects yields:

- Management control   INFLUENCING
- Existing business   FINAL (value)
      INTERMEDIATE (number)
- New business   FINAL (value)
      INTERMEDIATE (number)
- Quality of business   INFLUENCING (provided we measure value)
- Service quality   INTERMEDIATE (it could be argued that this should be classified as 'INFLUENCING' if service quality only achieves branch business)
- Workload   INTERMEDIATE (it is 'half way between'; it may influence, but it consumes resource—hence, in a sense, it is already accounted for by final inputs)
- Cross-selling capability   INFLUENCING

Applying our 'rules', then, leads to the elimination of factors for all aspects except 'Existing business', 'New business', and 'Service quality'.

The Input factors chosen were not product related but covered a wide variety of aspects. Thus, the sort of classification used for output factors could not be used here. However, there are three types of classification, similar to those for Output factors, that are appropriate.

(1) FINAL—a direct measure of resources actually consumed in the process of generating the output activities, e.g. 'Domestic cost'.

(2) INTERMEDIATE—not properly FINAL or INFLUENCE—an indirect measure of resource consumed, used as a substitute in the absence of a final input or to measure a factor which may influence achievement but whose resource consumption is accounted for by a final input. Our variable list contains examples of the latter only. The interest in variables of this type is usually to test if the factor does have the desired influence on achievement. For example, the variable 'Car parking facilities' is present to permit its

influence on achievement to be evaluated, but any resources which the provision of car parking facilities consumes are covered by 'Domestic costs'.

(3) INFLUENCE—a measure of a factor which may have an influence on achievement but does not consume resource, e.g. 'Competition'.

Table 8.4 shows the suggested input factors sorted according to this classification.

Table 8.4 Classification of input factors

Category	Factors
FINAL	Staff Costs
	Staff in post
	Domestic costs excluding staff costs
INTERMEDIATE	Staff grades
	Car parking available
	No. interview facilities
	Frontage
	No. tills
INFLUENCING	Distance to nearest automatic teller machine
	Competition
	Catchment area
	Staff—length of service
	Population of catchment
	Age of branch
	Pitch (location) quality
	Local unemployment

Where possible, all final inputs should be included in the model, subject to no double counting. Similarly, each intermediate input, for which no final input exists, should also be included—again subject to no double counting. Influencing factors are really 'possible influencing' factors and need to be tested, as described in the stepwise approach (Chapters 4 and 7).

Cost Efficiency Model Structures

Here we addressed the question:

'Given the level of business that we contract, how far could costs have been trimmed whilst maintaining that level of business?'

The study followed the stepwise approach, and consequently before model building commenced there was a further task to be undertaken. This concerned a further refinement of the list of factors where data were either unavailable or too expensive to collect. Naturally, it is important to explain any omissions to the managers who proposed the excluded factors. In this study, it was found that data for most factors were available, or could be extracted, but the coverage was patchy across the branches. Consequently, 13 branches were dropped from the study, leaving 47 branches for the analysis.

Careful examination of the input factors (Table 8.4) led to the conclusion that the most straightforward way to proceed in the first instance would be to use the single input of branch 'domestic cost', combining both staff and non-staff components. (Note that there is a high degree of correlation between 'staff costs' and 'staff in post' and so to include both would be double counting.) This is consistent with the approach of building a series of models starting with the highest level. Each new model, which further breaks out the high level factors, provides information for different aspects of decision making.

Continuing this theme, the highest level of aggregation of output factors was chosen to be 'total volume of business', incorporating both new and existing accounts. The implicit assumption was that the work (and therefore cost) required to maintain an existing account is the same as that required to open and service a new account. Analysis showed this not to be the case and so the structure for the first (highest level) model was:

- Input: Domestic cost (i.e. staff costs plus controllable non-staff costs)

- Outputs: Total existing business
  Total new business

Table 8.5 Model structures (outputs), excluding service factor

Structure 1	
New business	Existing business
Structure 2	
New business	Existing cheque account business
	Existing investment account business
	Existing mortgage account business
Structure 3	
New cheque account business	Existing business
New investment account business	
New mortgage account business	
Structure 4	
New cheque account business	Existing cheque account business
New investment account business	Existing investment account business
New mortgage account business	Existing mortgage account business

Data for the factor 'service quality' were obtained from a continuing market research programme. Although 'service quality' is not a subset of 'existing business' or 'new business' it was excluded from the first model so that it could be analysed against the efficiency scores of that model. However, in the event, no relationship was found and so the factor was dropped from the analysis.

Table 8.5 shows the model structures that were investigated, each using different disaggregations of high level factors and with the input always being cost. Further low level structures incorporating 'commission' and 'other lending' were also considered. However, after conducting correlation analysis along the lines outlined above, the final recommended model was that of Structure 2. In deciding on this it was recognized that it would be necessary to re-analyse new account openings over a longer time period than the three months used in the study. It was felt that data collected over a period as short as three months showed insufficient stability from one time period to the next.

Results of the Cost Efficiency Models

There was a wide range of efficiency scores in the results and it was interesting to note the variations between branches from the two merging Societies (see Figure 8.15). Possible explanations for this variation were:

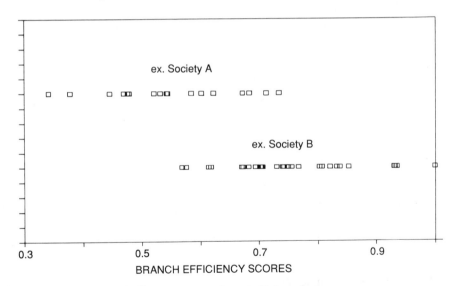

Figure 8.15 Range of efficiency scores from initial analysis

- Product mix—the mix of products offered by the two Societies was different in the initial stages of the merger. However, even after accounting for this, the variation still existed—as shown in Figure 8.16.
- Uncontrollable cost factors—but these, including rent (real or notional) and maintenance, had been excluded.

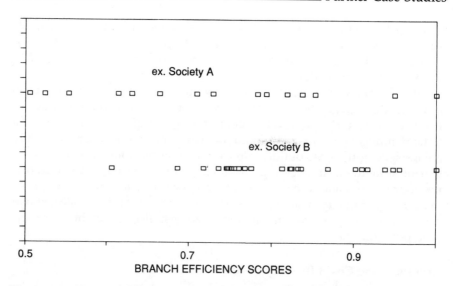

Figure 8.16 Range of efficiency scores after allowance for product mix

- Economies of scale—but there was no obvious correlation between size of branch and efficiency.
- Different administrative processes—a factor that could not be measured directly.

This last point refers principally to the organization of 'back office' processes. The variations highlighted by the DEA results constituted a significant finding of the study and have led to a further investigation of the relative merits of localized and centralized arrangements.

The models described here were specifically designed to examine the cost implications of inefficiencies in the branch network. A significant post-DEA analysis estimated that the potential savings from improving efficiency were:

Branches from Society A: £1.4m (17 branches)
Branches from Society B: £1.1m (30 branches)
Total potential saving: £2.5m (47 branches)

Market Potential Efficiency

Of equal importance to the sponsors of the study was the investigation of market potential efficiency. This addresses the question:

> 'Given our levels of staffing and given the conditions within which we operate, what increase in the level of business should we be achieving?'

For this latter approach, an assessment of 'market efficiency', one output factor was chosen—'growth in total business'—and several input factors were examined. After preliminary analysis the model structure agreed was:

Output: Growth in business in time period (i.e. new accounts)

Inputs: Staff costs
          Existing cheque account business
          Existing investment account business
          Existing mortgage account business
          Number of competitor (bank and building society) branches in catchment area
          Pedestrian traffic flow

The DEA efficiencies resulting from this model had a similar span to those for the cost efficiency models; i.e. 0.56 to 1. As might be expected, since they were addressing quite different questions, there was no direct relationship between the two sets of results, as can be seen in Figure 8.17.

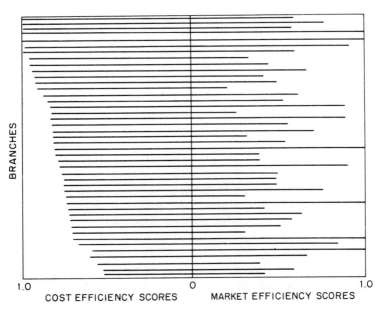

Figure 8.17 Comparison of results from cost and market efficiency models

Whereas the cost efficiency model can indicate the sorts of savings that could be achieved in the operation of the branch network, the market efficiency model is an aid to defining:

- performances of individual branches in the light of the available market potential;
- market factors that influence branch performance.

Comment

This study was initiated because a real problem needed to be tackled and management were searching for an approach or technique that would assist them. Once the project had been initiated, the steps described in Chapter 7 were all carried out and different levels of management, together with the planning analysts, were involved throughout. The thoroughness of this approach inevitably exposes gaps in the provision of important management information. This study proved to be no exception since the basic data required for the DEA models were of variable quality and often incomplete. One benefit of the study, then, was to identify the areas where data recording needed to be improved, with a view to assisting a variety of analyses, not just DEA.

The study was undertaken at a critical period for the Society. The merger had just been completed and the management were trying to establish:

- the right corporate focus;
- uniform operating procedures;
- appropriate delivery channels for their products;
- the role and shape of the branch network.

DEA specifically addressed the last of these points but, by following the stepwise approach (Chapter 7), it also provided input to the debates on the other topics. In the event, there were two major outcomes for DEA:

- The technique was accepted as a fair, objective appraiser of (comparative) branch performance.
- The participative nature of the approach was valuable in defining the objectives of branches within the network, and identifying problems that prevent the attainment of those objectives.

In carrying the study forward the Society will carry out the analysis at Sales Area level, where a Sales Area incorporates a group of branches that share certain common facilities, such as marketing support and back office functions. This reflects the discussion in Section 7.2 on defining the units that are most appropriate for a model designed to answer specific questions. Here, we will be dealing not with branches but with 'aggregate branches'. (See also the discussion on building separate models for cost and market efficiency in Section 4.7.)

The issues addressed by both the cost and market efficiency models were important to the Society but the difficulty of defining 'profit' in a branch operation, where benefits accrue from having a *network* of branches rather than a number of individual units, led them to favour the cost efficiency approach. The Operations Director has endorsed this and he will sponsor the next stages of the study along these lines.

Appendix A

Detailed Mathematical Formulation

A1 THE PROBLEM

In Section 3.1 we derived an efficiency measure for a unit based on two outputs O_1 and O_2 and one input I, of the form:

$$\frac{aO_1 + bO_2}{cI}$$

where a, b and c gave the maximum possible value of the ratio for the unit subject to the value of the ratio for any other unit being constrained to a maximum of 1.

This can be generalized to the larger problem of comparing the performances of n units with:

  s outputs denoted by y_j, $j = 1, \ldots, s$
  r inputs denoted by x_i, $i = 1, \ldots, r$

The equivalent efficiency measure for unit o is:

(1)
$$\max e_o = \frac{\sum_{j=1}^{s} w_j y_{jo}}{\sum_{i=1}^{r} v_i x_{io}}$$

  subject to:

$$\frac{\sum_{j=1}^{s} w_j y_{jm}}{\sum_{i=1}^{r} v_i x_{im}} \leq 1; \ m = 1, \ldots, n$$

$$w_j \geq 0; \ j = 1, \ldots, s$$

$$v_i \geq 0; \ i = 1, \ldots, r$$

Where the value of the ratio for unit o is less than 1, the subset of units whose ratio value is equal to 1 is the reference set for unit o.

A2 LINEAR PROGRAMMING PRIMAL FORMULATION

This problem can be solved by one of two linear programming (LP) formulations.

Firstly, the denominator of the function to be maximized, i.e. the weighted sum of inputs, can be constrained to 1. Since it is possible in the above formulation to multiply all v_i and all w_j by a constant whilst leaving all the ratios unchanged, there is no loss of generality in introducing this additional constraint. The problem can then be expressed as the following LP:

(2)
$$\max e_o = \sum_{j=1}^{s} w_j y_{jo}$$

subject to:

$$\sum_{i=1}^{r} v_i x_{im} - \sum_{j=1}^{s} w_j y_{jm} \geq 0; \ m = 1, \ldots, n$$

$$\sum_{i=1}^{r} v_i x_{io} = 1$$

$$w_j \geq 0; \ j = 1, \ldots, s$$

$$v_i \geq 0; \ i = 1, \ldots, r$$

Every LP has both primal and dual formulations which have identical solutions. Charnes Cooper and Rhodes introduced the above formulation as the primal in their original paper [6].

A3 LINEAR PROGRAMMING DUAL FORMULATION

It is not our intention to cover the theory of LP within this book since there are many standard texts on the subject. Any of these will provide adequate background for a reader not familiar with the concept of duality. We will therefore merely state the dual formulations of the primal formulations expressed.

The dual of problem (1) is:

(3)
$$\min f_o$$

subject to:

$$-\sum_{m=1}^{n} L_{om} x_{im} + f_o x_{io} \geq 0, \ i = 1, \ldots, r$$

$$\sum_{m=1}^{n} L_{om} y_{jm} \geq y_{jo}, \ j = 1, \ldots, s$$

If we reorganize these equations slightly, we can make a very direct practical interpretation, as follows:

Mathematics	Interpretation
min f_o	For the unit o, find the minimum proportion f_o
subject to:	which allows a weighted combination (i.e. the L_{om}) of the performance of all units to be found such that
$\sum_{m=1}^{n} L_{om} x_{im} \leq f_o x_{io}, i = 1, \ldots, r$	for each input, the weighted combination of input does not exceed the proportion f_o of the input of unit o
$\sum_{m=1}^{n} L_{om} y_{jm} \geq y_{jo}, j = 1, \ldots, s$	and for each output, the weighted combination of output is at least as great as that of unit o.

We can see that the minimum value of f_o will never be greater than 1 since a value of 1 can always be obtained via the performance of unit o itself by choosing the weighted combination given by $L_{oo} = 1$ and all other $L_{om} = 0$.

A minimum value of f_o of less than 1 determines the existence of a weighted combination of the actual performance of other units such that no output of unit o exceeds the corresponding output of the weighted combination whilst, at the same time, it is possible to reduce all of the inputs of unit o to the proportion f_o of its existing value without any input falling below the corresponding input of the weighted combination. In other words, the weighted combination produces at least as much output in every respect for less input in every respect and f_o is a measure of how much we can reduce ALL of the inputs of unit o in the same proportion to produce a performance in line with the weighted combination.

This corresponds exactly with our alternative view of efficiency in Section 3.2, the L_{om} being the dual weights established in Section 3.2. The weighted combination established for the Newcastle shop in that case was the point B which was a weighted combination of the performances of the reference shops Reading and Northampton only. Accordingly, when we solve the dual LP problem (3) above for the Newcastle shop in the same two-output, one-input case, the L_{om} are all zero except for the two values of m which correspond to the Reading and Northampton shops. By analogy, it is true in general that the L_{om} are zero except for those corresponding to the reference units. Table 3.2 confirmed that the values obtained by this process are the same values which were derived for L_1 and L_2 in Section 3.2.

The value of f_o for any unit o which appears in the reference set for any other unit p will be 1. This can be proved simply by assuming otherwise and substituting the weighted combination which determines f_o in place of unit o in the weighted combination which determines f_p, thereby establishing a new f value less than f_p and hence a contradiction. Efficiency of units can therefore be interpreted in the sense that no other unit or weighted combination of units can perform as well in every respect across the complete range of inputs and outputs.

A4 SLACKS

Returning now to the discussion of inefficient units, we observed in Section 3.3 that, in the case of the Bromley shop, we can reduce Bromley's input by the factor OC/OD (equivalent to f_o) to arrive at the point D on the frontier, at which point we can no longer reduce the input without going beyond the frontier. We can, however, make an additional improvement in *Total revenue* without detriment to *Revenue growth*. We referred to that additional improvement as the 'slack' for the output *Total revenue*. On making that improvement, we arrive at a point coincident with the Northampton shop itself. Accordingly, when we solve the dual LP problem (3) for the Bromley shop, the L_{om} are all zero except for that which corresponds to the Northampton shop.

In the LP formulation (3) above, it is clear from the mathematics that the inputs of unit o can be reduced to the proportion f_o of their existing value at which point some of the input and output constraints are satisfied as equalities and to reduce all inputs further would result in violation of those constraints. However, equality may not be achieved in all constraints, in which case unit o will still have some inputs greater than the inputs of the weighted combination or some outputs less than the outputs of the weighted combination, indicating that additional improvements are possible in those aspects.

The magnitude of the additional possible improvements is simply the amount by which the relevant constraint fails to achieve equality. These amounts can be included in the LP formulation as s_i^-, $i = 1,...,r$, and s_j^+, $j = 1,...,s$, as follows:

(4)
$$\min f_o$$

subject to:

$$-\sum_{m=1}^{n} L_{om}x_{im} + f_o x_{io} - s_i^- = 0, i = 1, \ldots, r$$

$$\sum_{m=1}^{n} L_{om}y_{jm} - s_j^+ = y_{jo}, j = 1, \ldots, s$$

The s_i and s_j are called 'slack variables' which is standard LP terminology for additional variables introduced to convert inequality constraints to equality constraints. This is also the terminology used in the DEA sense when referring to the additional improvements possible in specific inputs or outputs.

In their introductory paper on DEA, Charnes, Cooper and Rhodes [6] introduced the simple example reproduced in the graph in Figure A1. The example depicts a DEA for six units each having a single output with value one unit and two inputs with differing values as plotted on the graph. The main point of the example is that, for P6, there are two possible minima. The minimum value of f_6 is 1, but this can be achieved for either $L_{63} = 1$ and all other L_{6m} and slacks zero; or $L_{66} = 1$, $s_2 = 1$ all other L_{6m} and slacks zero. In other words, for P6 best performance is exhibited either by P3 or by P6, but in the case of P6 with a reduction of one unit possible in Input 2. In fact, this amounts to the same thing since on reducing Input 2 by one unit, P6 would become coincident with P3. Hence in practical terms there is no ambiguity although in mathematical terms there are dual minima.

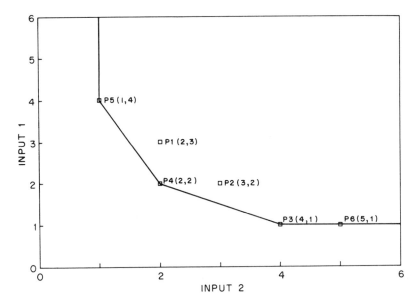

Figure A1 Alternative minima (reproduced from Charnes, Cooper & Rhodes, 1978, by permission of Elsevier Science Publishers BV)

Charnes, Cooper and Rhodes sought to remove the mathematical ambiguity by amending the objective function to maximize the slack values too, but in a manner which did not impair the minimization of f. This resulted in the following amended objective function which has become the form usually quoted when the DEA dual formulation is presented:

$$\min \left\{ f_o - \delta \left(\sum_{i=1}^{f} s_i^- + \sum_{j=1}^{s} s_j^+ \right) \right\}$$

where δ is a very small constant usually chosen to be 10^{-6}.

The case of P6 is covered by Charnes, Cooper and Rhodes [6] in their definition of efficiency which we presented originally in Section 1.7.

A5 RECIPROCAL FORMULATION

Let us now take another view of the original formulation in (1). We saw in Section 3.4 that we could invert our efficiency measure to obtain an equivalent result with the efficiency measure becoming the reciprocal of its former value. Mathematically, this transforms the original formulation in (1) to:

(5)
$$\min e'_o = \frac{\sum_{i=1}^{r} v_i x_{io}}{\sum_{j=1}^{s} w_j y_{jo}}$$

subject to:

$$\frac{\sum_{i=1}^{r} v_i x_{im}}{\sum_{j=1}^{s} w_j y_{jm}} \geq 1; \ m = 1, \ldots, n$$

$$w_j \geq 0; \ j = 1, \ldots, s$$

$$v_i \geq 0; \ i = 1, \ldots, r$$

The constraints determine that the e'_o will be at least 1 with efficiency achieved as before when $e'_o = 1$.

Again, the denominator of the function to be minimized, this time the weighted sum of outputs, can be constrained to 1 without loss of generality resulting in the following LP:

(6)
$$\min e'_o = \sum_{i=1}^{r} v_i x_{io}$$

subject to:

$$\sum_{i=1}^{r} v_i x_{im} - \sum_{j=1}^{s} w_j y_{jm} \geq 0; \ m = 1, \ldots, n$$

$$\sum_{j=1}^{s} w_j y_{jo} = 1$$

$$w_j \geq 0; \ j = 1, \ldots, s$$

$$v_i \geq 0; \ i = 1, \ldots, r$$

As before, we can dualize this problem and rearrange, giving us the following interpretation:

Mathematics	Interpretation
$\max f'_o$	For the unit o, find the maximum multiplier f'_o
subject to:	which allows a weighted combination (i.e. the L'_{om}) of the performance of all units to be found such that
$\sum_{m=1}^{n} L'_{om} x_{im} \leq x_{io}, \ i = 1, \ldots, r$	for each input, the weighted combination of input does not exceed that of the input of unit o

$\sum_{m=1}^{n} L'_{om} y_{jm} \geq f_o y_{jo}, j = 1, \ldots, s$ and for each output, the weighted combination of output is at least as great as f'_o times that of unit o.

We can see that the maximum value of f'_o will never be less than 1 since a value of 1 can always be obtained via the performance of unit o itself by choosing the weighted combination given by $L'_{oo} = 1$ and all other $L'_{om} = 0$.

If we introduce slack variables, as before, the equations become:

(7) $$\max f'_o$$

subject to:

$$\sum_{m=1}^{n} L'_{om} x_{im} + S_i^- = x_{io}, i = 1, \ldots, r$$

$$- \sum_{m=1}^{n} L'_{om} y_{jm} + f'_o y_o + S_j^+ = 0, j = 1, \ldots, s$$

Hence the problem has transformed from 'Given the outputs, by how much can we reduce the inputs?' to 'Given the inputs, by how much can we increase the outputs?', and perhaps not surprisingly the answer to one is the reciprocal of the other. However, whilst the two formulations are equivalent in terms of measuring efficiency, the choice of formulation is critical to the calculation of the L_{om}. We saw in Section 3.2 that L_1 and L_2 differ by a factor equal to the efficiency score depending on whether we choose to minimize input or maximize output. We can deduce the equivalent relationship between the L_{om} in (3) and the L'_{om} in (6) by direct comparison of the sets of equations (3) and (6). The interpretations associated with these equations indicate that, strictly, the original formulation (equations 1 to 3) applies only to input minimization and the reciprocal formulation (equations 4 to 6) applies only to output maximization. Note also the result in Section 3.3, that a different value for slack is obtained depending on which of these formulations is used.

Note that the dual gives by far the clearest interpretation of what is happening in terms of input minimization and output maximization. In this respect, CCR's choice of which formulation to introduce as the primal was unfortunate. It is a source of constant confusion (and error) amongst practitioners who work with the primal that input minimization is achieved through the formulation which maximizes the objective function whilst output maximization is achieved through the formulation which minimizes the objective function.

A6   BUDGETS AND TARGETS

In Chapter 2, we introduced input minimization and output maximization in the context of either setting reduced input budgets for a unit whilst maintaining its current level of output or setting increased output targets for a unit whilst maintaining its current level of input. Specifically, we illustrated that the budgets or targets were based on the point B in Figure 2.3 for the Newcastle shop and Northampton for the Bromley shop.

We indicated in the mathematical development above that these points are given by the weighted averages of the reference units; i.e. for reduced input budgets:

$$\sum_{m=1}^{n} L_{om}x_{im}, i = 1, \ldots, r$$

$$\sum_{m=1}^{n} L_{om}y_{jm}, j = 1, \ldots, s$$

For the Newcastle shop all L_{om} are zero except those in respect of the Reading and Northampton shops, resulting in the weighted combination being equivalent to the point B; and for the Bromley shop, all L_{om} are zero except for that in respect of the Northampton shop, resulting in the weighted combination being equivalent to the Northampton shop itself.

Alternatively, for increased output targets, we have:

$$\sum_{m=1}^{n} L'_{om}x_{im}, i = 1, \ldots, r$$

$$\sum_{m=1}^{n} L'_{om}y_{jm}, j = 1, \ldots, s$$

Hence we can derive our budget or target values directly from the computed L_{om} or L'_{om} values.

However, from (4) and (7), we can see that the following calculations are equivalent. For reduced input budgets:

$$f_o x_{io} - s_i^-, i = 1, \ldots, r \quad \text{and} \quad y_{jo} + s_j^+, j = 1, \ldots, s$$

and for increased output targets:

$$x_{io} - S_i^-, i = 1, \ldots, r \quad \text{and} \quad f'_o y_{jo} + S_j^+, j = 1, \ldots, s$$

Hence an equivalent calculation for target values can be obtained by first factoring the inputs or outputs (depending on whether we are setting input budgets or output targets) by the efficiency score, and then subtracting all input slacks and adding all output slacks.

A7 UNCONTROLLABLE INPUTS

In Section 3.5 we also examined the effect of having uncontrollable inputs where reductions cannot be achieved. From our graphical analysis, we derived a modified weighted sum ratio in which only the controllable input remained in the numerator with the uncontrollable input being incorporated into the denominator.

For consistency with the development above, we will begin with the outputs in the numerator and generalize to a problem of n units with:

s outputs denoted by y_j, $j = 1, \ldots, s$

r controllable inputs denoted by x_i, $i = 1, \ldots, r$

t uncontrollable inputs denoted by z_k, $k = 1, \ldots, t$

The equivalent efficiency measure for unit o is:

$$(8) \qquad \max e_o = \frac{\sum_{j=1}^{s} w_j y_{jo} - \sum_{k=1}^{t} u_k z_{ko}}{\sum_{i=1}^{r} v_i x_{io}}$$

subject to:

$$\frac{\sum_{j=1}^{s} w_j y_{jm} - \sum_{k=1}^{t} u_k z_{km}}{\sum_{i=1}^{r} v_i x_{im}} \leq 1; \ m = 1, \ldots, n$$

$$w_j \geq 0; \ j = 1, \ldots, s$$

$$v_i \geq 0; \ i = 1, \ldots, r$$

$$u_k \geq 0; \ k = 1, \ldots, t$$

As before, this can be rearranged as an LP as follows:

$$(9) \qquad \max e_o = \sum_{j=1}^{s} w_j y_{jo} - \sum_{k=1}^{t} u_k z_{ko}$$

subject to:

$$\sum_{i=1}^{r} v_i x_{im} + \sum_{k=1}^{t} u_k z_{km} - \sum_{j=1}^{s} w_j y_{jm} \geq 0; \ m = 1, \ldots, n$$

$$\sum_{i=1}^{r} v_i x_{io} = 1$$

$$w_j \geq 0; \ j = 1, \ldots, s$$

$$v_i \geq 0; \ i = 1, \ldots, r$$

The dual of this LP is:

$$(10) \qquad \min f_o$$

subject to:

$$-\sum_{m=1}^{n} L_{om}x_{im} + f_o x_{io} \geq 0, i = 1, \ldots, r$$

$$-\sum_{m=1}^{n} L_{om}z_{km} \geq -z_{ko}, k = 1, \ldots, t$$

$$\sum_{m=1}^{n} L_{om}y_{jm} \geq y_{jo}, j = 1, \ldots, s$$

which can be rearranged and interpreted as follows:

Mathematics	*Interpretation*
$\min f_o$	For the unit o, find the minimum proportion f_o
subject to:	which allows a weighted combination (i.e. the L_{om}) of the performance of all units to be found such that
$\sum_{m=1}^{n} L_{om}x_{im} \leq f_o x_{io}, i = 1, \ldots, r$	for each controllable input, the weighted combination of input does not exceed the proportion f_o of the input of unit o
$\sum_{m=1}^{n} L_{om}z_{km} \leq z_{ko}, k = 1, \ldots, t$	for each uncontrollable input, the weighted combination of input does not exceed that of unit o
$\sum_{m=1}^{n} L_{om}y_{jm} \geq y_{jo}, j = 1, \ldots, s$	and for each output, the weighted combination of output is at least as great as that of unit o.

Hence again, the dual provides a direct interpretation in that the weighted combination produces at least as much output in every respect for less input in every respect and f_o is a measure of how much we can reduce ALL of the CONTROLLABLE inputs in the same proportion to produce a performance in line with the weighted combination. The only difference between this and formulation (3) is that f_o is applied only to the controllable inputs which is consistent with the definition of controllable and uncontrollable. In fact, (3) is simply a special case of (10) where $t=0$.

This development is included in a later paper by Charnes and Cooper [7] where they make use of the terms discretionary and non-discretionary inputs—equivalent to our controllable and uncontrollable inputs.

Moving now to the inverted efficiency measure, we have:

$$(11) \qquad \min e'_o = \frac{\sum_{i=1}^{r} v_i x_{io}}{\sum_{j=1}^{s} w_j y_{jo} - \sum_{k=1}^{t} u_k z_{ko}}$$

subject to:

$$\frac{\sum_{i=1}^{r} v_i x_{im}}{\sum_{j=1}^{s} w_j y_{jm} - \sum_{k=1}^{t} u_k z_{km}} \geq 1;\ m = 1, \ldots, n$$

$$w_j \geq 0;\ j = 1, \ldots, s$$

$$v_i \geq 0;\ i = 1, \ldots, r$$

$$u_k \geq 0;\ k = 1, \ldots, t$$

As before, this can be rearranged as an LP as follows:

(12)
$$\min e_o' = \sum_{i=1}^{r} v_i x_{io}$$

subject to:

$$\sum_{i=1}^{r} v_i x_{im} + \sum_{k=1}^{t} u_k z_{km} - \sum_{j=1}^{s} w_j y_{jm} \geq 0;\ m = 1, \ldots, n$$

$$\sum_{j=1}^{s} w_j y_{jo} - \sum_{k=1}^{t} u_k z_{ko} = 1$$

$$w_j \geq 0;\ j = 1, \ldots, s$$

$$v_i \geq 0;\ i = 1, \ldots, r$$

with the dual of this LP being:

(13)
$$\max f_o'$$

subject to:

$$\sum_{m=1}^{n} L_{om} x_{im} \leq x_{io},\ i = 1, \ldots, r$$

$$\sum_{m=1}^{n} L_{om} z_{km} - f_o' z_{ko} \leq 0,\ k = 1, \ldots, t$$

$$-\sum_{m=1}^{n} L_{om} y_{jm} + f_o' y_{jo} \leq 0;\ j = 1, \ldots, s$$

which can be rearranged and interpreted as follows:

Mathematics	*Interpretation*

$\max f_o'$

For the unit o, find the minimum proportion f_o'

subject to:

which allows a weighted combination (i.e. the L_{om}) of the performance of all units to be found such that

$\sum_{m=1}^{n} L_{om} x_{im} \leq x_{io}, i = 1, \ldots, r$

for each controllable input, the weighted combination of input does not exceed that of unit o

$\sum_{m=1}^{n} L_{om} z_{km} \leq f_o' z_{ko}, k = 1, \ldots, t$

for each uncontrollable input, the weighted combination of input does not exceed f_o' times that of unit o

$\sum_{m=1}^{n} L_{om} y_{jm} \geq f_o' y_{jo}, j = 1, \ldots, s$

and for each output, the weighted combination of output is at least as great as f_o' times that of unit o.

Again, we have a direct interpretation; but in this instance it is of little practical value for we have established that, if we use this formulation for output maximization, we would be factoring the uncontrollable inputs as well as the outputs. Clearly, we wish to factor only the outputs and so, in this case, the reciprocal formulation is inappropriate. However, where we seek to maximize output and maintain input, we are effectively not distinguishing between controllable and uncontrollable input. We should therefore continue to use one of the formulations (5) to (7).

The formulations from (8) to (13) are appropriate for input minimization in the presence of uncontrollable inputs, but for output maximization we must use one of the formulations (5) to (7). A consequence of this is that, when uncontrollable inputs are present, the input minimization and output maximization efficiency scores are no longer reciprocal.

Finally, the targets for outputs and controllable inputs are calculated in an identical manner to that when uncontrollable inputs are not present. Formulations (8) to (13) may identify slack in respect of an uncontrollable input and, clearly, by the very definition of an uncontrollable input, this cannot be converted to a target and we must settle for the interpretation that best use is not being made of that uncontrollable input. A typical example in practice would occur when seeking output maximization where the output is revenue, the controllable input is staff and the uncontrollable input is catchment population. If a slack is identified for catchment population this should be interpreted as meaning that the potential of the catchment population has been under-exploited and that greater staff resources would be needed to exploit it. The latter is evident from our graphical illustration of slack (Figure 3.3) which showed that improvements which are possible relative to both inputs are the basis of the efficiency score itself, and only additional improvement in respect of one of the inputs is reflected in slack.

A8 VARIABLE RETURNS TO SCALE

In Section 5.4 we developed a variable returns to scale model based on input minimization. From our graphical analysis, we derived a modified weighted sum ratio in which an additional constant appeared in the numerator. This can be generalized to our standard problem of comparing the performances of n units with:

s outputs denoted by y_j, $j = 1, \ldots, s$

r inputs denoted by x_i, $i = 1, \ldots, r$

The equivalent efficiency measure for unit o is:

(14)
$$\max e_o = \frac{\sum_{j=1}^{s} w_j y_{jo} + c_o}{\sum_{i=1}^{r} v_i x_{io}}$$

subject to:

$$\frac{\sum_{j=1}^{s} w_j y_{jm} + c_o}{\sum_{i=1}^{r} v_i x_{im}} \leq 1; \quad m = 1, \ldots, n$$

$$w_j \geq 0; \quad j = 1, \ldots, s$$

$$v_i \geq 0; \quad i = 1, \ldots, r$$

The problem can then be expressed as the following LP:

(15)
$$\max e_o = \sum_{j=1}^{s} w_j y_{jo} + c_o$$

subject to:

$$\sum_{i=1}^{r} v_i x_{im} - \sum_{j=1}^{s} w_j y_{jm} - c_o \geq 0; \quad m = 1, \ldots, n$$

$$\sum_{i=1}^{r} v_i x_{io} = 1$$

$$w_j \geq 0; \quad j = 1, \ldots, s$$

$$v_i \geq 0; \quad i = 1, \ldots, r$$

The dual of this LP is:

(16)
$$\min f_o$$

subject to:

$$-\sum_{m=1}^{n} L_{om} x_{im} + f_o x_{io} \geq 0, \quad i = 1, \ldots, r$$

$$\sum_{m=1}^{n} L_{om} y_{jm} \geq y_{jo}, j = 1, \ldots, s$$

$$\sum_{m=1}^{n} L_{om} = 1$$

which can be rearranged and interpreted as follows:

Mathematics	*Interpretation*
min fo	For the unit o, find the minimum proportion f_o
subject to:	which allows a weighted combination (i.e. the L_{om}) of the performance of all units to be found such that
$\sum_{m=1}^{n} L_{om} x_{im} \leq f_o x_{io}, i = 1, \ldots, r$	for each input, the weighted combination of input does not exceed the proportion f_o of the input of unit o
$\sum_{m=1}^{n} L_{om} y_{jm} \geq y_{jo}, j = 1, \ldots, s$	and for each output, the weighted combination of output is at least as great as that of unit o
$\sum_{m=1}^{n} L_{om} = 1$	and the L_{om} sum to 1.

Hence the dual is identical to the dual in (3) but with the additional constraint that the L_{om} sum to 1. This is the condition referred to at the end of Section 5.4 where it was shown that scale conversion no longer applies.

In Section 5.4, we also developed a modified model based on output maximization. At the time we stressed the importance of using the reciprocal formulation to determine the solution. The reason for this will become clear if we first generalize the measure without inverting it. The efficiency measure for unit o would be:

(17)
$$\max e_o = \frac{\sum_{j=1}^{s} w_j y_{jo}}{\sum_{i=1}^{r} v_i x_{io} - c_o}$$

subject to:

$$\frac{\sum_{j=1}^{s} w_j y_{jm}}{\sum_{i=1}^{r} v_i x_{im} - c_o} \leq 1; m = 1, \ldots, n$$

$$w_j \geq 0; j = 1, \ldots, s$$

$$v_i \geq 0; i = 1, \ldots, r$$

The problem can then be expressed as the following LP:

(18)
$$\max e_o = \sum_{j=1}^{s} w_j y_{jo}$$

subject to:

$$\sum_{i=1}^{r} v_i x_{im} - \sum_{j=1}^{s} w_j y_{jm} - c_o \geq 0; m = 1, \ldots, n$$

$$\sum_{i=1}^{r} v_i x_{io} - c_o = 1$$

$$w_j \geq 0; j = 1, \ldots, s$$

$$v_i \geq 0; i = 1, \ldots, r$$

The dual of this LP is:

(19)
$$\min f_o$$

subject to:

$$-\sum_{m=1}^{n} L_{om} x_{im} + f_o x_{io} \geq 0, i = 1, \ldots, r$$

$$\sum_{m=1}^{n} L_{om} y_{jm} \geq y_{jo}, j = 1, \ldots, s$$

$$\sum_{m=1}^{n} L_{om} - f_o = 0$$

which can be rearranged and interpreted as follows:

Mathematics	Interpretation
$\min f_o$	For the unit o, find the minimum proportion f_o
subject to:	which allows a weighted combination (i.e. the L_{om}) of the performance of all units to be found such that
$\sum_{m=1}^{n} L_{om} x_{im} \leq f_o x_{io}, i = 1, \ldots, r$	for each input, the weighted combination of input does not exceed the proportion f_o of the input of unit o
$\sum_{m=1}^{n} L_{om} y_{jm} \geq y_{jo}, j = 1, \ldots, s$	and for each output, the weighted combination of output is at least as great as that of unit o

$$\sum_{m=1}^{n} L_{om} = f_o \qquad\qquad \text{and the } L_{om} \text{ sum to } f_o.$$

The net effect of this procedure is that we have generated the correct efficiency score for output maximization but have proceeded in a manner consistent with input minimization in that we have kept output constant and reduced input. In doing so, we arrive at a set of L_{om} which do not sum to 1, which has the consequence that the weighted combination is not even on the frontier.

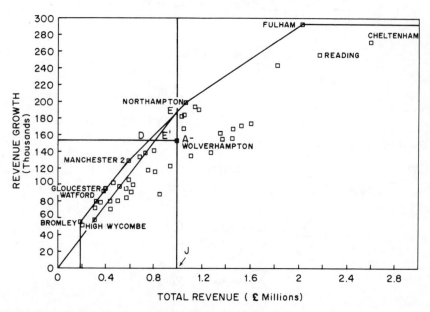

Figure A2 Output maximization: decreasing returns

This is illustrated by Figure A2 which is a replica of the graph of Figure 5.3. The resultant efficiency measure is with respect to the point E', yielding the same efficiency measure as the point E but with a reduced scale of operation. As such, E' is not a valid target point since, in the absence of constant returns to scale, the revised scale of operation does not render E' efficient.

It is clear, then, that we must use the reciprocal formulation for output maximization. This generalizes to:

$$(20) \qquad\qquad \min e'_o = \frac{\sum_{i=1}^{r} v_i x_{io} - c_o}{\sum_{j=1}^{s} w_j y_{jo}}$$

subject to:

$$\frac{\sum_{i=1}^{r} v_i x_{im} - c_o}{\sum_{j=1}^{s} w_j y_{jm}} \geq 1; \; m = 1, \ldots, n$$

$$w_j \geq 0; j = 1, \ldots, s$$

$$v_i \geq 0; i = 1, \ldots, r$$

The problem can then be expressed as the following LP:

(21)
$$\min e'_o = \sum_{i=1}^{r} v_i x_{io} - c_o$$

subject to:

$$\sum_{i=1}^{r} v_i x_{im} - \sum_{j=1}^{s} w_j y_{jm} - c_o \geq 0; \; m = 1, \ldots, n$$

$$\sum_{j=1}^{s} w_j y_{jm} = 1$$

$$w_j \geq 0; j = 1, \ldots, s$$
$$v_i \geq 0; i = 1, \ldots, r$$

The dual of this LP is:

(22)
$$\max f'_o$$

subject to:

$$-\sum_{m=1}^{n} L'_{om} x_{im} \geq -x_{jo}, \; i = 1, \ldots, r$$

$$\sum_{m=1}^{n} L'_{om} y_{jm} - f_o y_{jo} \geq 0, j = 1, \ldots, s$$

$$\sum_{m=1}^{n} L'_{om} = 1$$

which can be rearranged and interpreted as follows:

Mathematics	Interpretation
$\max f'_o$	For the unit o, find the maximum multiplier f'_o
subject to:	which allows a weighted combination (i.e. the L'_{om}) of the performance of all units to be found such that

$\sum_{m=1}^{n} L'_{om}x_{im} \leq x_{io}, i = 1, \ldots, r$ for each input, the weighted combination of input does not exceed that of the unit o

$\sum_{m=1}^{n} L'_{om}y_{jm} \geq f_{o}y_{jo}, j = 1, \ldots, s$ and for each output, the weighted combination of output is at least as great as f'_{o} times that of unit o.

$\sum_{m=1}^{n} L'_{om} = 1$ and the L'_{om} sum to 1.

A9 SUMMARY

Finally, on the basis of the developments in this Appendix, we can present two completely general models which incorporate both uncontrollable inputs and variable returns to scale. One model is required where the objective is input minimization and the other is required where the objective is output maximization. The practitioner will find that much possible confusion is eliminated by recognizing that there are only these two possible model forms. All other requirements can be met as a special case of one of these two forms. For example:

- for constant returns to scale, restrict $c = 0$;
- for decreasing returns to scale, restrict $c < 0$; and
- in the absence of uncontrollable inputs, set $t = 0$.

As this is a composite of the models already derived, we will present here the original formulation and the interpreted dual, but exclude the intermediate steps.

The models assume n units with:

s outputs denoted by $y_j, j = 1, \ldots, s$

r controllable inputs denoted by $x_i, i = 1, \ldots, r$

t uncontrollable inputs denoted by $z_k, k = 1, \ldots, t$

The input minimization efficiency measure for unit o is:

(23)
$$\max e_o = \frac{\sum_{j=1}^{s} w_j y_{jo} - \sum_{k=1}^{t} u_k z_{ko} + c_o}{\sum_{i=1}^{r} v_i x_{io}}$$

subject to:

$$\frac{\sum_{j=1}^{s} w_j y_{jm} - \sum_{k=1}^{t} u_k z_{km} + c_o}{\sum_{i=1}^{r} v_i x_{im}} \leq 1; m = 1, \ldots, n$$

$$w_j \geq 0; j = 1, \ldots, s$$

$$v_i \geq 0; i = 1, \ldots, r$$

$$u_k \geq 0; k = 1, \ldots, t$$

The dual problem with interpretation is:

Mathematics	Interpretation
min f_o	For the unit o, find the minimum proportion f_o
subject to:	which allows a weighted combination (i.e. the L_{om}) of the performance of all units to be found such that
$\sum_{m=1}^{n} L_{om} x_{im} \leq f_o x_{io}, i = 1, \ldots, r$	for each controllable input, the weighted combination of input does not exceed the proportion f_o of the input of unit o
$\sum_{m=1}^{n} L_{om} z_{km} \leq z_{ko}, k = 1, \ldots, t$	for each uncontrollable input, the weighted combination of input does not exceed that of unit o
$\sum_{m=1}^{n} L_{om} y_{jm} \geq y_{jo}, j = 1, \ldots, s$	and for each output, the weighted combination of output is at least as great as that of unit o
$\sum_{m=1}^{n} L_{om} = 1$	and the L_{om} sum to 1.

The output maximization efficiency for unit o is

$$(24) \qquad \min e'_o = \frac{\sum_{i=1}^{r} v_i x_{io} + \sum_{k=1}^{t} u_k z_{ko} - c_o}{\sum_{j=1}^{s} w_j y_{jo}}$$

subject to:

$$\frac{\sum_{i=1}^{r} v_i x_{im} + \sum_{k=1}^{t} u_k z_{ko} - c_o}{\sum_{j=1}^{s} w_j y_{jm}} \geq 1; \ m = 1, \ldots, n$$

$$w_j \geq 0; \ j = 1, \ldots, s$$

$$v_i \geq 0; \ i = 1, \ldots, r$$

$$u_k \geq 0; \ k = 1, \ldots, t$$

The dual of this problem is

Mathematics	Interpretation
max f'_o	For the unit o, find the maximum multiplier f'_o
subject to:	which allows a weighted combination (i.e. the L'_{om}) of the performance of all units to be found such that
$\sum_{m=1}^{n} L'_{om} x_{im} \leq x_{io}, i = 1, \ldots, r$	for each controllable input, the weighted combination of input does not exceed that of the unit o

$\sum_{m=1}^{n} L'_{om} z_{km} \leq z_{ko}, k = 1, \ldots, t$ for each uncontrollable input, the weighted combination of input does not exceed that of unit o

$\sum_{m=1}^{n} L'_{om} y_{jm} \geq f_o y_{jo}, j = 1, \ldots, s$ and for each output, the weighted combination of output is at least as great as f'_o times that of unit o

$\sum_{m=1}^{n} L'_{om} = 1$ and the L'_{om} sum to 1.

This reflects our earlier discussion that there is no need to distinguish between controllable and uncontrollable inputs when the objective is output maximization.

Appendix B

Additional Mathematical Proofs

In Section 4.3, we quoted without proof that the best performer in terms of the ratio of any single output factor to any single input factor will be efficient in any Data Envelopment Analysis which includes these factors.

We can see this easily if we take the general DEA ratio in equation 23 of Appendix A:

$$\frac{\sum_{j=1}^{s} w_j y_{jo} - \sum_{k=1}^{t} u_k z_{ko} + c_o}{\sum_{i=1}^{r} v_i x_{io}}$$

Suppose the unit o is such that

$$\frac{y_{ao}}{x_{bo}} > \frac{y_{am}}{x_{bm}}, m = 1, \ldots, n, m \neq o$$

Then we can choose

$$w_j = 0, j = 1, \ldots, s, j \neq a$$

$$u_k = 0, k = 1, \ldots, t$$

$$v_i = 0, i = 1, \ldots, r, i \neq b$$

and

$$c_o = 0$$

to reduce the ratio to

$$\frac{w_a y_{ao}}{v_b x_{bo}}$$

and we can further choose w_a and v_b such that the value of this ratio is 1. And since

$$\frac{y_{ao}}{x_{bo}} > \frac{y_{am}}{x_{bm}}, m = 1, \ldots, n, m \neq o$$

it follows that

$$\frac{w_a y_{ao}}{v_b x_{bo}} > \frac{w_a y_{am}}{v_b x_{bm}} \quad m = 1, \ldots, n, m \neq o$$

Hence we have a weighted ratio for which the value for unit o is 1 and the value for all other units is less than 1.

References

1. Taffler, R. J. (1983), The Z-score Approach to Measuring Company Solvency, *The Accountant's Magazine*, March 1983.
2. *Relationship of Expenditure to Needs*, Eighth Report from the Expenditure Committee, Session 1971/72.
3. *Efficiency and Effectiveness in the Civil Service*, Cmnd 8616, September 1982.
4. *Managing the Crisis in Council Housing*, The Audit Commission for Local Authorities in England and Wales.
5. Farrell, M. J. (1957), The Measurement of Productive Efficiency, *Journal of the Royal Statistical Society*, Series A, **120**, 253–290.
6. Charnes, A., Cooper, W. W. and Rhodes, E. (1978), Measuring the Efficiency of Decision Making Units, *European Journal of Operational Research*, **2**, 429–444.
7. Charnes, A. and Cooper, W. W. (1985), Preface to Topics in Data Envelopment Analysis, *Annals of Operations Research*, **2**, 59–94.
8. Grosskopf (1986), The Role of Reference Technology in Measuring Productivity Efficiency, *The Economic Journal*, **96**, 499–513.
9. Hildenbrand (1983), Numerical Computation of Short-Run Production Functions, In *Quantitative Studies on Production and Prices* (ed. W. Eichhorn et al.), 173–180, Würzburg, West Germany: Physica Verlag.
10. Sherman, H. D. (1984), Data Envelopment Analysis as a New Managerial Audit Methodology—Test and Evaluation, *Auditing: A Journal of Practice and Theory*, **4**, 35–53.
11. Lewin, A. Y. and Morey, R. C. (1981), Measuring the Relative Efficiency and Output Potential of Public Sector Organizations: an Application of Data Envelopment Analysis, *International Journal of Policy Analysis and Information Systems*, **5**, 267–285.
12. Bowlin, W. F. (1985), *A Data Envelopment Analysis Approach to Performance Evaluation in Not-for-Profit Entities with an Illustrative Application to the U.S. Air Force*, PhD Thesis, The University of Texas Graduate School of Business, Austin, Texas.
13. Lewin, A. Y., Morey, R. C. and Cook, T. J. (1982), Evaluating the Administrative Efficiency of Courts, *Omega*, **10**, 401–411.
14. Bessent, A. M., Bessent, E. W., Cooper, W. W. and Thorogood, N. C. (1983), Evaluation of Educational Program Proposals by Means of DEA, *Educational Administration Quarterly*, **19**, 82–107.
15. Banker, R. D. and Morey, R. C. (1986), The Use of Categorical Variables in Data Envelopment Analysis, *Management Science*, **32**, 1613–1627.

16. Banker, R. D., Conrad, R. F. and Strauss (1986), A Comparative Application of Data Envelopment Analysis and Translog Methods: an Illustrative Study of Hospital Production, *Management Science*, **32**, 30–44.

17. Banker, R. D. (1984), Fuel Productivity and Scale Efficiency of Coal-Fired Steam-Electric Plants. Working paper, Carnegie-Mellon University.

18. Charnes, A., Cooper, W. W. and Rhodes, E. (1981), Evaluating Program and Managerial Efficiency: an Application of Data Envelopment Analysis to Program Follow Through, *Management Science*, **27**, 668–697.

19. Banker, R. D. and Morey, R. C. (1986), Efficiency Analysis for Exogenously Fixed Inputs and Outputs, *Operations Research*, **34**, 513–521.

20. Thanassoulis, E., Dyson, R. G. and Foster, M. J. (1987), Relative Efficiency Assessments using Data Envelopment Analysis: an Application to Data on Rates Departments, *Journal of the Operational Research Society*, **38**, 397–411.

21. Levitt, M. S. and Joyce, M. A. S. (1987), The Growth and Efficiency of Public Spending, Cambridge University Press, Cambridge.

22. Ganley, J. and Cubbin, J. (1987), Performance Indicators in Prisons, *Public Money*, December, 57–59.

23. Cubbin, J., Domberger, S. and Meadowcroft, S. (1988), Competitive Tendering and Refuse Collection: Identifying the Sources of Efficiency Gains, *Fiscal Studies*.

24. Jesson, D., Mayston, D. and Smith, P. (1987), Performance Assessment in the Education Sector: Educational and Economic Perspectives, *Oxford Review of Education*, **13**, 249–266.

25. Banker, R. D. (1984), Estimating Most Productive Scale Size using Data Envelopment Analysis, *European Journal of Operational Research*, **17**, 35–44.

26. Working for Patients—The Health Service 'Caring for the 1990's'.

Index